The Value of Close Calls in Improving Patient Safety:

Learning How to Avoid and Mitigate Patient Harm

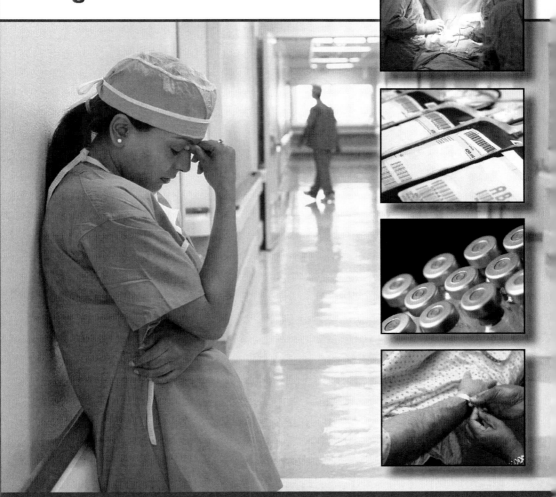

Joint Commission Resources

Joint Commission International

Edited by
Albert W. Wu, M.D., M.P.H.

Foreword by
James Reason, Ph.D.

Executive Editor: Steven Berman
Project Manager: Bridget Chambers
Manager, Publications: Paul Reis
Associate Director, Production: Johanna Harris
Executive Director: Catherine Chopp Hinckley, Ph.D.
Joint Commission/JCR Reviewers: Gerry Castro, M.P.H.; Jerod Loeb, Ph.D.; Paul Reis; Paul Schyve, M.D.; Paul vanOstenberg, D.D.S., M.S.

JOINT COMMISSION RESOURCES MISSION

The mission of Joint Commission Resources (JCR) is to continuously improve the safety and quality of care in the United States and in the international community through the provision of education and consultation services and international accreditation.

JOINT COMMISSION INTERNATIONAL

A division of Joint Commission Resources, Inc.
The mission of Joint Commission International (JCI) is to improve the safety and quality of care in the international community through the provision of education, publications, consultation, and evaluation services.

Joint Commission Resources educational programs and publications support, but are separate from, the accreditation activities of the Joint Commission and Joint Commission International. Attendees at Joint Commission Resources educational programs and purchasers of Joint Commission Resources publications receive no special consideration or treatment in, or confidential information about, the accreditation process.

The inclusion of an organization name, product, or service in a Joint Commission Resources publication should not be construed as an endorsement of such organization, product, or services, nor is failure to include an organization name, product, or service to be construed as disapproval.

Printed in the U.S.A. 5 4 3 2 1
Requests for permission to make copies of any part of this work should be mailed to
Permissions Editor
Department of Publications
Joint Commission Resources
One Renaissance Boulevard
Oakbrook Terrace, Illinois 60181 U.S.A.
permissions@jcrinc.com

ISBN: 978-1-59940-415-8
Library of Congress Control Number: 2010938403

For more information about Joint Commission Resources, please visit http://www.jcrinc.com.

For more information about Joint Commission International, please visit http://www.jointcommissioninternational.org.

Contents

Contributors

Editor

Albert W. Wu, M.D., M.P.H., is Professor of Health Policy and Management, Epidemiology, and International Health, Johns Hopkins Bloomberg School of Public Health, Baltimore; Professor of Medicine and Surgery, Johns Hopkins School of Medicine, Baltimore; former Senior Adviser to the World Health Organization (WHO) Safety program; and a member of *The Joint Commission Journal on Quality and Patient Safety's* Editorial Advisory Board.

Chapter 1. Close Calls in Health Care

Fiona Pathiraja, M.B.B.S., D.H.M.S.A., D.R.C.O.G., is Clinical Advisor to Professor Sir Bruce Keogh, National Health Service (NHS) Medical Director, Department of Health (England), London. **Marie-Claire Wilson, M.A.(Cantab), M.B.B.S.,** is Independent Consultant, London. **Peter J. Pronovost, M.D., Ph.D.,** is Professor, Quality and Safety Research Group, Department of Anesthesiology and Critical Care Medicine, and Department of Surgery, The Johns Hopkins University School of Medicine, Baltimore; Department of Health Policy and Management, The Johns Hopkins Bloomberg School of Public Health; and a member of *The Joint Commission Journal on Quality and Patient Safety* Editorial Advisory Board.

Chapter 2. Reporting and Learning from Close Calls

Alan Fayaz, M.A.(Cantab), M.B.B.S., M.R.C.P., formerly Clinical Advisor to Medical Director, National Patient Safety Agency, London, is Specialist Trainee in Anaesthesia and Intensive Care, North East London Rotation. **Laura Morlock, Ph.D.,** is Professor and Associate Chair for Health Management Programs, Department of Health Policy and Management, Johns Hopkins Bloomberg School of Public Health, Baltimore.

Chapter 3. Promoting Meaningful Close-Call Reporting: Lessons from Aviation

Sidney W.A. Dekker, Ph.D., formerly Professor and Director, Leonardo da Vinci Laboratory for Complexity and Systems Thinking, Lund University, Sweden, is Professor and Director, Key Centre for Ethics, Law, Justice and Governance, Griffith University, Mt. Gravatt, Queensland, Australia.

Chapter 4. Human Factors Applications to Understanding and Using Close Calls to Improve Health Care

Tosha B. Wetterneck, M.D., M.S., is Associate Professor of Medicine, Division of General Internal Medicine, University of Wisconsin (UW) School of Medicine and Public Health; and Researcher,

Center for Quality and Productivity Improvement, UW–Madison. **Ben-Tzion Karsh, Ph.D.,** is Associate Professor of Industrial and Systems Engineering, UW–Madison.

Chapter 5. Disclosing Close Calls to Patients and Their Families

Albert W. Wu, M.D., M.P.H., is Professor of Health Policy and Management, Epidemiology, International Health, Department of Medicine and Surgery, Johns Hopkins Bloomberg School of Public Health, Baltimore. **Thomas H. Gallagher, M.D.,** is Associate Professor of Medicine, Department of General Internal Medicine, University of Washington School of Medicine, Seattle. **Rick Iedema, Ph.D.,** is Professor of Organizational Communication and Director, Centre for Health Communication, University of Technology, Sydney, Australia.

Chapter 6. Outpatient Endoscopy: Closing the Loop on Colonoscopy Orders

Lydia C. Siegel, M.D., M.P.H., is Associate Physician, Brigham and Women's Hospital, Boston; and Instructor, Harvard Medical School. **Tejal K. Gandhi, M.D., M.P.H.,** is Director of Patient Safety, Partners Healthcare, Boston; Associate Physician at Brigham and Women's Hospital, Boston; and Associate Professor of Medicine, Harvard Medical School, Boston.

Chapter 7. Medication Safety: Neuromuscular Blocking Agents

David U, M.Sc.(Pharm.), is President and Chief Executive Officer, Institute for Safe Medication Practices Canada (ISMP Canada), Toronto. **Bonnie Salsman, B.Sc.(Pharm.),** is Consultant Pharmacist, ISMP Canada.

Chapter 8. Oncology: The Patient's Family Speaks Up

Saul N. Weingart, M.D., Ph.D., is Vice President for Quality Improvement and Patient Safety, Dana-Farber Cancer Institute, Boston; and Associate Professor of Medicine, Harvard

Medical School, Boston. **Audrea Szabatura, Pharm.D., B.C.O.P.,** is Medication Safety Officer; **Deborah Duncombe, M.P.H.,** is Risk Manager; and **Sarah Kadish, M.S.,** is Director of Process Improvement, Dana-Farber Cancer Institute. **Amy Billett, M.D.,** is Director of Safety and Quality, Division of Pediatric Hematology/ Oncology, Dana-Farber Cancer Institute and Children's Hospital, Boston; and Associate Professor of Pediatrics, Harvard Medical School. **Sylvia Bartel, R.Ph., M.P.H.,** is Vice President of Pharmacy, Dana-Farber Cancer Institute.

Chapter 9. Surgery: Safety Culture, Site Marking, Checklists, and Teamwork

Andrew M. Ibrahim is Doris Duke Clinical Research Fellow, Department of Surgery, Johns Hopkins University School of Medicine, Baltimore. **Martin A. Makary, M.D., M.P.H.,** is Associate Professor of Surgery and Health Policy and Management, Johns Hopkins University School of Medicine; and Co-Director, The Quality and Safety Research Group, Johns Hopkins Hospital.

Chapter 10. Transfusion Medicine: The Problem with Multitasking

Barbara Rabin Fastman, M.H.A., M.T.(A.S.C.P.)S.C., B.B. is Assistant Professor and **Harold S. Kaplan, M.D.,** is Professor, Health Evidence and Policy, Mount Sinai School of Medicine, New York City.

Chapter 11. Radiotherapy: Using Risk Profiling to Identify Errors and Close Calls in the Process of Care

Michael B. Barton, M.B.B.S., M.D., is Professor of Radiation Oncology, South West Clinical School, University of New South Wales (NSW); and Senior Staff Specialist, Liverpool Cancer Therapy Centre, Liverpool, NSW, Australia. **Geoffrey P. Delaney, M.B.B.S., M.D., Ph.D.,** is Clinical Professor, South West Clinical School, University of NSW; and Area Director of Cancer Services, Sydney South West

Area Health Service, NSW, Australia. **Douglas J. Noble, B.M., B.Ch., M.P.H.,** is Public Health Registrar, London Deanery, London; and Research Fellow, Green Templeton College, University of Oxford, Oxford, United Kingdom.

Chapter 12. Health Information Technology: Look-Alikes in the Drop-Down Menu

Erika Abramson, M.D., M.Sc., is Assistant Professor of Pediatrics; and Associate Program Director, Pediatric Graduate Medical Education, Division of Quality and Medical Informatics, Weill Medical College of Cornell University, New York City; and Assistant Attending Pediatrician, New York-Presbyterian Hospital (NYPH), New York City. **Rainu Kaushal, M.D., M.P.H.,** is Associate Professor of Pediatrics, Medicine and Public Health, Weill Cornell Medical College; Chief of the Division of Quality and Medical Informatics, Department of Pediatrics; Director of Pediatric Quality and Safety, Komansky Center for Children's Health, NYPH; and Executive Director, Health Information Technology Evaluation Collaborative (HITEC), New York City.

Chapter 13. Pediatrics: "Wrong Patient" Breast-Milk Administration in the Neonatal Intensive Care Unit

Michael L. Rinke, M.D., is Instructor of Pediatrics, Division of Quality and Safety, Johns Hopkins University School of Medicine, Baltimore. **Julie Murphy, R.N., B.S.N., I.B.C.L.C.,** is a Registered Nurse and Certified Lactation Consultant, Neonatal Intensive Care Unit, Johns Hopkins Hospital, Baltimore. **David G. Bundy, M.D., M.P.H.,** is Assistant Professor of Pediatrics, Johns Hopkins University School of Medicine, Baltimore.

Chapter 14. Psychiatry: Mistaken Identity in a Patient with Schizophrenia

Geetha Jayaram, M.D., M.B.A., is Associate Professor, Department of Psychiatry, Johns Hopkins Hospital, Baltimore; and Associate Professor, Department of Health Policy and

Management, Johns Hopkins Bloomberg School of Public Health, Baltimore. **Jennifer Meuchel, M.D.,** is Clinical Associate, Community Psychiatry Program, Johns Hopkins Hospital.

Chapter 15. Anesthesia: Administration of Sedatives to Patients Receiving Epidural Analgesia

Stephen Pratt, M.D., formerly Clinical Director, Obstetric Anesthesia, Department of Anesthesia, Critical Care, and Pain Medicine, is Chief, Division of Quality and Safety, Department of Anesthesia, Critical Care and Pain Medicine, Beth Israel Deaconess Medical Center, Boston.

Chapter 16. Emergency Medicine: Medication Displacement in an Automated Medication Dispensing System

Sommer Gripper, M.D., is Emergency Medicine Physician; **Elizabeth Fang, Pharm.D., B.C.P.S.,** is Pharmacy Resident, Department of Pharmacy; **Sneha Shah, M.D.,** is Emergency Medicine Resident, Department of Emergency Medicine; **Melinda Ortmann, Pharm.D., B.C.P.S.,** is Clinical Pharmacist, Department of Emergency Medicine; **Michelle Patch, R.N., M.S.N.,** is Safety Officer, Department of Emergency Medicine; and **Jordan Sax, M.D.,** is Emergency Medicine Resident, Department of Emergency Medicine, Johns Hopkins Hospital, Baltimore. **Julius Cuong Pham, M.D., Ph.D.,** is Assistant Professor, Departments of Emergency Medicine, Anesthesia and Critical Care, and Surgery, Johns Hopkins School of Medicine, Baltimore.

Chapter 17. Obstetrics: Pulmonary Edema Following a Failed Handoff

Susan Mann, M.D., formerly Director of Quality Improvement, Department of Obstetrics and Gynecology, is Director of Team Training and Simulation, Department of Obstetrics and Gynecology, Beth Israel Deaconess Medical Center, Boston. **Stephen Pratt, M.D.,** formerly Clinical Director,

Obstetric Anesthesia, Department of Anesthesia, Critical Care, and Pain Medicine, is Chief, Division of Quality and Safety, Department of Anesthesia, Critical Care and Pain Medicine, Beth Israel Deaconess Medical Center.

Chapter 18. Radiology: A Chance Discovery of Retained Sponges

Anthony Fotenos, M.D., Ph.D., is Radiology Resident, Russell H. Morgan Department of Radiology and Radiological Science, Johns Hopkins Hospital, Baltimore. **John Eng, M.D.,** is Associate Professor of Radiology and Health Sciences Informatics, Russell H. Morgan Department of Radiology and Radiological Science, Johns Hopkins University School of Medicine, Baltimore.

Chapter 19. Geriatrics: Improving Medication Safety in the Nursing Home Setting—The Case of Warfarin

Jerry H. Gurwitz, M.D., is Executive Director, Meyers Primary Care Institute, Worcester, Massachusetts; and Professor of Medicine and of Family Medicine and Community Health, University of Massachusetts Medical School,

Worcester. **Terry Field, D.Sc.,** is Associate Director, Meyers Primary Care Institute; and Associate Professor of Medicine, University of Massachusetts Medical School. **Jennifer Tjia, M.D., M.S.C.E.,** is Assistant Professor of Medicine, and **Kathleen Mazor, Ed.D.,** is Associate Professor of Medicine, University of Massachusetts Medical School.

Chapter 20. Laboratory Medicine/ Pathology: Improving Diagnostic Safety in Papanicolaou Smears

Lee Hilborne, M.D., M.P.H., is Professor of Pathology and Laboratory Medicine, David Geffen School of Medicine at University of California at Los Angeles, Los Angeles; Medical Director, Quest Diagnostics, West Hills, California; and Deputy Director, Global Health, RAND, Santa Monica, California. **Maria Olvera, M.D.,** is Senior Pathologist, Quest Diagnostics, West Hills, California; **Dereck C. Counter, M.B.A.,** is Six Sigma Black Belt; and **Toni L. Kick, Ph.D.,** is Six Sigma Master Black Belt. **Stephen C. Suffin, M.D.,** is Chief Laboratory Officer, Quest Diagnostics, Madison, New Jersey.

Foreword

The patient safety problem is huge and exists everywhere. Estimates of the frequency of adverse events vary from country to country, although the majority of these numbers tend to distribute themselves around 10%, plus or minus 2. That is, around 1 in 10 patients in acute care hospitals are likely to be harmed or even killed as the result of iatrogenic errors. The potentially most harmful of these generally occur at the patient–caregiver interface. However, most proximal unsafe acts have a causal history that may implicate the team, the workplace, the organization, the health system at large, and the prevailing socioeconomic climate.

As in other hazardous domains, human fallibility dominates the risks of an adverse patient event. But health care has a number of singular characteristics that sets it apart from, say, aviation—a realm that is frequently invoked as a model of safe operation. Unlike pilots, physicians and nurses are faced with a huge variety of equipment and activities. Unlike passengers, patients are especially vulnerable by virtue of illness and injury, and so are more susceptible to harm. Health professionals, unlike aviators (or nuclear power plant operators, for that matter), deliver their services in a one-to-one or a few-to-one fashion. It is "hands-on" work, and the more close up and personal it is, the greater is the opportunity for something to go wrong. Whereas aviation accidents are closely investigated and the results made available to all, bad events in health care usually happen to isolated individuals scattered over a wide range of institutions and locations. They are rarely studied in any systemic depth and, until recently, the results of these investigations were not shared across institutions and specialties. These features in combination make health care one of the most error-provoking activities on the planet—although it has to be acknowledged that aircraft maintenance is fairly close.

Now we arrive at the paradox lying at the heart of the patient safety problem. Health care, by its very nature, makes slips, lapses, and mistakes highly likely. Yet health care professionals—and physicians in particular—are taught very little about the varieties of human fallibility and the conditions likely to provoke them. They are raised in a culture of trained perfectibility. After a long, arduous, and expensive education, physicians expect (and are expected) to get it right. Errors are marginalized and stigmatized. They are equated to incompetence. All of this means that unsafe acts—unless they result in patient harm—are hardly ever discussed or shared with other members of the profession. And this, too, is in stark contrast to commercial aviation, an activity that was predicated from its outset on the assumption that people make errors. Was it Wilbur or was it Orville Wright who came up with the first checklist? Error detection and error management are essential features of flight training, both from its outset and throughout a pilot's career.

The foregoing should begin to explain why this book about close calls is both exceedingly valuable and very timely. Close calls (or near misses) are "free lessons" about the varieties of human error, the local circumstances that trigger them, and the "upstream" systemic factors that can give rise to them. Close calls, as defined in this book, are unsafe acts—errors or procedural violations—that could seriously harm a patient but in the event did not. Three possible types of close call are discussed in the book. First, an error occurred but its adverse consequence did not reach the patient. Second, an error happened and may have reached the patient but did not cause harm. Third, an error happened and its effects reached the patient but did not cause serious harm.

To deliver its patient safety benefits, a close call must be recorded, analyzed (both in regard to the local factors and any upstream systemic issues that contributed to it), and the results must be collated and disseminated. One of the most important things that can be revealed by this procedure is the nature and location of recurrent "error traps." A crucial feature of human fallibility is that the same tasks or situations keep producing the same types of error in *different* people. Thus, we are talking about error-prone situations, not error-prone people. The first rule of effective error management is to discover the error traps and then to direct inevitably limited remedial resources toward removing or ameliorating them. Trying to deal with errors singly is akin to swatting mosquitoes individually. Kill one, and another arrives. As with errors, the best defense is to drain the "swamps" in which they breed. In health care (or any other hazardous domain), this means finding the systemic error traps and then dealing with them.

We cannot eliminate human fallibility. It is deeply rooted in the human condition. And error can have benign as well as damaging outcomes. (Think about the value of trial-and-error learning: The therapeutic properties of both radium and penicillin were the result of serendipitous discoveries arising out of unintended actions.) But while we cannot change the human condition, we can change the conditions under which people work to make them less error-provoking and more forgiving.

A vital tool for the clinical risk/error manager is a well-designed close-call reporting system. There are many reasons for this, but mentioning three will suffice here. First, they allow for the detection of error traps. Second, they tell you where the "edge" lies without necessarily having to fall over it. Third, consideration of their possibly damaging consequences stops health care practitioners from forgetting to be afraid. I will say a little more about this below.

High-reliability organizations (HROs) are systems operating in potentially hazardous environments that sustain fewer than their "fair" share of bad events. They have been extensively studied by research teams at the University of California, Berkeley, and at the University of Michigan. HROs have many characteristics in common, but perhaps the most important is a great respect for the hazards of their business. They expect errors to happen and things to go wrong. They seek to learn the systemic lessons from past events and then "brainstorm" possible new accident scenarios. In short, they are characterized by chronic unease—something that does not necessarily burn out the gastric mucosa but that depends on cultural reminders.

Chronicling, analyzing, debating, and disseminating stories about close calls are prerequisites for achieving the unrelenting vigilance and informed wariness that are vital steps along the path to improving patient safety. And this excellent book will tell you how to do it. Buy it, read it, and discuss it: Following its messages will reduce patient harm and save lives.

James Reason, Ph.D.
Emeritus Professor, University of Manchester, United Kingdom

Introduction

Albert W. Wu, M.D., M.P.H.

In the past decade, patient safety has emerged as a common and important health priority in all nations.[1] Policymakers, health care leaders, and health care providers and workers—and patients and their families—increasingly expect health care to be safe and effective. Strides have been made in patient safety.[2,3] There is now broad awareness among clinicians and managers about the challenge of patient safety, as well as a greater understanding that problems in patient safety reflect systems rather than individuals alone. However, capturing information about these problems depends on reliable reporting systems. The current emphasis on incident reporting was presaged by The Joint Commission's Sentinel Event Policy, which since 1995 has mandated that accredited organizations investigate incidents that result in serious harm or the risk thereof.[4] But these were only the worst cases.

There is another whole layer of incidents that underlie sentinel events: close calls. Close-call incidents—more commonly referred to as "near misses" in health care and other high-risk industries—are an important vehicle for understanding both failures and recovery in health care systems (*see* Sidebar 1, right). Close calls are indicators of problems in health care operations, weaknesses that we often did not even suspect. Capturing and addressing them has the potential to reduce adverse events. If the underlying

Sidebar 1. *Near Misses* Versus *Close Calls*

There is internal debate among patient safety experts about whether we should refer to these incidents as near misses or close calls. In aviation, the term *near miss* is readily understandable as an incident involving two moving aircraft. Historically, this term has been used most often in health care. However, some argue that *near miss* is a more appropriate term when you are trying to hit something (like a target) rather than when you are trying to avoid something (for example, getting hit by a bullet, harming a patient). The same individuals argue that the term *close call* is preferable, also reflecting the fact that it can include both a near miss, in which the error did not reach the patient, and a "harmless hit," in which the error reached the patient but did not result in harm. For this reason, in this book, for the most part the term *close call* is used. However, it should be understood to be largely interchangeable with *near miss*. Both terms have also been used along with *potential adverse event*, and even *potential error*.

hazards can be identified and remedied, the likelihood of recurrence can be reduced or even eliminated. However, close calls are widely ignored and rarely acted on. The failure to investigate and manage the situation leaves the underlying hazards unchanged. Even when a fix is made, it is most often only at a single institution, and the potential for a serious consequence remains.

It would be unacceptable for an organization to say in public, "We won't investigate and take corrective action until a serious injury or major damage occurs." But in reality, this is how health care organizations handle close calls today. Most close calls are not investigated, as in the case shown in Sidebar 2 (right).[5-7]

Most organizations do not even have a system to capture close calls, much less act on them. This is not surprising; many of the necessary resources go instead to investigating and reporting sentinel events. An unintended consequence has been that organizations focus on "reviewable" events (all of which represent adverse events) to the exclusion of other information-rich incidents such as close calls.

In the remainder of this introduction, I address the importance of close calls, review definitions to propose a working definition for *close call* for the purposes of this book, and briefly highlight the topics and issues addressed in the book.

WHY ARE CLOSE CALLS IMPORTANT?

Close calls are important for several reasons. First, they provide information on active and latent errors in the health care system. "Active errors" occur where health care, usually in the form of a frontline health care worker, comes into direct contact with a patient. They are generally readily apparent—unlike "latent errors" (also referred to as "latent conditions"), which are features of an organization or design that are less apparent but that allow errors to occur. For example,

---

Sidebar 2. Patients with a Penicillin Allergy

Receiving or Nearly Receiving a Penicillin Drug

A patient with a documented penicillin allergy underwent debridement of a wound infection. The surgical resident ordered Zosyn, using the hospital's computerized provider order entry system. He did not recall that Zosyn contains a combination of tazobactam and piperacillin, a semi-synthetic penicillin. The medication was dispensed, but just before administering the injection, the nurse recognized the error, and the dose was not administered. The resident was relieved. There was no investigation. Six months later, in a similar case, the error was not recognized, and this time the patient received the injection—and went on to develop hives and a systemic reaction. Luckily, he was treated successfully. The nurse entered the case into the hospital's online error reporting system. The ensuing investigation revealed that the computerized order entry system did not identify the component drugs in the combination. A change was made to the listing so that it reads "Zosyn—a penicillin drug," reducing the risk of this type of incident. However, a similar incident occurred six months later at a nearby hospital that was not aware of the original problem or the solution.

---

administration of the wrong medication is an active error, whereas the packaging of different medications in look-alike vials is a latent error.[8,9]

Close calls can also provide information on factors that contribute to these errors. Importantly, the causes of close calls in health care appear to be very similar to the causes of incidents that cause harm.[10] On the other hand, reports of close calls can identify points of failure within systems that are not present in reports about events with more serious outcomes. Second, close calls are more frequent than adverse events and provide more information about errors from the perspective of health care workers in different positions—who come into contact with processes and equipment at all levels of the health care system. Third, they are less complicated to investigate because they are divorced from worries about liability claims. Health care workers are more likely to be forthcoming about these incidents than those in which there is patient injury, and there are fewer complications such as the imperative to mitigate harm and conduct investigations in a timely fashion. Fourth, it is possible to capture and study recovery strategies in context. This is more difficult in cases where recovery was absent or unsuccessful. Understanding recovery can lead to designing systems that are more resilient and more effective at capturing errors before they cause harm.[11]

A culture of safety should promote reporting of errors, close calls, and incidents that cause harm by all health care workers rather than those strictly concerned with "safety." As might be depicted in a "safety pyramid," errors (as the most common) would form the base, followed by close calls, with incidents that cause harm at the top. Of course, to improve safety, more than the simple identification of close calls is required. Information on close calls must be analyzed in terms of contributing factors and trends over time. Solutions must be proposed to reduce their recurrence, these solutions must be implemented, and implementation must be evaluated.[12,13]

A new appreciation of the importance of close calls is reflected in the planned revisions of the Joint Commission Sentinel Event Policy.[14] Under the current policy, reviewable sentinel events are the only type of incident that requires root cause analysis.[15] An unintended consequence has been that organizations have focused on reviewable

events to the exclusion of close calls and other potentially informative incidents. The planned revisions to the policy are intended to promote the analysis and reporting of close calls and no-harm events. Current Joint Commission International medication management and quality and patient requirements call for proper analysis of and response to near-miss events.[16]

DEFINITIONS

Part of the failure to capitalize on the wealth of close-call incidents can be explained by the lack of a consistent definition.[5,17,18] Frontline clinicians have trouble identifying close calls because of their unfamiliarity with the concept, making it unlikely that they will post them to incident reporting systems.[19] All involved stakeholders—health care organizations, patient safety researchers, and software developers—would benefit from standard definitions to identify errors and related factors. Without such definitions, it is difficult to count and evaluate these mistakes. Standard definitions would allow comparisons to be made across disciplines and between organizations and would also facilitate trending of incident data, investigation and analysis of the role of system and human factors in patient safety, determination of applications and limitations of strategies to reduce risk, and development of priorities and safety solutions. These arguments undergird the common formats adopted for use by the Patient Safety Organization (PSO) reporting program.[20]

HOW ARE CLOSE CALLS RELATED TO ERRORS?

Human beings will always make errors. An adverse event is an injury caused by medical care. Identifying something as an adverse event does not imply error, negligence, or poor quality of care. Rather, it indicates an undesired outcome that results from diagnosis or treatment, as opposed to the underlying disease process.

Errors, bad outcomes, negligence, and lawsuits are distinct entities that are often confused,

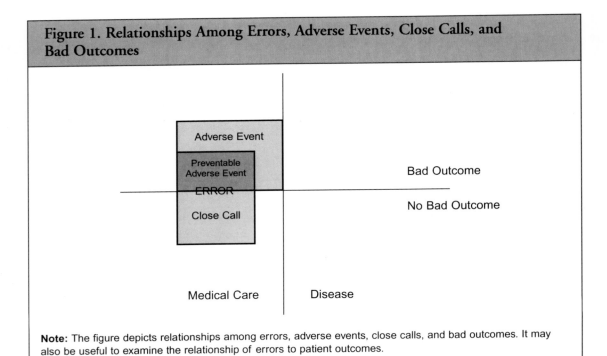

Figure 1. Relationships Among Errors, Adverse Events, Close Calls, and Bad Outcomes

Note: The figure depicts relationships among errors, adverse events, close calls, and bad outcomes. It may also be useful to examine the relationship of errors to patient outcomes.

particularly in the minds of physicians involved in adverse events. In fact, not all errors are negligent, and lawsuits may occur in the setting of a bad outcome despite the absence of any error. Some errors result in patient harm, while others do not (Figure 1, above). Close calls are errors that do not result in harm.

WHAT IS A CLOSE CALL?

To understand the extent and importance of a problem in health care, it is essential to have precise definitions. However, researchers from various specialties and disciplines apply different definitions to the term *close call*. This situation is further complicated by the fact that *close call* (or *near miss*) is in common use outside health care. Two factors are used to distinguish types of incidents: whether the incident "reached" the patient (patient reached), and whether the patient was harmed (patient harmed).[21] Combining these two characteristics yields three types of incidents:

1. Incidents that never reached the patient.

2. Incidents that reached the patient but did not cause harm.

3. Incidents that reached the patient and caused harm.

Definition 1. An Error That Happened but Did Not Reach the Patient

The first type of close call includes events, situations, or errors that never reached the patient. This is the definition that is used by the Institute for Safe Medication Practices (ISMP),[22] which further specifies that the failure was captured and corrected before reaching the patient, either through chance or purposefully designed system controls that have been put in place.[23,24] It is also consistent with the provisional definition applied by WHO (World Health Organization) Patient Safety.[25] Nashef created a gradient of near misses to distinguish between errors recognized by the system and those recognized by luck.[26] This definition has a practical benefit related to reporting: Reporting close calls can help to evaluate whether the circumstances of error capture are fortuitous—which would imply that system controls are inadequately designed or functioning poorly—or if error capture was part of the system design, implying that controls are functioning well.

Human factors engineers would argue that the term *close call* implies that nothing bad happened, but something bad already did happen—an error occurred (*see* Chapter 3). It is just that no person or thing (for example, patient, operator, equipment, system) was harmed.[27,28]

Definition 2. An Error That Happened and May Have Reached the Patient but Did Not Result in Harm

Definition 2 describes an incident that may have reached the patient and does not specify why the incident did not cause harm. This is exemplified by the U.S. Agency for Healthcare Research and Quality's (AHRQ's) definition[29] and is similar to the definitions used by other researchers.[30–32] An advantage of Definition 2 is that it is based on the severity of the outcome and corresponds to real-world and legal judgments, which tend to be based on the presence or absence of harm. A criticism of this definition is that it does not differentiate between incidents that reach the patient and those that do not reach the patient. Kessels-Habraken and colleagues found that the error-handling process used for incidents that did not reach the patient differed from those that did reach the patient.[21] This definition may also be more difficult to use to monitor systems for capturing errors because a period of follow-up may be needed to ascertain the outcome.

Definition 3. An Error That Happened and May Have Reached the Patient but Did Not Result in Serious Harm

Extending the definition further, the term *near miss* has been used in obstetrics and gynecology to refer to a patient safety incident that did not result in maternal or neonatal mortality (*see* Chapters 1 and 17). This definition of *near miss* encompasses adverse outcomes, including other injuries of lesser severity, and corresponds to that used in the 2004 Institute of Medicine (IOM)

report on medical errors—which also included incidents that did not cause serious harm.[5]

There are several classification schemes to grade the extent of harm, including the AHRQ Harm Score (version 1.1),[33] the National Coordinating Council for Medication Error Reporting and Prevention's index for categorizing errors (which also evaluates the preventability of the incident),[34] WHO's international classification for patient safety that includes harm outcomes (in development),[35] and the grading scheme developed by the U.S. Department of Veterans Affair, which considers the extent of harm as well as the probability of recurrence of an incident as an aid to prioritizing action.[36]

Proposed Definition

As I have argued, health care organizations do not take full advantage of close calls, which are "information rich." In the interest of learning how to capture as much useful information as possible about close calls, as well as about the failed, missed, or successful opportunities for recovery that they may represent, events should be considered to be close calls whether or not they reach the patient. Accordingly, I propose the following definition:

> An event or a situation that did not produce patient harm because it did not reach the patient, either due to chance or to capture before reaching the patient; or if it did reach the patient, due to robustness of the patient or to timely intervention (for example, an antidote was administered).

This definition is consistent with the IOM definition of *near miss*—"…an error of commission or omission that could have harmed the patient, but serious harm did not occur as a result of change, prevention, or mitigation."[5] It is also corresponds with the definition of *near miss* used in The Joint Commission's current Sentinel Event Policy—"Any process variation that did not affect an outcome but for which a recurrence carries a significant chance of a serious adverse outcome."[15] In the planned revisions to the Sentinel Event Policy, a "patient safety incident" is an event or circumstance that could have resulted, or did result, in unnecessary harm to a patient.[14] Patient safety incidents include the following:

Adverse event—An incident that resulted in harm to a patient.

No harm event—An incident that reached a patient but no discernable harm resulted.

Close call—An incident that did not reach the patient (also called "near miss").

Hazardous circumstance—A situation in which there was potential for harm, but no incident occurred. Includes hazards, unsafe conditions, and unusual occurrences.[14]

Close calls are considered the most information-rich incidents because of the potential benefit from the learning without the consequence of patient harm. No-harm events, however, point to more serious system vulnerabilities than close calls because they represent a failure of error-recovery systems (resulting in the incidents reaching the patient).

WHO SHOULD READ THIS BOOK?

The Value of Close Calls in Improving Patient Safety: Learning How to Avoid and Mitigate Patient Harm was developed for leaders and practitioners in health care organizations, including medical directors, patient safety officers, risk managers, physicians, nurses, performance improvement professionals, physician assistants, nurse practitioners, nurses, and pharmacists. Indeed, the book is relevant to health care staff in both clinical and nonclinical areas, including office mangers, medical records clerks, laboratory technicians, and environmental services staff.

A GUIDE TO THIS BOOK

This book consists of two parts. Part 1 (Chapters 1–5) provides a guide to what the literature tells us about the concept of close calls and their identification, relationship with errors, and use in assessing and improving the safety and reliability of health care (and aviation). Part II (Chapters 6–20) provides 15 detailed case studies from a variety of clinical disciplines and specialties to show how the health care organizations in which the close calls occurred used them to identify, investigate, and solve patient safety problems.

Part I
Chapter 1. **Close Calls in Health Care**
This chapter explains how close calls relate to current models of quality of care and error causation. It focuses on how concepts and tools used by high-reliability organizations (HROs) in other industries might be adapted to understand and manage safety in health care. It reviews mechanisms for using close calls to identify hazards and to design interventions to improve patient safety. Finally, it describes barriers to learning from close calls and proposes strategies to overcome them and enhance learning.

Chapter 2. **Reporting and Learning from Close Calls**
Reporting systems are necessary to capture information about errors and close calls so that it can be used to improve safety. This chapter reviews the role of reporting systems in health care organizations and focuses on systems that collect information on close calls. It also addresses how this information can be used to improve systems and safety.

Chapter 3. **Promoting Meaningful Close-Call Reporting: Lessons from Aviation**
Close calls have been collected and used to improve safety in a number of high-risk industries. This chapter describes the importance of confidential, nonpunitive, and protected reporting in aviation. In his engaging account, Professor

Dekker, who is also a working commercial airline pilot, explores the many issues that need to be considered in reporting, aggregating, and analyzing close-call information to change actual processes and behaviors.

Chapter 4. Human Factors Applications to Understanding and Using Close Calls to Improve Health Care

The field of human factors brings a wealth of knowledge about human performance and how systems can be designed to reduce the risk of error. This chapter introduces the theory and basic principles of human factors, including how issues in care processes, equipment, environment of care, and the workplace can be designed to avoid patient harm.

Chapter 5. Disclosing Close Calls to Patients and Their Families

This chapter explains the obligations of health care organizations and health care providers to disclose adverse events, along with a subset of close-call events, to patients and their families. It suggests ways in which disclosure of close-call events can be conducted to best meet patients' medical, emotional, and informational needs.

Part II

The 15 case-study chapters are grouped on the basis of where they fall according to the three characteristics in the IOM definition of close-call events[5]:

1. Prevention (for example, a potentially lethal overdose was prescribed, but a nurse identified the error before administering the medication)—"Event Prevented Before Reaching the Patient."

2. A act of commission or omission that could have caused harm, but serious harm did not occur as a result of chance (for example, the patient received a contraindicated drug but did not experience an adverse drug reaction)—"Event Reached the Patient but did No Harm."

3. Mitigation (for example, a lethal drug overdose was administered but discovered early and countered with an antidote)—"Event Reached the Patient, but Harm was Mitigated"

Although close calls contain more information about the successful recovery mechanisms, case studies involving harm that reached the patient can also reveal system vulnerabilities, as argued earlier.

Event Prevented Before Reaching the Patient

Many errors occur in the ambulatory setting. In Chapter 6, Siegel and Gandhi describe a series of related incidents that highlight barriers to patients attempting to complete screening colonoscopy. Interviews with frontline staff revealed an inefficient and error-prone referral process. The solution was the redesign of the process in a way that consolidated parallel scheduling efforts and relieved primary care physicians of responsibilities that could be handled more reliably by others.

Look-alike packaging of medications is common and can lead to disaster when high-risk neuromuscular blocking agents are involved. In Chapter 7, U and Salsman report a narrowly averted incident in which two simultaneous changes in packaging resulted in look-alike vials of sodium chloride and succinylcholine. A nationwide safety bulletin in Canada and discussions with the manufacturer of the products led to changes to packaging and labeling. This case provides an example of a high-level solution that substantially mitigated a hazard.

In Chapter 8, Weingart and colleagues describe a near-overdose of chemotherapy in oncology. Notably, the pharmacy technician's transcription error was detected by the patient's parents, who noticed an unfamiliar-looking dose. A root cause analysis (RCA) identified difficulty by pharmacy staff in reading a handwritten and faxed prescription. Illegibility was compounded by a curious feature of the tamper-proof prescription blanks that produced the word "VOID" across the paper when it was faxed. Solutions included a plan for electronic prescribing and replacement of the prescription forms, with notification of its manufacturer. The case identifies transcription as a high-risk point in the medication use process. In addition, it highlights the rule that no "innovation" is 100% benign and that patients and families can be vigilant partners in patient safety.

Wrong-site surgery is another archetypal sentinel event. In Chapter 9, Ibrahim and Makary describe a case in which a patient's wrong knee came close to being replaced. The RCA revealed several contributing factors, which included the fact that the surgeon who had initialed the correct knee the night before was not present in the operating room (OR) when the patient was draped. Several strategies, including use of a preoperative checklist and increased emphasis on reporting, were implemented, resulting in a decrease in surgical adverse events. However, it is acknowledged that it is difficult to detect decreases in uncommon events such as wrong-site surgery.

Wrong blood events are the signature error in transfusion medicine. In Chapter 10, Rabin Fastman and Kaplan describe a close call that was found to be largely due to "excessive multitasking demands." The corrective action focused on limiting the need for and use of multitasking in the steps involved the transfusion process. Follow-up audits suggested that the fixes had been implemented successfully, and no errors in blood unit issue have since occurred.

Event Reached the Patient but Did No Harm
The radiotherapy-dosing errors described by Barton, Delaney, and Noble in Chapter 11 are somewhat different from the other cases presented in this book. This example is instructive in that the close calls, along with several no-harm events, inspired a new procedure, risk

profiling, for mapping the process of radiotherapy care to guide safety efforts. Remedial actions included redesign of the process, resulting in a reduction in repeat incidents.

Health information technology (IT) is recommended as the solution for many problems in patient safety. However, every solution brings its own problems. In Chapter 12, Abramson and Kaushal describe a drop-down list error associated with use of the hospital's computerized prescription order entry system which resulted in a neonate receiving a dose of the wrong antibiotic. Several IT and non-IT interventions were implemented to make it more difficult to pick the wrong medication.

Misappropriation of expressed breast milk is a well-known problem in pediatrics, if not to those outside this field. In Chapter 13, Rinke, Murphy, and Bundy present a case of a breast-milk swap for two babies in a neonatal intensive care unit. As the authors report, there are many steps (more than 35, as it turned out) in the process of safely delivering breast milk to an infant—and many opportunities for error. The problem proved surprisingly resistant to a series of different interventions, culminating in the adoption of a bar-coding system.

Patients are not always believed by health care workers, a problem that can be especially pronounced in psychiatry. In Chapter 14, Jayaram and Meuchel describe as case in which a patient being admitted on an emergency petition was mistakenly assigned the identity of another patient. This error was detected only after she received more than a week's worth of the other patient's medications—fortunately, with no ill effects. A series of errors and contributing factors, including examination of the medical record rather than face-to-face examination of the patient, was identified. Corrective actions, including using at least two patient identifiers and encouraging person-to-person handoffs, were taken to prevent further patient identification errors.

Event Reached the Patient, but Harm Was Mitigated

In anesthesia, epidural analgesia is an effective form of pain relief but can cause respiratory depression, particularly when co-administered with other sedative medications. In Chapter 15, Pratt describes a recurring series of cases, which were due to resident physicians' lack of knowledge about the problem and their desire for autonomy. Solutions included IT fixes to make it difficult to order inappropriate sedating medications in patients on epidural anesthesia—and education about the changes. As a result, the problem was virtually eliminated.

The emergency department is an environment where medication errors can easily be made. In Chapter 16, Gripper and colleagues describe the case of a patient with chest pain who received a medication that sped up her heart rate rather than the intended medication to slow it. Review of the case revealed that vials of the two medications had been mixed in the same compartment of the automated medication dispensing system—devices that are particularly prone to such "medication displacement." The solution was redesign of the medication bins, with plans for bar-coding of medications and patients.

In Chapter 17, Mann and Pratt describe a hand-off failure in obstetrics—from labor and delivery to the postpartum unit. The investigation identified the lack of standard processes in several areas of clinical management and in handoffs. Solutions included reexamination of the processes and establishment of protocols for common problems (such as decreased urine output) and handoffs.

The event described by Fotenos and Eng in Chapter 18 is a classic example of a retained foreign body after surgery, which was not seen by the radiology resident. Following discovery of the error, the patient was returned to the OR, and the sponges were removed. As in all other such cases, responsibility was shared with surgeons and the OR, technologists, and nurses. In addition, the time-critical task of foreign-body readings was distributed among many radiologists. Solutions included concentrating responsibility for real-time readings to attending radiologists and encouraging direct communication between surgeon and radiologist.

Errors are common in geriatrics, but the full extent of this problem in long term care settings is not well studied. Anticoagulants are a high-risk medication for all age groups. In Chapter 19, Gurwitz and colleagues describe a case involving a warfarin overdose that resulted from a series of errors in communication between the nursing home and covering physicians. The solution offered was structured telephone communication between nurses and physicians; this solution is appealing in that it is "low tech" and readily replicable in almost any setting. A randomized trial of this intervention resulted in a significant improvement of International Normalized Ratio (INR) values within the therapeutic range.[37]

Laboratory medicine is a specialty that for many years has made error reduction a priority, with the majority of emphasis placed on the analytic phase of the "total testing process." In Chapter 20, the case presented by Hilborne and colleagues involved a Papanicolaou smear that was misinterpreted as benign by a medical assistant in the physician's office. This error in the postanalytic phase of testing resulted in delayed diagnosis of cervical cancer. An important contributing factor was the assistant's lack of sufficient knowledge to correctly interpret the test results. One solution offered was for the clinician to "close the loop" by reviewing and responding to all test results.

LEARNING HOW TO AVOID AND MITIGATE PATIENT HARM

Overall, these 15 cases provide real-world illustrations of how health care organizations report incidents and learn from them. It is clear that organizations are making efforts to find the critical weaknesses in their defense systems and to improve patient safety by preventing or mitigating them. However, there is currently no commonly agreed way to do this and, indeed, no agreed framework for how to approach it, despite calls to standardize methods for investigation.[12,14] Investigations range from formal RCAs organized at the institutional level, such as that reported by Weingart and colleagues in Chapter 8; to "lighter" RCA, as reported by Ibrahim and Makary (Chapter 9); to still less structured methods, such as the multidisciplinary medication safety task force reported by Abramson and Kaushal (Chapter 12). There is even less consensus on how health care organizations should intervene to effect changes and improve safety. Many organizations are just beginning to develop the safety culture and infrastructure "that enable identification of system vulnerabilities and support the development of actions to reduce risk."[14(p. 4)] The experiences of the health care organizations, as represented in these cases, should help other organizations as they learn how to use close calls to avoid and mitigate patient harm.

References

1. World Health Assembly Resolution 55.18: *Quality of care: patient safety. 55th World Health Assembly.* Geneva, May 18, 2002.
2. Leape L.: Is hospital patient care becoming safer? A conversation with Lucian Leape. Interview by Peter I. Buerhaus. *Health Aff (Millwood)* 26:w687–w696, Nov.–Dec. 2007.
3. Wachter R.M.: Patient safety at ten: Unmistakable progress, troubling gaps. *Health Aff (Millwood)* 29:165–73, Jan.–Feb. 2010.
4. The Joint Commission: *Sentinel Event Policies and Procedures.* http://www.jointcommission.org/ SentinelEvents/PolicyandProcedures/se_pp.htm (accessed Oct. 6, 2010).
5. Institute of Medicine: *Patient Safety: Achieving a New Standard for Care.* Washington, DC: National Academies Press, 2004. http://www.nap.edu/openbook.php?record_id= 10863&page=332 (accessed Sep. 1, 2010).
6. Parnes B., et al.: Stopping the error cascade: A report on ameliorators from the ASIPS collaborative. *Qual Saf Health Care* 16:12–16, Feb. 2007.
7. Patel V.L., Cohen T.: New perspectives on error in critical care. *Curr Opin Crit Care* 14:456–459, Aug. 2008.
8. Reason J.T.: *Human Error.* New York: Cambridge University Press, 1990.
9. Reason J.: Human error: Models and management. *West J Med* 172:393–396, Jun. 2000.
10. Morlock L., et al.: Comparing near miss and harmful medication errors. *BMJ,* forthcoming.
11. Habraken M.M., van der Schaaf T.W.: If only…: Failed, missed and absent error recovery opportunities in medication errors. *Qual Saf Health Care* 19:37–41, Feb. 2010.
12. Wu A.W., Lipshutz A.K., Pronovost P.J.: Effectiveness and efficiency of root cause analysis in medicine. *JAMA*; 299:685–687, Feb. 13 ,2008.
13. Pronovost P.J., et al.: Reducing health care hazards: Lessons from the commercial aviation safety team. *Health Aff (Millwood)* 28:w479-w89, May–Jun. 2009. Epub Dec. 11, 2009.
14. Looking at sentinel events along the continuum of patient safety: A future direction for the Sentinel Event Policy. *Jt Comm Persp* 30:3–5, Aug. 2010.
15. The Joint Commission: *2010 Comprehensive Accreditation Manual for Hospitals: The Official Handbook.* Oak Brook, IL: Joint Commission Resources, 2009.
16. Joint Commission International: *Joint Commission International Accreditation Standards for Hospitals,* 4th ed. Oak Brook, IL: Joint Commission Resources, 2010.
17. Affonso D., Jeffs L.: Near misses: Lessons learned in the processes of care. *International Nursing Perspectives* 4:15–122, Sep.–Oct. 2004.
18. Yu K.H., Nation R.L., Dooley M.J.: Multiplicity of medication safety terms, definitions and functional meanings: When is enough enough? *Qual Saf Health Care* 14:358–363, Oct. 2005.
19. Etchegaray J.M., et al.: Differentiating close calls from errors: A multidisciplinary perspective. *J Patient Saf* 1:133–137, 2005.
20. Clancy C.M.: Common formats allow uniform collection and reporting of patient safety data by patient safety organizations. *Am J Med Qual* 25:73–75, Jan.–Feb. 2010.
21. Kessels-Habraken M., et al.: Defining near misses: Towards a sharpened definition based on empirical data about error handling processes. *Soc Sci Med* 70:1301–1308, May 2010.
22. Institute for Safe Medication Practices (ISMP): ISMP survey helps define and near miss and close call! *ISMP Medication Safety Alert! Acute Care* 14:1–2, Sep. 24, 2009. http://www.ismp.org/newsletters/acutecare/ articles/20090924.asp (accessed Oct. 27, 2010).
23. Barnard D., et al.: Implementing a good catch program in an integrated health system. *Healthc Q* 9(Spec.):22–27, Oct. 2006.
24. Kaplan H.S., Rabin Fastman B.: Organization of event reporting data for sense making and system improvement. *Qual Saf Health Care* 12(Suppl. 2):ii68–ii72, Dec. 2003.

25. Runciman W., et al.: Towards an international classification for patient safety: Key concepts and terms. *Int J Qual Health Care* 21:18–26, Feb. 2009.

26. Nashef S.A.: What is a near miss? *Lancet* 361(9352): 180–181, Jan. 11, 2003.

27. Alper S.J., Karsh B.T.: A systematic review of safety violations in industry. *Accid Anal Prev* 41:739–754, Jul. 2009. Epub Apr. 18, 2009.

28. Bogner M.S. (ed.): *Human Error in Medicine.* Hillsdale, NJ: Lawrence Erlbaum Associates, Inc. 1994.

29. Agency for Healthcare Research and Quality: *Patient Safety Network.* http://www.psnet.ahrq.gov. (accessed Sept. 9, 2010).

30. Barach P., Small S.D., Kaplan H.: Designing a confidential safety reporting system: In depth review of thirty major medical incident reporting systems, and near-miss safety reporting systems in the nuclear, aviation and petrochemical industries. *Anesthesiology* 91:A1209, 1999.

31. Barach P., Small S.D.: Reporting and preventing medical mishaps: Lessons from non-medical near miss reporting systems. *BMJ* 320(7237):759–763, Mar. 2000.

32. Gurwitz J.H., et al.: Incidence and preventability of adverse drug events in nursing homes. *Am J Med* 109:87–94, Aug. 2000.

33. U.S. Agency for Healthcare Research and Quality: *Concepts Underlying Common Formats Event Descriptions.* http://www.pso.ahrq.gov/formats/eventdesc.htm (accessed Oct. 7, 2010).

34. National Coordinating Council for Medication Error Reporting and Prevention: *NCC MERP Index for Categorizing Medication Errors.* http://www.nccmerp.org/pdf/indexColor2001-06-12.pdf (accessed Sep. 9, 2010)

35. World Health Organization *Draft Guidelines for Adverse Event Reporting and Learning Systems: From Information to Action.* http://www.who.int/patientsafety/events/05/Reporting_Guidelines.pdf (accessed Sep. 9, 2010)

36. Veterans Health Administration National Center for Patient Safety: *Presentation to the National Committee on Vital and Health Statistics, Subcommittee on Populations, Work group on Quality.* Ann Arbor, MI: Veterans Health Administration, National Center for Patient Safety, 2001.

37. Field T.S., et al.: Randomized trial of a warfarin communication protocol for nursing homes: An SBAR-based approach. *Am J Med,* in press.

PART I

Close Calls and Patient Safety

CHAPTER 1

Close Calls in Health Care

Fiona Pathiraja, M.B.B.S., B.Sc., D.H.M.S.A., D.R.C.O.G.; Marie-Claire Wilson, M.A. (Cantab), M.B.B.S.; Peter J. Pronovost, M.D., Ph.D.

Despite advances in modern medicine, patients around the world are still placed at risk by the very organizations designed to alleviate their illness. Patient safety is a rapidly emerging field in medicine that has learned from high-reliability organizations (HROs) in other industries, such as aviation and nuclear power, where the potential for error and subsequent disaster is high. A basic component of any HRO is the ability to identify and mitigate hazards. This is typically accomplished with error-reporting systems in which frontline operators report both errors that result in and harm or close calls. Close calls are generally several times more common than harmful errors, making them a rich source of information about improving patient safety. In this chapter, we describe a model for learning from close calls and review strategies for using them to understand and manage safety in health care.

DEFINITION OF *CLOSE CALL*

As discussed in the Introduction, the proposed definition of *close call* for the purposes of this book is "An event or a situation that did not produce patient harm because it did not reach the patient, either due to chance or to capture before reaching the patient; or if it did reach the patient, due to robustness of the patient or to timely intervention (for example, an antidote was administered)." However, different operational definitions are employed in the context of different branches of medicine, as shown in the following examples:

- Operation site wrongly labeled initially but corrected before to the start of operation by the operating room team (surgery)
- ABO mismatch (mismatch among blood types A, B, and O) between patient and blood prepared for transfusion recognized by physician before transfusion and therefore not transfused (transfusion medicine)
- Wrong patient brought for a procedure, but the patient alerts medical staff before being taken from the ward (intervention)
- Prescription-dosing error by physician written in patient's chart, which is recognized by a pharmacist. Medication is not administered until the dose is corrected and rechecked (drug error)

EPIDEMIOLOGY OF CLOSE CALLS

It is difficult to obtain an accurate impression of the incidence and prevalence of close calls because of the lack of standardization of nomenclature and definitions, combined with varying interpretations in different specialties, organizations, and countries. Another contributing factor is that detection of close calls depends almost entirely on voluntary reporting.

There is greater consensus about the burden of adverse events in health care. An Institute of

Medicine (IOM) report stated that health care in the United States is not as safe as it could be, with between 44,000 and 98,000 preventable deaths (as derived from hospital records) and many more injuries occurring in hospitals in the United States each year.[1] This annual burden is more than the combined number of deaths and injuries from motor and air crashes, suicides, falls, poisonings, and drowning.[2] The estimated cost of deaths in hospital in the United States is between $17 and $29 billion.[1] In the United Kingdom, the National Health Service (NHS) reported 974,000 patient safety incidents and close calls—not including health care–associated infections, which would have increased the total by an estimated 300,000.[3] Patient safety incidents alone cost the NHS an estimated £2 billion per year in extra bed days, with health care–associated infection costing an estimated further £1 billion. Because adverse events are known to be underreported by 50% to 96%, these figures are likely to be underestimates.[4]

Although close calls are significantly more common than adverse events, they are even less likely to be recorded. It has been estimated that for each preventable death, there are between 7 and 100 close calls that occur before it.[5] It is recommended that close calls be reported via local and national reporting systems.[2,6] Although this recommendation is not implemented widely, there are some local cases of success. For example, the Pennsylvania Patient Safety Reporting System (PA-PSRS) collects more than 200,000 reports per year, 97% of which are close-call events.[7,8]

THEORETICAL BASIS: HOW HEALTH CARE COULD LEARN FROM CLOSE CALLS

The traditional approach to medicine was based on the knowledge and skills of the individual clinician and his or her interaction with the patient. A corollary of this approach was the expectation that a trained and competent clinician does not make errors—error was the reserve

of those who were incompetent, and blame and punitive measures were needed to keep the incompetent few in check. Individual factors such as fatigue, interruptions, and overreliance on memory are important considerations when improving patient safety. Health care professionals can easily recognize and understand these factors as potential causes of adverse events.

Modern thinking about medicine has evolved beyond the individual patient–physician interaction to the reality of multidisciplinary teams working within organizations. The delivery of health care takes place within this system, and patient safety can be understood as a property of system that includes many structures, processes, and professionals. It is necessary to move toward integrating individual factors into a systems-based model, considering the processes, behaviors, and interactions that can lead to particular outcomes.

The complexity inherent in such systems presents multiple points where failures can occur. James Reason proposed a Swiss cheese model of how system accidents occur with health care processes. In this model, there are multiple layers, each of which serves as a mechanism that defends against an error leading to patient harm. Holes in each layer of cheese represent opportunities for failures to progress and reach the patient (*see* Figure 1-1, page 5).[9] When all of the holes in various layers align, an error can reach the patient.

Some of the holes occur at the "sharp end" of the system—at the frontline of patient care, such as, the operating room (OR) or emergency department (ED).[10] They may lead to active errors. An example of an active error would be the wrong dose of a drug being administered in the ED, to which the patient has a severe allergy (for example, penicillin). In general, an incident that causes patient harm involves a cascade of error and events.

Reason also describes latent conditions that reside in systems.[9] These latent conditions are

Figure 1-1. James Reason's Swiss Cheese Model

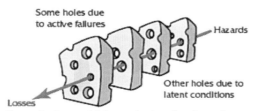

The Swiss Cheese Model of Accident Causation

Some holes due to active failures

Hazards

Other holes due to latent conditions

Losses

Successive layers of defenses, barriers, & safeguards

Source: Reason J.: Human error: Models and management. *BMJ* 320(7237):768–770, Mar. 18, 2000. Used with permission from the BMJ Publishing Group.

errors that are "waiting to happen" and may contribute to active failures. These latent conditions occur at the blunt end of a system and become intangible and therefore difficult to identify. For example, the active error of penicillin being administered to an allergic patient in the ED may have been allowed by a latent error in the system, such as the use of an unfamiliar color-coded sticker for penicillin allergy placed in the patient's chart. The stickers may have been introduced recently, with their use not widely publicized.

To prevent further occurrences of error, simply reminding ED staff of the need to ask patients about allergies may not be sufficient. The latent errors, which could include inconsistent documentation procedures between departments and poor communication between managers and frontline staff, would need to be addressed in a systematic manner.

A "hole in the cheese" could lead to a close call, which is subsequently blocked by slices more proximal to the patient. Identifying these "holes" can provide valuable information on where the system is likely to go wrong again; close calls and adverse events often demonstrate the same underlying patterns of failure.[11]

Improving system resilience—the ability to recognize and react to failure within a care process—can help to prevent harm. For example, studies on medication errors have demonstrated that nursing staff were responsible for intercepting 86% of all medication errors before the medication was given.[12] Thus, empowering and educating groups of staff to their role in close-call identification could improve patient safety.

Although it is likely impossible to reduce the number of medical errors to zero, it is important that health care organizations attempt to ensure that systems are designed to drive error rates toward zero. This is because even a small margin for error will lead to significant consequences. For example, it has been estimated that a 600-bed teaching hospital with 99.9% error-free drug procurement, dispensing, and administration will still experience 4,000 drug errors a year.[13]

High-Reliability Organizations

Complex, high-risk, high-impact industries such as aviation and nuclear power—where the potential for error and subsequent disaster is very high—put systems in place that consistently attain quality outcomes despite facing many unexpected events. They recognize and respond to weak danger signals and are particularly attuned to close-call events.[14] The objective behind high-reliability philosophy is to create a culture and processes that reduce system failures and respond effectively and appropriately when failures do occur. Health care systems, which are inherently complex, incorporating many interacting layers and a variety of subsystems, need to become HROs with systems in place to eliminate error.

Human Factors Engineering

Human factors engineering (HFE) is another field of study that has contributed to our understanding of errors in health care. Human factors engineers consider close calls as one type of outcome of errors or violations. They also consider them to be special because the system defenses may have prevented harm—that is, the error may have been detected and corrected before harm could occur or by chance the error may not have caused harm. Evaluating close calls allows us to see the traps that we fall into over and over again that have not caused harm to determine how to prevent harm from occurring at some point. Close calls that do not arise from chance can inform HFE professionals about error recovery pathways present in the work system—the mechanisms in the system that help detect close calls—and correct them to prevent errors from reaching the patient or causing harm. These recovery pathways can be characterized and incorporated formally as a system defense to promote recovery in the future. Close calls are also an important reminder to health care organizations that their systems contain the preconditions for unsafe acts, (that is, errors). Therefore, the potential value of information on close calls suggests that organizations should compile reports of close calls and disseminate this information regularly to all staff so that staff are reminded to remain sensitive to error occurrence at all times.[15,16]

Recent research suggests that there is a difference in error recovery efforts between events that (1) do not reach the patient and those that (2) reach the patient but do not cause harm.[17] This suggests that whatever the definition used, it is important to identify errors and violations that do not cause harm, whether or not they reach the patient, as understanding error recovery mechanisms is important for error management.

MODEL FOR LEARNING FROM CLOSE CALLS

In order to learn from close calls, an organization can apply the following four steps: (1) identify hazards, (2) prioritize risks, (3) investigate events and intervene to reduce risks, and (4) evaluate whether risks were reduced.[18] These steps are now described in more detail.

Identify Risks and Hazards
As described in detail in Chapter 2, patient

safety reporting systems are a valuable tool for identifing and helping mitigate hazards.[19] Typically, these systems are used to describe individual incidents in detail, identify causes and contributing factors, and occasionally identify mitigating factors. This method can be helpful at the local level, within a hospital or health care organization, as well as higher, ranging up to country level.[20] Reporting systems are generally Web based but may also collect data on paper or by telephone. Some organizations make very effective use of 24-hour phone hotlines, staffed by trusted personnel, to capture reports about patient safety incidents.[21]

In addition to formal reporting systems, the wisdom of frontline health care staff can also be tapped efficiently by simply asking them how the next patient will be harmed. Information from different perspectives, ranging from frontline clinicians to risk managers to even patients, can provide complementary information.[22] All of these systems can accommodate close calls as well as events that cause significant harm.

Prioritize Risks
As discussed in Chapter 2, where incident reporting has been adopted successfully, a new dilemma is that the responsible organizations are now drowning in reports. For example, Johns Hopkins Medicine receives more than 1,000 reports per month through its online incident reporting system.[23] It is not possible to investigate all of them, much less fix all the problems underlying these cases. A mechanism is needed to prioritize them, yet there is no established way to do this. In the investigation of hazards within a health system, Reason suggests asking three questions to predict where unforeseen events are most likely to occur[9]:

1. *The "hands-on" question:* Which activities involve the most direct human interaction with the system?

2. *The "criticality" question:* Which activities, if executed inadequately, have the greatest potential for harm?

3. *The "frequency" question:* How often are these activities performed in routine operations?

These questions can be applied to incidents submitted to a reporting system and could be particularly useful to help identify close calls that deserve to be investigated. It might be useful to investigate errors with a high potential to cause harm that reached the patient but did not cause harm due to chance alone. In these cases, the error was not caught because defenses failed, while in others there may have been no defenses present at all.

The National Reporting and Learning System, which is deployed in the United Kingdom for the reporting of patient safety incidents, poses an extreme case, with more than 1 million incidents reported since its inception. To help prioritize among these, investigators have developed the "Harm Susceptibility Model," a statistical method to identify organizations or work areas with low resiliency, for example, in which a high proportion of errors result in harm.[24]

Investigate Events and Intervene to Reduce Risks

In the next step, incidents that are assigned a sufficiently high priority are subjected to a detailed investigation. The findings of this investigation are used to select an intervention, which is then implemented to reduce risks.

The initial investigation requires an understanding of the role of systems in patient safety, as well as the systems involved in the case of the specific care processes where failure occurred. The nested hierarchy developed by Vincent reflects the recognition that an adverse events may be due to several interlocking factors (*see* Figure 1-2, page 8).[25] The model also accounts for latent failures being transmitted through the system. Stratification of the key factors that influence clinical practice provides a framework to structure investigations into close calls and adverse events. Information for the investigation is obtained from multiple sources, including

interviewing staff, examining medical records, reviewing the literature, and re-enacting events.

Reducing risk requires identifying important hazards, prioritizing the most important among them, and targeting interventions to defend against those risks.[26]

Nolan outlines key measures for reducing errors and adverse events across a system, which fall into the following five categories[27]:

1. Reducing complexity in processes

2. Optimizing information processing

3. Automating wisely (for example, judicious use of robotic packaging for medications)

4. Using constraints (for example, physical, procedural, and cultural) when necessary

5. Mitigating the unwanted side effects of the change

Interventions vary in their strength and the probability that they will reduce risks.[28] In general, the intervention that is likely to have the biggest impact on outcome should be selected. Health care systems are complex, with potential for error on multiple levels, from the frontline to strategy. Interventions to reduce error should therefore address the various levels, including streamlining of systems to reduce errors on the macro level, and individual education at the practitioner level, covering topics such as the factors involved in decision-making processes. Investigations into close calls should likewise involve analysis at all levels, from the patient through the institution. This is greatly facilitated in a culture that places importance on safety and openness.

Evaluate Whether Risks Were Reduced

This is a challenging task because it is difficult to measure reduction in events, and it is rarely possible to measure recurrent incidents as rates. In a few clinical areas, it is possible to identify rate-based measures, such as the incidence of bloodstream infection. In other cases, it is possible to

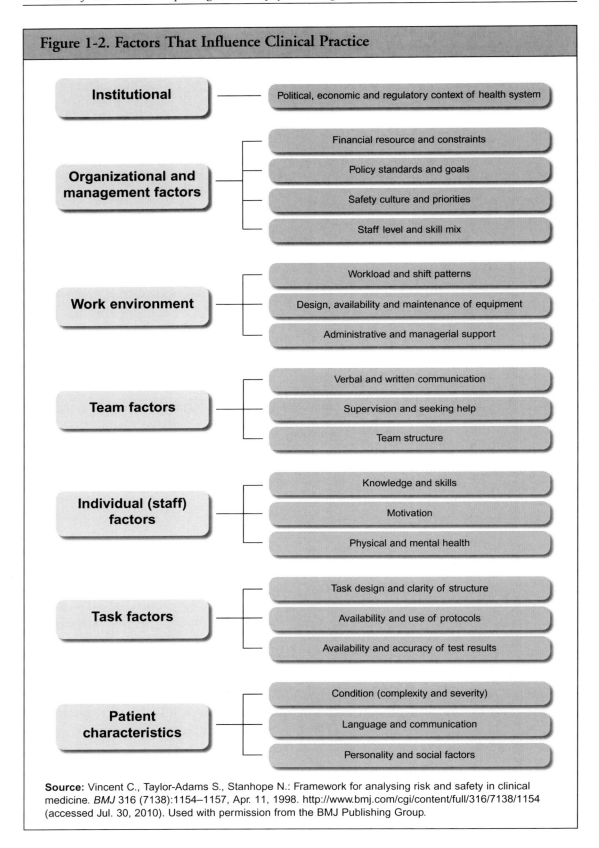

Figure 1-2. Factors That Influence Clinical Practice

Institutional — Political, economic and regulatory context of health system

Organizational and management factors —
- Financial resource and constraints
- Policy standards and goals
- Safety culture and priorities
- Staff level and skill mix

Work environment —
- Workload and shift patterns
- Design, availability and maintenance of equipment
- Administrative and managerial support

Team factors —
- Verbal and written communication
- Supervision and seeking help
- Team structure

Individual (staff) factors —
- Knowledge and skills
- Motivation
- Physical and mental health

Task factors —
- Task design and clarity of structure
- Availability and use of protocols
- Availability and accuracy of test results

Patient characteristics —
- Condition (complexity and severity)
- Language and communication
- Personality and social factors

Source: Vincent C., Taylor-Adams S., Stanhope N.: Framework for analysing risk and safety in clinical medicine. *BMJ* 316 (7138):1154–1157, Apr. 11, 1998. http://www.bmj.com/cgi/content/full/316/7138/1154 (accessed Jul. 30, 2010). Used with permission from the BMJ Publishing Group.

develop measures to evaluate the reliability with which the intervention itself is delivered. There are additional sources of information that can be employed. Listed from the least valid and least resource intensive to the most valid and most resource intensive, it is possible to measure the creation of a policy or procedure; staff awareness of that policy; whether or not the policy or procedure is being executed as intended (by audit or direct observation of practice); and whether staff believe risks were reduced (by standardized survey of staff about perceptions of risks reduction).

The overall premise of learning from close calls is reinforced by recent findings that the system factors that contributed to adverse events are the same for both near misses and adverse events.[29]

BARRIERS TO LEARNING FROM CLOSE CALLS

There are several important barriers that prevent health care organizations from using close calls to improve patient safety: lack of familiarity of the science of safety in general, underappreciation of the importance the of close calls in particular, lack of accountability for patient safety, and resource limitations.

Although understanding of the science of safety is growing among health care workers, many do not fully appreciate the dual role played by individual providers operating within a larger system of care. There is a persistent tendency to want to blame individual providers for the errors they make in care. What is required is accomplishing a shift in the question asked after a safety incident from "Who was responsible?" to "Why did this happen?"[12] One advantage of close-call events is that because there was no harm, these events are easier to report and can be handled with less anxiety about blame.

Many clinicians and leaders of health care organizations do not appreciate the important threat posed by close calls and the corresponding opportunity to improve safety. HROs pay close attention to close calls, worrying about why a close call has challenged their system. Less sophisticated organizations often view a close call as reassuring proof of the system's resilience.[14] In fact, studies have shown that following a close call, organizations may develop a false sense of security regarding the system's reliability and ability to recover from potentially harmful events.[30] However, closer examination reveals just the contrary. For example, examination of the 2% subset (266 of 12,303 total reports in one study) of all transfusion service event reports that were considered as high risk by the reporting institutions showed that fully 90% of these events were considered to be close calls.[31] Although it is understandable that top-level managers are more highly motivated to act by conspicuous events that cause harm, they need to be persuaded that at least some close calls also warrant action.

An additional problem is that frontline clinicians and unit-level managers may not feel empowered or able to act to reduce hazards suggested by close calls.[32] They may judge that this is the responsibility of the organization's patient safety department.

One solution to overcome this barrier is to deploy interventions to improve safety at multiple levels of the health care system: senior leaders, local team leaders, and frontline staff. Although some projects should be dictated from the "top down," such as making changes to a hospital computerized provider entry system, other projects are best conducted at the unit level. An example of this is the Comprehensive Unit-based Safety Program (CUSP), which allows health care organizations to develop broad strategy to improve safety but at the same time incorporates local concerns and the wisdom of staff in individual care areas.[33] One proposal might be for local unit teams to focus on learning from near misses, while hospital risk and safety departments take primary responsibility for handling harmful events.

Finally, health care organizations often have limited financial and human resources to work with, including resources available to devote to patient safety. Greater appreciation for the importance of close calls can help organizations to more fully exploit this important source of information.

STRATEGIES FOR HOW HEALTH CARE ORGANIZATIONS CAN LEARN FROM CLOSE CALLS

There are several concrete strategies that health care organizations can take to enhance learning from errors and close calls. These include increasing clinician engagement, increasing executive involvement and accountability, enriching educational activities, and creating institutional policies and structures.

Increasing Clinician Engagement

Clinicians often view patient safety initiatives and protocols as being removed from their daily duty of attending to the patients sitting in front of them. However, the very concept of patient safety engages clinicians on one of the central tenets of medical professionalism: "Above all, do no harm." This simple statement, often attributed to Hippocrates[34] (and cited by Lucian Leape in an influential article[35]), strikes at the core value of nonmaleficence. Medicine is a value-driven culture where nonmaleficence is highly prioritized as one of the core values that comprise one's professional integrity. Therefore, if patient safety initiatives are to be truly successful, they need to engage clinicians on this value. To accomplish this, local cases that demonstrate the emotional impact of medical errors on patients can be especially effective.

One goal is to increase safety awareness by making more people aware of safety concerns more of the time and by placing responsibility of identifying close calls and hazards to all health care workers, rather than those strictly concerned with safety. Cases of close calls can be introduced systematically into the clinical routine. Work rounds could include a routine query about

errors, including close calls, that occurred during the previous shift. Frontline providers can also be asked on a regular basis about hazards, perhaps most directly about how they think that the next patient is likely to be injured.[18]

It should be emphasized that health care workers other than physicians and nurses can also play an important role in reporting hazards. An important goal would be to shift the task of identifying unsafe operations from frontline clinicians to a larger workforce that has contacts with processes and equipment at all levels of the health care system.

Increasing Executive-Level Involvement and Accountability

Patient safety should be included as a regular agenda item at a health care organization's executive board meetings.[36] Just as the board would expect to know about financial flows and business processes, it should expect robust information about patient safety in its part of the health system, especially as organizations are increasingly held accountable for patient outcomes. After the investigation of an adverse event or a significant close call, the board can serve to "close the loop" in determining whether the prescribed intervention was deployed—and to what effect.

Enriching Education

Medical education has traditionally taught that if one learns diligently, keeps up to date, has a good knowledge base, and applies it precisely, then one will not make mistakes.[37] A recent report, *Unmet Needs: Teaching Physicians to Provide Safe Patient Care*, reveals that the medical education system does not provide for the teaching of safety science nor equip new doctors with the interpersonal skills they need to practice safely.[38] The report recommends that medical schools and teaching hospitals create "learning cultures that emphasize patient safety, model professionalism, enhance collaborative behavior, encourage transparency, and value the individual learner."[38,p. 2]

Close calls present numerous, fertile opportunities for teaching and learning around system thinking and safety culture.[39] There are few settings where physicians routinely discuss error, such as morbidity and mortality programs and conferences, which were adapted at some institutions to promote safety. For example, a program in anesthesiology was redesigned to focus on cases that do not involve harm, including close calls, to identify trends and implement policies to prevent future error and harm (online extras available at http://www.jcrinc.com/VNM10/Extras).[40] Also, a teaching hospital established a patient safety morbidity and mortality conference as a forum for informing frontline providers about adverse events that occur at the hospital and engage participants' input in root cause analysis, thereby encouraging reporting and promoting systems-based thinking among clinicians (online extras available at http://www.jcrinc.com/VNM10/Extras).[41] This conference also involves presentation of a "Good Catch" award, given to an individual who has reported an error or error-prone situation caught before it reached a patient.

Creating Institutional Policies and Structures

Health care organizations can set expectations by developing policies, procedures, and other structures for handling adverse events, including close calls. Policies should be established to assure health care workers that reporting a close call should be confidential and should carry no risk of reprisal; indeed, it should be linked to reward, where appropriate. Organizations should create an expectation that it is a clinical responsibility for frontline health care professionals and explain what is to be reported.

Mechanisms should be put into place so that the reporting process is simple and not time consuming or bureaucratic. It is important that it not be viewed as yet another burden. Although online reporting should comprise the mainstay of a reporting system, other channels should be provided for incident reporting, including a telephone hotline.

Organizations should demonstrate how information on close calls and other incidents is being used. Ideally, there should be demonstrable changes that are important to patients and health care professionals. Mechanisms should be put in place for information sharing, both at the level of individual institutions, and at the level of state, professional, and national organizations so that more individuals can benefit from the findings of any particular hospital or clinic.

CONCLUSIONS

Health care organizations and clinicians have learned from other industries to gain a growing understanding the role of system factors in patient safety. However, in health care, events that cause harm claim the majority of attention, to the exclusion of valuable information posed by close calls. We now know that harmful events and close calls are caused by essentially the same system factors and that the occurrence of harm is most often due simply to chance.[29] Theory from HROs supports the value of learning from close calls, which can provide information about both hazards and strategies for recovery.

Understanding of close calls can provide practitioners, institutions, and government agencies with valuable information on weaknesses in their health care systems. Reporting and learning from close calls must not be restricted to the hospital but should be applied across the health care continuum, including care delivered in ambulatory settings and elsewhere in the community. In the end, both close calls and incidents involving patient harm provide vital and complementary information—and both deserve the resources to be investigated and remedied.

References

1. Institute of Medicine: *To Err Is Human: Building a Safer Health System.* Washington, DC: National Academy Press, 2000.
2. Baker S.P., et al.: *The Injury Fact Book,* 2nd ed. New York City: Oxford University Press, 1992.
3. National Audit Office: *A Safer Place for Patients: Learning to Improve Patient Safety.* London: National Audit Office, 2005.

4. Barach P., Small, S.D.: Reporting and preventing medical mishaps: Lessons from non-medical near miss reporting systems. *BMJ* 320:759–763, Mar. 18, 2000.

5. Institute of Medicine: *Patient Safety: Achieving a New Standard for Care.* Washington, DC: National Academies Press, 2004.

6. Department of Health: Safety first: A report for patients, clinicians and healthcare managers. London: Department of Health, England, 2006.

7. Marella W.M.: Why worry about near misses? *Patient Safety & Quality Healthcare* 4:22–26, Sep./Oct. 2007.

8. Greenberg C.C.: Learning from adverse events and near misses. *J Gastrointest Surg* 13:3–5, Mar. 2009. Epub Sep. 17, 2008.

9. Reason J.: Human error: Models and management. *BMJ* 320:768–770, Mar. 18, 2000. http://www.ncbi.nlm.nih.gov/pmc/articles/PMC1117770/ (accessed Jul. 30, 2010).

10. Emanuel L., et al.: What exactly is patient safety? *Advances in Patient Safety: New Directions and Alternative Approaches*, Vol. 1., Aug. 2008. Rockville, MD: Agency for Healthcare Research and Quality. http://www.ahrq.gov/downloads/pub/advances2/vol1/advances-emanuel-berwick_110.pdf (accessed Oct. 19, 2010).

11. Lamb B.W., Nagpal K.: Importance of near misses [letter]. *BMJ* 339:3032, Jul. 21, 2009.

12. Hughes R.G.: First, do no harm: Avoiding the near misses. *Am J Nurs* 104:83–84, Aug. 2004.

13. Leape L.: The preventability of medical injury. In Bogner M.S. (ed.).: *Human Error in Medicine.* Hillsdale, NJ: Lawrence Erlbaum Associates, 1994, pp.13–25.

14. Weick K.E., Sutcliffe K.M.: *Managing the Unexpected: Assuring High Performance in an Age of Complexity.* San Francisco: Jossey-Bass, 2001.

15. Alper S.J., Karsh B.T.: A systematic review of safety violations in industry. *Accid Anal Prev* 41:739–754, Jul. 2009.

16. Bogner M.S. (ed).: *Human Error in Medicine.* Hillsdale, NJ: Lawrence Erlbaum Associates, Inc. 1994.

17. Kessels-Habraken M., et al.: Defining near misses: Towards a sharpened definition based on empirical data about error handling processes. *Soc Sci Med* 70:1301–1308, May 2010.

18. Pronovost P.J., et al.: Creating high reliability in health care organizations. *Health Serv Res* 41(4 Pt. 2):1599–1617, Aug. 2006.

19. Vincent C.: Incident reporting and patient safety. *BMJ* 334:51, Feb. 8, 2007.

20. National Patient Safety Agency: *Patient Safety Incident Reports in the NHS: National Reporting and Learning System (NRLS)*, Data Summary, Issue 9. London: National Patient Safety Agency, 2008.

21. McDonald T.B., et al.: Responding to patient safety incidents: The "seven pillars." *Qual Saf Health Care* (Epub ahead of print), Mar. 1, 2010.

22. Weingart S., et al.: What can hospitalized patients tell us about adverse events? Learning from patient-reported incidents. *J Gen Intern Med* 20:830–836, Sep. 2005.

23. Personal communication between the author and [A.W.W.] and Lori Paine, R.N., M.S., Director of Patient Safety, Johns Hopkins Hospital, Baltimore, Oct. 11, 2010.

24. Pham J.C., et al.: The harm susceptibility model: A method to prioritise risks identified in patient safety reporting systems. *Qual Saf Health Care* (Epub ahead of print), Apr. 28, 2010.

25. Vincent C., et al.: Framework for analysing risk and safety in clinical medicine. *BMJ* 316:1154–1157, Apr. 11, 1998.

26. Pham J.C., et al.: ReCASTing the RCA: An improved model for performing root cause analyses. *Am J Med Qual* 25:186–191, May–Jun. 2010.

27. Nolan T.W.: System changes to improve patient safety. *BMJ* 320:771–773, Mar. 18, 2000.

28. Woodward H.I., et al.: What have we learned about interventions to reduce medical errors? *Annu Rev Public Health* 31:479–497, Apr. 21, 2010.

29. Morlock L.L.: Comparing near miss and harmful medication errors. *BMJ*, in press.

30. Hubbard D.: *The Failure of Risk Management: Why It's Broken and How to Fix It.* Hoboken, NJ: John Wiley and Sons, Inc., 2009.

31. Personal communication between the author [A.W.W.] and Harold S. Kaplan, M.D., Professor of Clinical Pathology and Director of Transfusion Medicine, Columbia University Medical Center, New York City, Oct. 19, 2010.

32. Sexton J.B., et al.: The Safety Attitudes Questionnaire: Psychometric properties, benchmarking data, and emerging research. *BMC Health Serv Res* 6:44, Apr. 3, 2006.

33. Pronovost P.J., et al.: A web-based tool for the Comprehensive Unit-based Safety Program (CUSP). *Jt Comm J Qual Patient Saf* 32:119–129, Mar. 2006.

34. Smith C.M.: Origin and uses of *primum non nocere:* Above all, do no harm! *Clin Pharmacol* 45:371–377, Apr. 2005.

35. Leape L.L.: Error in medicine. *JAMA* 272:1851–1857, Dec. 21, 1994.

36. Reinertsen J.L.: Let's talk about error: Leaders should take responsibility for mistakes. *BMJ* 320:730, Mar. 11, 2000.

37. Schyve P. M.: An interview with Lucian Leape. John M. Eisenberg Patient Safety and Quality Awards. *Jt Comm J Qual Patient Saf* 30:653–658, Dec. 2004.

38. National Patient Safety Foundation: *New Lucian Leape Institute Report Finds That U.S. Medical Schools Are Falling Sort in Teaching Physicians How to Provide Safe Patient Care* (news release). http://www.npsf.org/pr/pressrel/2010-03-10.php (accessed Jul. 28, 2010).

39. McCafferty M.H., Polk H.C.: Addition of "near-miss" cases enhances a quality improvement conference. *Arch Surg* 139:216–217, Feb. 2004.

40. McDonnell C., et al.: Redesigning a morbidity and mortality program in a university-affiliated pediatric anesthesia department. *Jt Comm J Qual Patient Saf* 36:117–125, Mar. 2010.

41. Szekendi M.K., et al.: Using patient safety morbidity and mortality conferences to promote transparency and a culture of safety. *Jt Comm J Qual Patient Saf* 36:3–9, Jan. 2010.

CHAPTER 2

Reporting and Learning from Close Calls

Alan Fayaz, M.A.(Cantab), M.B.B.S., M.R.C.P.; Laura Morlock, Ph.D.

In its 1999 report, *To Err Is Human*, the Institute of Medicine (IOM) recommended that health care organizations use two types of error reporting systems: mandatory reporting systems and voluntary reporting systems.[1] Mandatory systems typically focus on errors associated with serious injury or death. In the United States, reports of such errors are generally reviewed by state regulatory agencies that can conduct investigations into specific incidents. The types of errors captured in mandatory reporting systems typically are rare and represent a very small subset of errors. In contrast, voluntary reporting systems focus on errors that have resulted in no patient harm, according to the IOM[1] (or minimal or no harm, according to other reporting systems)—and thereby capture close calls.

The IOM recommendations regarding reporting provoked a mixed response in the health care community. Concerns about mandatory reporting's possible negative repercussions, such as a possible chilling effect on reporting and its overall impact on the safety culture within health care organizations, were balanced by the concurrent call to invest in voluntary systems for the main purpose of *learning* from medical error.

As discussed in the Introduction and Chapter 1 of this book, the perceived value of reporting close calls is based on the premise that close calls

occur much more frequently than harmful events but are similar to harmful events in regard to their causal and contributing factors. For these reasons, close calls are helpful for detecting patterns of risk that will lead to a better understanding of error prevention, recovery from errors, and, consequently, harm reduction.[2]

The reporting-system strategies in health care have been modeled on those widely credited with improving safety in aviation and several other high-risk industries.[3]

This chapter discusses examples of adverse event and medical error reporting systems, with a focus on the role of close calls in reporting, data analysis, and prioritization of areas for improvement, as well as dissemination and learning. This chapter also reviews some of the main challenges in using close-call information most effectively in health care.

REPORTING SYSTEMS

Around the world, incidents are being reported on paper (often in predesigned forms) or via e-mail through secure servers or through custom-made Internet portals. Demonstration projects on telephone reporting, which is intended to minimize inconvenience for the reporter, have been conducted in the United Kingdom and the United States.[4] Given the current trend toward more "intelligent" mobile devices, how long can it be before an application is designed to report incidents directly from a cell phone? Despite these efforts, underreporting of incidents remains a serious issue in health care, and perhaps only 5%–20% of incidents are ever reported[5] (versus 4%–50%, as stated in Chapter 1; but, after all, these are estimates).

In an attempt to combat underreporting, some institutions have started collecting data proactively—notably in cardiac surgery and intensive care—by employing human factors and risk experts who observe practice and gather data in real time to compile lists of errors and close calls that may then be used to improve clinical safety.[6,7] Where used appropriately, such "active" reporting systems have been demonstrated to identify a greater number of safety issues than "passive" reporting alone.[8,9] In practice, the majority of reporting systems rely on staff members, or occasionally patients and their relatives, to identify and record incidents themselves.

Generally, "what," "who," and "how" information is collected and is usually defined by "why" information—insofar as a truly successful system will be geared to meet particular objectives. To this end, systems are often regarded as falling broadly into one of two categories: accountability and learning.

Accountability systems, often state led and created with the purpose of maintaining a fiduciary responsibility to the stakeholder population, tend to collect a subset of data. Incident reporting is often compulsory and may be associated with disincentives or punitive responses, depending on the gravity of the incident reported. Learning systems as such are geared to data collection for the purposes of hazard/risk identification, provision of information on system weaknesses and successful barriers to harm, and targeting of improvement efforts. The primary objective is learning, with the subsequent dissemination of these lessons to the reporting population.

In reality, both learning and accountability systems provide the potential for learning, which is usually a product of the standard of data analysis rather than the data collection. In many ways it is the response to the incident(s), more than the reporting system, that accomplishes the reporting system's primary objective.

Reporting in Aviation and Other Industries

More than 50 years ago, Flanagan described the critical incident technique (CIT) as a means of "collecting direct observations of human behavior in such a way as to facilitate their potential usefulness in solving practical problems."[10(p. 327)] A product of the aviation psychology program of the U.S. Army Air Forces, the CIT was used to examine military aircraft training accidents and subsequently formed the basis of the Aviation Safety Reporting System (ASRS).

The ASRS database holds the largest public repository of aviation incidents in the world and remains the inspiration for similar reporting systems across many other disciplines and countries.[11] The ASRS was founded in 1976 in the United States through an agreement between the aviation regulatory body, the Federal Aviation Administration (FAA), and an independent, respected research organization, the National Aeronautics and Space Administration (NASA), with the intention of eliminating unsafe conditions in aviation practice. The reporting system is confidential and voluntary, and it ensures immunity in the absence of deliberate violation and on the condition that the reporter has submitted the incident within 10 days of its occurrence. Much of the success of the project is attributed to the nonpunitive approach to hazard identification as well as to the ongoing, bidirectional communication between NASA and the system's stakeholders.

The ASRS database receives more than 30,000 reports annually, which have been used to redesign aircrafts, restructure training, and improve control systems and airports, as well as to implement a host of other measures aimed at minimizing human error. The development of a healthy reporting culture in the aviation industry has been accompanied by stark improvements in safety. It is important to note that in contrast to health care, in aviation harmful events are now rare enough that the system has the privilege of relying almost entirely on close-call data as a resource for safety improvements.

A focus on close calls is not exclusive to aviation; similar parallels can also be found in nuclear power technology, steel production, and military operations.[12–15] In fact, there is compelling evidence for the need for systematic review of close calls in the science of transportation safety; the error precipitating the Paddington (Ladbroke Grove) rail crash in 1999 in the United Kingdom, which claimed 31 lives, had been flagged as a close call on eight previous occasions during a six-year period.[16] Related close-call events had also been reported in advance of the 1986 Space Shuttle *Challenger* explosion; the 1997 Hindustan, India, refinery explosion; and a variety of high-profile aviation accidents.[17,18]

Reporting Systems in Health Care

In contrast to its application in other industries, the analysis and use of close-call information in health care is at a preliminary stage. This is due in part to the overwhelming volume of data on incidents involving patient harm that invariably take priority in analysis and to the lack of a standard definition of what actually constitutes a close call. In cardiac surgery, for example, the term *near miss* has been used to denote both a serious complication that would normally have led to death but did not in that instance[19] and the need to go back to the bypass machine after a failed "wean."[20] Maternal medicine (obstetrics/gynecology) has classified *near misses* as serious events with significant morbidity, such as the loss of a limb following meningococcal septicemia, that did not result in death (essentially a "near death"),[21] whereas in blood transfusion, a *near miss* refers to an error that might have resulted in the transfusion of incompatible blood.[22]

Despite these challenges, attitudes to reporting close calls are improving. In the United States, where reporting systems are often operated by state regulatory programs, the number of states with mandatory reporting systems has increased from 15 to 27 (plus the District of Columbia) in the past decade.[23,24] This trend in large part reflects the response to the calls of *To Err Is Human* for better documentation of events resulting in patient harm and close calls[1] and has been supported by the creation of Patient Safety Organizations (PSOs).

Created following the Patient Safety and Quality Improvement Act of 2005, PSOs are independent entities, which may be private or public, for profit or nonprofit. They aim to supplement local quality improvement efforts by allowing health care organizations to confidentially report information about patient safety events without fear of legal discovery and to receive feedback about how to reduce the frequency of such events.

As previously mentioned, reporting systems currently in operation vary considerably, ranging from highly specific, specialty-based event reporting (as found in many developed blood transfusion units) to more open-ended databases, which collect unfiltered information from a variety of sources within defined geographic areas. National reporting systems, as described by the World Health Organization (WHO), exhibit great variation in sponsorship, support, participation, and function; reporting tends to be voluntary, but only a few reporting systems specifically include close calls (Denmark, Australia, Japan, and Sweden).[25]

A sample of selected reporting systems currently in operation that include reporting of close calls—including the aviation-based ASRS—is provided in Table 2-1 (*see* page 16).

Table 2-1. A Sample of Selected Reporting Systems Currently in Operation That Include Close-Call Reporting

REPORTING SYSTEM	Launch Date	Data Type	Reporting Demographic	Voluntary	Anonymous	Immunity	Dissemination	Estimated Reports	Incidents Analyzed
ASRS	1976	All	Aviation related	Yes	De-identified	Conditional	Newsletters and direct feedback	700,000 to date; mostly near misses	All events
MEDMARX	1998	All	Medication errors (National)	Yes	Yes	Not specified	Annual reports, toolkits for member institutions	1.3 million errors through 2007	All events
National Patient Safety Agency	2001	All	England and Wales	Yes (until 2010)	De-identified	No	Reports, alerts, toolkits, national projects	Over 4 million to date; 66% near misses	Deaths and severe harms routinely
Pennsylvania Patient Safety Authority	2004	All	Statewide	No	Yes	Yes	E-newsletters backed by clinical evidence	Over 200,000 annually; 96% near misses	All events
Maryland Patient Safety Center	2003 (designated PSO in 2008)	All	Regional (Delmarva Peninsula)	Yes	De-identified	Yes	Newsletters, educational initiatives through the Maryland hospital educational institute	23,000 reports to date	Topic based
ACP New York chapter	2007	Near misses only	Statewide, internal medicine trainees only	Yes	Yes	Yes	Newsletters, stakeholder access to raw data	Approx. 300 near misses to date	All events

Note: The National Patient Safety Agency's reporting is conducted through "Patient Safety," formerly known as the National Reporting and Learning Service (NLRS); ASRS, Aviation Safety Reporting System; PSO, Patient Safety Organization; ACP, American College of Physicians.

The National Reporting and Learning Service (NRLS), also known as Patient Safety, a division of the National Patient Safety Agency (NPSA), collects patient safety incidents on behalf of the entire National Health Services in England and Wales.[26] Reports on both incidents and close calls may be filed directly (and anonymously) to the NRLS via its Web resource and can be filed by health care staff and by patients or their relatives. In practice, however, the majority of reports are forwarded directly from health care organizations, all of which are responsible for structuring their own local data collection systems. The national collation of the data under the auspices of the NPSA allows for wider dissemination of lessons from the analysis of these data. Other sources of data, including a database of serious untoward incidents (SUIs) that are routinely reported to the strategic health authorities in England,* coroners' reports, and risks

---

* Strategic health authorities, which now number 10, were created in 2002 to manage the local NHS on behalf of the secretary of state.
Source: National Health Service (NHS): *About the NHS: Strategic Health Authorities.*
http://www.nhs.uk/NHSEngland/thenhs/about/Pages/authoritiesandtrusts.aspx (accessed Jul. 28, 2010).

identified by safety organizations in other countries, are also scanned for potentially serious safety issues.

Reporting systems are by no means exclusively geographically based. The anesthesia,[27] intensive care,[28] and hematology[29] specialties have all developed high-profile reporting systems with some conformity to international terminologies and taxonomies, which has allowed for greater dissemination of information, potentially leading to safer practices from their respective incident data.

The Medication Event Reporting System for Transfusion Medicine (MERS-TM) is a "no-fault," confidential, voluntary, and anonymous event-reporting system first launched in February 1999 at the Women's Health Sciences Centre (now part of the Sunnybrook Health Sciences Centre, Toronto).[29] MERS-TM is designed to capture harmful incidents and close calls related to transfusion medicine. The system has been used extensively to monitor errors associated with blood transfusion across the United States, Canada, the United Kingdom, and Europe.

In 1991, the U.S. Pharmacopeia (USP) began analyzing incidents involving medication errors in cooperation with the Institute for Safe Medication Practices (ISMP) through a confidential reporting program—the Medication Errors Reporting Program (MER). Experience with MER led the USP to launch an Internet-accessible reporting program in 1998 called MEDMARX.[30] (In 2008, MEDMARX was acquired by Quantros, Inc.) The MER and MEDMARX databases were used to produce annual and other summary reports focusing on a variety of issues, ranging from medication errors in pediatric and intensive care units to errors associated with look-alike/sound-alike drugs.

Both the MER and MEDMARX programs received reports on close calls, which constituted approximately 98% of all incidents reported.

Armed with these data, the USP had valuable information regarding no-harm incidents from which to make recommendations (such as the change of a drug name to avoid potential confusion with similar sounding drugs, following anecdotal reports of phonetic similarities). Key to the success of these two reporting programs was a nationally recognized taxonomy for the classification of medical errors, which was developed by the National Coordinating Council for Medication Error Reporting and Prevention (NCC MERP).[31] The harm index created by NCC MERP has allowed pooling of more than 1.3 million MEDMARX error reports into a database available for analyses, dissemination of results, and benchmarking by participating organizations to target areas for safety improvements.

CLOSE CALLS IN HEALTH CARE

New York and Maryland are two states that have invested time and finances in developing reporting systems focused specifically on close calls. In New York, a small group of clinical directors helped champion a registry to collect incident data from internal medicine residents.[32] There are plans to extend this program to other training directorates by late 2010. The Web-based data-collecting tool has been formatted to collect "near-miss" reports only; the New York chapter of the American College of Physicians (NYACP) has defined *near misses* as "those events that might have resulted in harm to a patient but were discovered and corrected before they reached the patient." The tool has also been designed to work alongside local risk-management systems currently collecting data on adverse events with harm. Reporters are discouraged from entering any identifiable information in the survey, thus maintaining an anonymous, risk-free system that promises state protection for any person supplying de-identified data. As an added incentive, on completion of a survey, residents are awarded a certificate that could be used to assist them in meeting their practice-based learning and improvement system training requirements. Between 2007 and 2009, approximately 3,300 internal medicine interns and residents from 46 training programs were trained in patient safety and the use of the Near Miss Reporting System (NMRS).[32] The near-miss reports are reviewed by a specialized team composed of clinical representatives, quality improvement experts, and biostatisticians.[33] Current findings include the following[33]:

- Most near-miss events reported occurred after one day of admission, on a weekday, and during the day—and were discovered immediately or within one to three hours.

- One in every eight near-miss events is not reported to the hospital or program.

- Two-thirds of the near-miss events reported constituted slip (a mistake made in execution of a valid plan), and approximately one-third were a lapse (a mistake made by forgetting to do something that should have been done).

- The most common near-miss event type was drug administration (48.3%), followed by communication (15.7%) and wrong patient (13.3%).

- The primary team, nurse, pharmacist, and coverage team were the most cited preventive barriers for the near-miss event reaching the patient.

- Most (97.5%) of the interns and residents felt it was important that the survey be anonymous.

The Maryland Patient Safety Center (MPSC),[34] established by the Maryland legislature in 2003 was one of the first 25 organizations in the nation to be listed as a PSO. A not-for-profit organization, the MPSC collaborates with health care providers in the Delmarva Peninsula to collect safety data through its Adverse Events Reporting System (AERS). The data are then used to explore patterns and trends related to patient safety to establish best practices and various collaborative programs aimed at improving safety culture.

Reporting of close-call incidents to the ASRS and NPSA is predominantly voluntary; consequently, the information that these reporting systems are able to collect is heavily reliant on the willingness of reporters to provide information. The Pennsylvania Patient Safety Reporting System (PA-PSRS)—developed under contract with ECRI, a Pennsylvania-based independent, nonprofit health services research agency, in partnership with an international information technology firm and the ISMP—is unique in being the first mandatory reporting system of close calls as well as of serious events.[35] It is maintained by an independent state agency, the Pennsylvania Patient Safety Authority, and is funded in part by the Pennsylvania Department of Health. In 2009, the database collected 226,670 reports, of which approximately 96% were categorized as near misses (incidents that did not cause harm). Reporters use a Web-based Internet portal to answer 21 core questions that allow users to provide responses by checking boxes, selecting from drop-down menus, and supplying free-text narrative to provide the necessary information characterizing an incident. Reporters may also describe some of the potential contributory factors as well as system safeguards that might prevent a recurrence. Reports are anonymous; information is confidential, nondiscoverable, and, crucially, not admissible as evidence.

Many institutions, as described in two recent reports, have created "good catch" (so-named in order to provide a more positive connotation) awards[36] or programs[37] to promote the reporting of errors or error-prone situations that are caught before they reach the patient.

ANALYSIS AND PRIORITIZATION

After error reports have been collected, they must be coded and analyzed. Priorities must be established regarding how to select individual reports for in-depth or root cause analysis, as well as to identify the areas that most require focused improvement efforts. In addition, all reports must be aggregated and analyzed to determine trends, high-risk areas, and problem-prone activities.

In an ideal world, every report would be individually investigated to maximize the learning potential surrounding untoward events, and some reporting systems operate with this aim in mind. At NASA, each individual report is analyzed by two separate professionals from a cohort of retired pilots, air traffic controllers, and mechanics whose role is to flag potential hazards for immediate action and to classify reports according to their underlying causes and contributing factors in order to maintain a database that remains a rich resource for learning.

In health care, however, reporting systems that collect de-identified data from large populations may be overwhelmed by the volume of information reported. For example, in England and Wales, more than 3 million reports have been received since the NPSA's inception in 2003. In 2008 alone, more than 900,000 reports were sent to the organization, of which 66% were related to close calls. This is equivalent to the entire (30-year) output from the aviation industry, making it infeasible to review every reported incident at the level of the reporting system.

When reviewing every incident separately is impractical—close calls are not routinely reviewed by the NPSA—incidents must be prioritized. At the NPSA, a team of clinical experts individually reviews all the reported incidents of death and severe harm to extract the potential for wider learning, which includes detailed scrutiny of the free text within the incident report where the "patient story" is described. Understanding the patient's story is felt to be vital because it helps to identify the contributing factors that may have led to the incident and/or wider system failures.

From the initial monthly pool of up to 1,500 incidents of death and severe harm, approxi-

mately 50 trigger incidents are chosen for discussion at a weekly response meeting involving a range of clinical and human factors/design experts. Although reports are de-identified on entry into the database, enough information is retained to permit referral back to the reporting organization at any stage for further information about the incident or underlying safety issue. On the basis of initial evidence, the response team agrees which issues should be subject to a formal investigation (usually, 4 are chosen a month). It is at this "scoping" stage that the wider NRLS database is searched for relevant information about close calls to better quantify and describe the extent of the problem. The scoping process is described in Sidebar 2-1 (*see* page 20) with respect to epidural injections and infusions.

In the New York reporting system, the data-collecting tools were designed to incorporate improvement methodology aimed at maximizing the learning from individual incidents. Following the collection of necessary descriptive details, reporters are asked to detect systematic weaknesses and errors that may have preceded the near miss and to identify any protective barriers in place that helped to neutralize the errors. The New York data have been used to identify some safety trends (including the essential role of medication reconciliation as a barrier to harm in the vast majority of reported near misses), errors arising from overly complex protocols, and hazards associated with computerized provider order entry systems positioned in close proximity to busy nursing stations. The project leads are in the process of compiling updated statistics and drafting recommendations based on the data and intend to publish this information in late 2010.

In Maryland, the AERS went beyond compiling adverse event data to also incorporate data recording the *potential* for adverse events from its collection of what it terms "near hits" (close calls). The challenge of measuring what had not yet happened was met by two design strategies:

(1) incorporating proxy variables deemed to contribute to an event's occurrence and (2) allowing free-text space for almost all questions when a proxy variable was collected.

Sidebar 2-1. Scoping Process at the National Patient Safety Agency

In 2007, the National Patient Safety Agency (NPSA) in the United Kingdom focused on a series of high-profile incidents related to the incorrect administration of epidural anesthetic agents through intravenous routes. All (three) cases, each of which resulted in the patient's death, had occurred before the NPSA's inception and so had not been formally reported, but the thematic consistencies and shared, devastating outcomes were felt to warrant a review of the early database.

All reported incidents occurring between January 2005 and May 2006 were searched for terms that related to epidural injections and infusions. None of the identified 346 incidents had resulted in death, and only 1 had been thought to cause severe harm. In fact, 293 of the 348 incidents had been categorized as no harm ("near-miss incidents").

Detailed analysis of the incidents allowed identification of common themes or factors that were thought to contribute to the incident occurrence, and a safety alert was produced with recommendations regarding the storage, labeling, and administration of epidural medicines. Since the release of the alert, there have been no reported deaths resulting from incorrectly administered epidural mixtures.

Source: National Patient Safety Agency: *Epidural Injections and Infusions*, Mar. 28, 2007. http://www.nrls.npsa.nhs.uk/resources/patient-safety-topics/medication-safety/?entryid45=59807&p=4 and (accessed Sep. 1, 2010). Used with permission.

Annual analyses are conducted to determine trending over time of the most frequent adverse events. In addition, focused analyses are conducted using near-hit information on topics such as patient falls due to medical error and opioid management in relation to adverse events. For patient falls, the database (which includes more than 20,000 voluntarily reported events or near hits) was queried to identify the medications that each patient who fell was on during that hospitalization episode. Then the data on medications were further analyzed for the potential the medications have for increasing the risk of falling individually or through their interaction (for example, zolpidem prescribed with antihypertensive medications). Following the data analysis, an MPSC initiative on medication safety was supplemented with findings from the AERS, and a falls collaborative was launched statewide. These activities resulted in a noteworthy decrease in patient falls and an enhanced attention to medication errors.[38]

The free-text reporting is descriptive and rich, but the analysis of such unstructured descriptive reporting can be challenging. The free-text reports describe the near hits in more detail about the time, setting, patient, and so on but do have a subjective aspect to them that has to be considered during the extraction of information from these descriptive reports. Nevertheless, the supplemental information gleaned through the free-text reports helped identify the structural and process variables involved in the care of patients who may be at risk of falling. For example, it was apparent that timely or complete information about the patient was not always available to care providers because of incomplete patient record computerization or difficulty in accessing computerized patient records when available. Consequently, the MPSC has focused on adoption of health care information technology as a domain of patient safety improvement.[39] In the Pennsylvania program, the analytic tools within the event-recording system itself allow trend identification and event prioritization before automatically referring relevant incidents to the appropriate clinical teams. Teams are then responsible for identifying immediate hazards along with any improvements that might contribute to patient safety.

MERS-TM goes a little further in attempting to automate the prioritization process by employing a specifically designed Risk Assessment Index (RAI)[40] to identify potential risk by cross-referencing the author's estimate on probability of causing harm with the author's estimate of likelihood of recurrence. This allows events deemed to be of significant risk, in addition to new, unusual, or frequently occurring events, to be submitted to root cause analysis by the analytical team. Meanwhile, the descriptive data from incidents not submitted for further investigation are used to compile trend and pattern statistics for referral and additional evaluation.

DISSEMINATION AND LEARNING

The overall aim of a reporting system is to improve safety by learning from previous mistakes—echoing James Reason's argument that the most detrimental error is failing to learn from an error.[41] A crucial step in the process of learning from errors is the ability to extract lessons and communicate these lessons to the reporting community. In the absence of such feedback, an otherwise efficient reporting system will risk disincentivizing potential reporters and failing to maintain high levels of participation and support.

At NASA, all reports are responded to directly, with an immediate verbal or written response. Within days of report filing, the reporter is presented with a tear-off identification strip as an assurance of confidentiality, a letter of gratification, a recent copy of the monthly report publication, and two fresh reporting forms. Summaries of interesting incidents and recommendations are disseminated formally through a series of

monthly (*CALLBACK*) and quarterly (*ASRS Directline*) newsletters.

Where reports are collected over large areas or where numbers dictate a more pragmatic approach to result dissemination, summary statistics can be published to highlight the range and distribution of errors in question. To facilitate the coordinated translation of the information collected by the many independent PSOs, the U.S. Agency for Healthcare Research and Quality (AHRQ) has released a series of Common Formats,[42] which were developed using the AHRQ's database of existing reporting systems.

Common Formats apply to all patient safety concerns, including close calls, and register information relating to both generic issues (pertaining to all patient safety concerns) and a list of specific issues relating to eight patient safety events that occur frequently and/or are serious in nature, such as pressure ulcers and falls. Reporting is therefore both standardized and simplified. (The surgical/anesthesia event-specific form asks between 12–20 questions, depending on the type of incident, with minimal space for free text.)

De-identified data from PSOs that have agreed to submit information will be collated and presented in the AHRQ's annual National Healthcare Quality Report. The AHRQ plans to use the information gathered from the network of patient safety databases to analyze national and regional statistics about patient safety events in order to identify safety trends and patterns. Data can also be used to crudely estimate the efficacy of local and national safety interventions.

Reports disseminated in narrative form have also been shown to be effective in engaging the reporting population. In 2004, the Association of periOperative Registered Nurses (AORN) in the United States launched a voluntary and anonymous reporting system, exclusively for perioperative practitioners, with the purpose of submitting close calls that occurred in the operating room.[43] Members were encouraged to provide detailed personal narratives of clinical situations (type of procedure, aspects influencing the situation, human factors contributing to the error), which were then periodically analyzed for patient safety trends—looking at what, how, and why things happened and what interventions can be implemented to prevent further occurrences. These reports were disseminated through the AORN journal *SafetyNet*, describing in story format a process of events that did not proceed as planned and that resulted in the occurrence of a close call in which a patient or patients narrowly avoided harm.[43] (The program ended in 2006.)

At the NYACP, lessons are also disseminated through a quarterly newsletter. In addition, participating organizations have access to the database of all incidents entered by reporters across the various institutions and are encouraged to draw their own inferences from data analysis at the organizational level. In Pennsylvania, recommendations are disseminated by e-mail through advisories that combine incident data with supporting evidence on relevant safety improvements from the medical literature.

As noted earlier, the MERS-TM reporting system has been used to monitor errors associated with blood transfusion in the United States, Canada, the United Kingdom, and Europe. In the United States, the system has helped to map the distribution of both serious errors and close calls. Close-call trends have been used to improve the efficiency of local services, minimizing errors that result in wasted blood products or delays in transfusion. A good example is the implementation of bar-code expiration dates on products to promote maintenance of an up-to-date inventory.[44] In Ireland, MERS-TM was exclusively used to track close calls during a three-year period. The results helped to highlight some of the crucial system safeguards in place—frequently involving the "human check" of transfusion samples in the laboratory—that have helped to prevent incompatible blood transfusions. Reports have also helped identify risk factors that predispose certain institutions to having higher "potential harm" scores.[45] This information is then advanced to the pilot sites that had poorer safety records as a means of disseminating information that can lead to safer practices.

CHALLENGES

Although learning from error is the primary objective in systems that mandate reporting of any kind, immunity and confidentiality are crucial to maintaining stakeholder participation, but this guarantee remains the subject of much contention. Leading policymakers responsible for reporting systems around the world, coordinated by the World Alliance for Patient Safety (WAPS), met in 2008 to discuss their respective experiences with close-call reporting in health care. A consensus was achieved that education should be the priority of close-call reporting systems, although it was also recognized that this needed to be balanced with a degree of accountability.[46] It remains a fine balance for reporting institutions to maintain a proactive, healthy, nonjudgmental safety culture while also preserving the safety and well-being of the populations they serve. A multifaceted approach to learning effectively from close-call reporting systems is needed that extends beyond local collection of data and dissemination of learning to include clinical audit, pooling of data, better (and more rigorous) use of narrative data, and a system for proactive identification of risks. For reporting systems to be able to communicate effectively with one another, there needs to be standardization of both terminology and taxonomy.[46] At present, these challenges are present even at a national level, where logistical and political barriers may hamper wider adaptation of learning. Furthermore, reporting systems that do collect both harmful-incident and close-call data need to invest in information technology that allows predictive modeling to permit filtering of the close calls that require greater attention in order to obtain the greatest benefit from this valuable resource.

CONCLUSIONS

It is widely understood that reporting systems have no utility unless they lead to safety improvements. It can be argued that one hall-mark of an effective incident reporting system is analysis and feedback that lead to system changes, which would then enable health care providers to deliver safer patient care. Currently, reporting systems and institutions struggle with how best to provide analysis and feedback to maximize the benefit from error reporting. Evaluating the impact of error reporting and tar-geted interventions on patient safety are at early stages of development in most reporting systems and health care settings, but these activities remain key to future progress.

The author thanks C. Patrick Chaulk, M.D., M.P.H., executive director and president, Maryland Patient Safety Center, and Vahé A. Kazandjian, Ph.D., M.P.H., president, LogiQual Research Institute, Elkridge, Maryland, for information regarding the Maryland Patient Safety Center.

References

1. Institute of Medicine: *To Err Is Human: Building a Safer Health System.* Washington, DC: National Academies Press, 2000.
2. Institute of Medicine: *Patient Safety: Achieving a New Standard for Care.* Washington, DC: National Academies Press, 2004. http://www.nap.edu/openbook.php?record_id=10863&page=332 (accessed Sep. 1, 2010).
3. Barach P., Small S.D.: Reporting and preventing medical mishaps: Lessons from non-medical near miss reporting systems. *BMJ* 320:759–763, Mar. 18, 2000.
4. Fernald D.H., et al.: Event reporting to a primary care patient safety reporting system: A report from the ASIPS collaborative. *Ann Fam Med* 2:327–332, Jul.–Aug. 2004.
5. Null G., et al.: Death by medicine part I. *HealthE-LivingNews.* http://www.healthe-livingnews.com/articles/death_by_medicine_part_1.html (accessed Apr. 26, 2010).
6. Wong D.R., et al.: Prospective assessment of intraoperative precursor events during cardiac surgery. *Eur J Cardiothorac Surg* 29:447–455, Apr. 2006. Epub Feb. 23, 2006.
7. Oken A., et al.: A facilitated survey instrument captures significantly more anesthesia events than does traditional voluntary event reporting. *Anesthesiology* 107:909–922, Dec. 2007.
8. Weingart S.N., Ship A.N., Aronson M.D.: Confidential clinician-reported surveillance of adverse events among medical inpatients. *J Gen Intern Med* 15:470–477, Jul. 2000.
9. O'Neil A.C., et al.: Physician reporting compared with medical-record review to identify adverse medical events. *Ann Intern Med* 119:370–376, Sep. 1, 1993.
10. Flanagan J.C.: The critical incident technique. *Psychol Bull* 51:327–358, Jul. 1954.
11. Aviation Safety Reporting System (ASRS): *Program Overview: ASRS Concept and Mission.* http://asrs.arc.nasa.gov/overview/briefing/br_1.html (accessed Apr. 26, 2010).
12. Ives G.: Near miss reporting pitfalls for nuclear plants. In Van der Shaff et al. (eds.): *Near Miss Reporting as a Safety Tool.* Oxford, UK: Butterworth-Heineman, 1991, pp. 51–56.
13. Van Vuuren W.: *Organizational Failure: An Exploratory Study in the Steel Industry, and the Medical Domain* (Ph.D. thesis). Eindhoven, the Netherlands: Eindhoven University of Technology, 1998.
14. Sagan S.D.: *The Limits of Safety: Organizations, Accidents, and Nuclear Weapons.* Princeton, NJ: Princeton University Press, 1993.
15. Turner B.A., Pidgeon N.F.: *Man-Made Disasters,* 2nd ed. London: Butterworth-Heinemann, 1997.
16. Cullen W.D.: *The Ladbroke Grove Rail Inquiry.* Norwich, UK: Her Majesty's Stationary Office, 2000.
17. Vaughan D.: *The Challenger Launch Decision: Risk Technology, Culture, and Deviance at NASA.* Chicago: University of Chicago Press, 1996.
18. Khan F.I., Abbasi S.A.: The world's worst industrial accident of the 1990s—What happened and what might have been: A quantitative study. *Process Safety Progress* 18:135–145, Autumn 1999. Epub Apr. 16, 2004.
19. Carthey J., de Leval M.R., Reason J.T.: The human factor in cardiac surgery: Errors and near misses in a high technology medical domain. *Ann Thorac Surg* 72:300–305, Jul. 2001.
20. de Leval M.R., et al.: Analysis of a cluster of surgical failures: Application to a series of neonatal arterial switch operations. *J Thorac Cardiovasc Surg* 107:914–923, discussion 923–924, Mar. 1994.
21. Geller S.E., et al.: Defining a conceptual framework for near-miss maternal morbidity. *J Am Med Womens Assoc* 57:135–139, Summer 2002.
22. Callum J.L., et al.: Reporting of near-miss events for transfusion medicine: Improving transfusion safety. *Transfusion* 41:1204–1211, Oct. 2001.
23. Rosenthal J., Riley T., Booth M.: *State Reporting of Medical Errors and Adverse Events: Results of a 50-State Survey.* National Academy for State Health Policy, Apr. 2000. http://www.nashp.org/sites/default/files/adverse_events_survey_2000.pdf (accessed Sep. 7, 2010).
24. National Academy for State Health Policy: *Patient Safety Toolbox.* http://www.nashp.org/pst-welcome (accessed Sep. 7, 2010).
25. World Health Organization (WHO): WHO *Draft Guidelines for Adverse Event Reporting and Learning Systems: From Information to Action,* 2005. http://www.who.int/patientsafety/events/05/Reporting_Guidelines.pdf (accessed Sep. 7, 2010).

26. National Patient Safety Agency: *National Reporting and Learning Service.* http://www.nrls.npsa.nhs.uk (accessed Apr. 26, 2010).

27. Department of Anaesthesia, University of Basel, Switzerland: *Critical Incidents Reporting System: Critical Incidents in Anaesthesiology.* http://www.medana.unibas.ch/cirs/ (accessed Apr. 26, 2010).

28. Hart G.K., et al.: Adverse incident reporting in intensive care. *Anaesth Intensive Care* 22:556–561, Oct. 1994.

29. Battles J.B., et al.: The attributes of medical event-reporting systems: Experience with a prototype medical event-reporting system for transfusion medicine. *Arch Pathol Lab Med* 122:231–238, Mar. 1998.

30. U.S. Pharmacopeia: *MEDMARX.* http://www.usp.org/ hqi/patientSafety/medmarx/ (accessed Apr. 26, 2010).

31. National Coordinating Council for Medication Error Reporting and Prevention: *About Medication Errors.* http://www.nccmerp.org/medErrorTaxonomy.html (accessed Sep. 7, 2010).

32. New York chapter of the American College of Physicians: *Near Miss Registry: Project Overview.* http://www.nyacp.org/ i4a/pages/Index.cfm?pageID=3387 (accessed Sep. 1, 2010).

33. New York Chapter of the American College of Physicians: *Near Miss Project Update*—Jun. 2010. http://www.nyacp.org/ i4a/pages/index.cfm?pageid=3419 (accessed Sep. 1, 2010).

34. Maryland Patient Safety Center: *Adverse Event Reporting.* http://www.marylandpatientsafety.org/html/adverse_event _reporting.html (accessed Sep. 7, 2010).

35. Pennsylvania Patient Safety Authority: *Annual Reports.* http://patientsafetyauthority.org/PatientSafetyAuthority/ Pages/AnnualReports.aspx (accessed Sep. 1, 2010).

36. Strategies for Nurse Managers.com: *Good Catch Program Encourages Near-Miss Reporting.* http://www.strategies fornursemanagers.com/ce_detail/251366.cfm (accessed Sep. 7, 2010).

37. Szekendi M.K., et al.: Using patient safety morbidity and mortality conferences to promote transparency and a culture of safety. *Jt Comm J Qual Patient Saf* 36:3–9, Jan. 2010.

38. Kazandjian V.A., et al.: Enhancing medication use safety: Benefits of learning from your peers. *Qual Saf Health Care* 18:331–335, Oct. 2009.

39. Kazandjian V.A., Lipitz-Snyderman A.: Hit or miss: The application of health care information technology to managing uncertainty in clinical decision making. *J Eval Clin Pract*, in press. Epub Jul. 13, 2010.

40. Medical Event Reporting System–Transfusion Medicine: *Risk Assessment Index—RAI.* http://www.mers-tm.org/ support/topics/rai_case.html (accessed Apr. 26, 2010).

41. Reason J.: *Human Error.* New York City: Cambridge University Press, 1990.

42. Agency for Healthcare Research and Quality: *Patient Safety Organizations: Common Formats.* http://www.pso.ahrq.gov/formats/commonfmt.htm (accessed Sep. 23, 2010).

43. SafetyNet: Lessons learned from close calls in the OR. *AORN J* 84(Suppl. 1), Jul. 2006. http://www.aornjournal. org/issues/contents?issue_key=S0001-2092%2806%29X 0003-0 (accessed Apr. 26, 2010).

44. Callum J.L., et al.: Reporting of near-miss events for transfusion medicine: Improving transfusion safety. *Transfusion* 41:1204–1211, Oct. 2001.

45. Lundy D., et al.: Seven hundred and fifty-nine (759) chances to learn: A 3-year pilot project to analyse transfusion-related near-miss events in the Republic of Ireland. *Vox Sang* 92:233–241, Apr. 2007.

46. Pham J.C., et al.: Establishing a global community for incident reporting systems. *Qual Saf Health Care*, in press.

CHAPTER 3

Promoting Meaningful Close-Call Reporting: Lessons from Aviation

Sidney W.A. Dekker, Ph.D.

We are on an approach to the airport at 2,000 feet above the ground. The big jet is on autopilot, docile, and responsively following the instructions I have put into the various computer systems. It follows the heading I gave it and stays at the altitude I want it at. The weather is all right, but none too wonderful. Cloud base is at about 1,000 feet; there is mist, drizzle. We should be on the ground in the next few minutes. I call for flaps, and the other pilot selects them for me. The jet starts slowing down. Then we come to the top of our approach. The autopilot does as it was told and nudges the nose of the jet downwards, onto the glide slope toward the runway.

Then something strange happens. The thrust levers that control the power to the jet's two engines move all the way to the back to their idle stop. This is very little thrust for the situation we're in—not enough for keeping the jet aloft much longer. Inside of a split second, my eyes dart up to the computer display with the various mode annunciations, which tells me in what mode the various automatic systems are operating. The autopilot is doing what it's supposed to be doing: riding down the electronically beamed glide slope towards the runway.

The autothrottle, however, is another story. This is the computer that helps control how much thrust goes out of each engine. And it is in a mode that I've never seen in this situation before: fully

retarded. My eyes flutter down onto the display with flight information.

My airspeed is leaking out of the airplane as if the hull has been punctured, slowly deflating like a massive, wounded balloon. It looks bizarre and scary, and it's the split second that lasts an eternity. Yet, I have taught myself in situations like this to act first and question what is going on later. This, I will admit, is against my nature. Deep down I'm probably more an academic than a pilot. Instructors used to remind me to "stop thinking" more than once.

So I act. There's not a whole lot of air between me and the hard ground, after all. I switch off the autothrottle, shove the thrust levers forward. From behind, I hear the engines screech, shrill and piercing. They're still with me and I remind myself to breathe again. The jet responds: Airspeed is picking up, back to where it should be. I switch off the autopilot for good measure (or good riddance) and fly the jet down to the runway. It feels solid in my hands, and docile again. We land. Then everything comes to a sudden standstill. The screens freeze, the world outside stops moving.

We are in a simulator.

"Nice work," the instructor says from his little pedestal behind the two pilot seats. I turn around and smile at him, knowing that he knows what I know.

At that very time, I was helping to investigate the accident on which the scenario was based. A big jet crashed short of the runway because, in a one-in-a-million chance, the autothrottle was tricked into a wrong mode by some rare indication failure of the airplane's altimeter system. The radar altimeter erroneously told the autothrottle that the jet was on the ground (even though, pertinently, it *wasn't*) and that it was time to retard the thrust levers, to pull the power. The autothrottle computer never bothered to tell the autopilot about its brilliant intentions, however. The autopilot was happily doing its thing by riding down the glide slope to the runway, blissfully unaware that the other computer system had just robbed it of the only factor responsible for being able to fly at all: airspeed. None of the books about this jet available to pilots ever revealed this possibility. As far as pilots were concerned, it was an unknown unknown.

So I wasn't all that impressed with my own bravado, mind you. What did impress me, however, was the fact that I was sitting in a simulator, for one of the regular four-hour proficiency sessions that I need to do several times a year to keep my license valid, and here it was: The scenario that killed a bunch of people in the same jet but in another part of the world was being played through our flight, into our hands and minds. The official accident report wasn't even out yet, but plenty of pilots had realized that this could be really hazardous and decided to do something about it. For themselves, their colleagues, everybody. Now that's *double-loop learning.**

Yet, the accident revealed both the strengths and the weaknesses of learning from failure in this particular industry, aviation. Because, you see,

there had been trouble with radar altimeters on this kind of jet before. After the accident, it turned out that some pilots in the same airline, as well as in other airlines, had sometimes experienced funny things with the radar altimeter. Spurious warnings about proximity to the ground would be triggered, for example. In some cases, even the autothrottle would go into the wrong mode. But the failures would never repeat themselves on the next leg of the trip. They were impossible to re-create on the ground.

Engineers had no idea. Pilots did not write it up. These things were not seen as close calls at the time. If an unknown is unknown, then the symptoms of its trouble may go unrecognized; any symptoms may get rationalized as the necessary, unavoidable noise generated by a complicated system. Hey, we landed without incident, right? No harm, no incident. No close call, no report. No signal is seen among the noise. This is one of the biggest challenges: How do we decide what counts as bad news? What is "near" enough to a bad outcome to count as a close call? Social systems are expert at adapting their readings of risk to accommodate the seemingly normal and leave intervention only for the patently hazardous. Norms for what counts as risky get renegotiated all the time, particularly as operational experience with a particular system, particular procedure, or particular failure mode (or disease) accumulates. It is the kind of normalization of deviance ("Oh, we've seen this before, it's OK.") that eventually brings space shuttles down in flames.[1,2] If it's okay, it's not a close call. It will remain unknown as risky to everybody else. It is not strange that underreporting of adverse events in health care has been estimated to be between 50% and 96%,[3,4] even though this assumes a "norm" that can be agreed on about what constitutes an event relative to which people underreport. This is tricky.

---

*Single-loop learning constitutes adaptive learning; double-loop learning is reflection in and on action; and triple-loop learning is meta-learning.

RECONCILING THE HYPOTHESIS OF INFALLIBILITY WITH THE INEVITABILITY OF MISTAKES

It has been said that infallibility is the medical profession's working hypothesis. Lucien Leape, in reflecting on human error in medicine in 1994, stated the following:

> The most important reason physicians and nurses have not developed more effective methods of error prevention is that they have a great deal of difficulty in dealing with human error when it does occur. The reasons are to be found in the culture of medical practice. Physicians are socialized in medical school and residency to strive for error-free practice. There is a powerful emphasis on perfection, both in diagnosis and treatment. In everyday hospital practice, the message is equally clear: mistakes are unacceptable. Physicians are expected to function without error, an expectation that physicians translate into the need to be infallible. One result is that physicians, not unlike test pilots, come to view an error as a failure of character—you weren't careful enough, you didn't try hard enough.[4(p. 1851)]

There is nothing wrong with striving for perfection, of course. It is consistent with the idea of medicine as a vocation, a calling, rather than just normal technical work. As Charles Vincent pointed out for medicine:

> Those working in this environment foster a culture of perfection, in which errors are not tolerated, in which a strong sense of personal responsibility both for errors and outcome is expected. . . . With this background it is not surprising that mistakes are hard to deal with, particularly when so much else is at stake in terms of human suffering.[5(p. 142)]

Failures, then, can get to be regarded as nonexistent anomalies in the system. This makes them, in principle, not reportable; they cannot be talked about for what they are. The existence of a "hidden curriculum,"[6] which teaches medical students and residents a repertoire of actions and vocabulary of phrases to deal with the inevitable imperfections of medical practice, is another example of this culture. But there is a contradiction here. Almost everybody in health care will readily acknowledge that "nobody is perfect, you will make an error occasionally although you take all precautions to avoid it."[7(p. 192)]

So how do we reconcile infallibility as a working hypothesis with the inevitability of mistakes? There are least two ways, neither of which encourages reporting of close calls. The first way is by invoking incompetence —either remediable clinical inexperience or irredeemable unsuitability for the profession.[8] In the first case, the person involved in a close call was considered not good enough (yet) and still had a lot to do to achieve levels of perfection. It causes a senior practitioner to counsel, help, direct, or take over altogether. There is the expectation that the frequency of such events decreases as time goes on and as the individual's experience accumulates. Again, infallibility could be preserved as a working hypothesis. Achieving it just gets pushed into the future a bit.

If the individual did not discharge role obligations diligently and created unnecessary extra work for colleagues, then his or her performance would be considered normatively erroneous. Bosk found how senior surgeons continuously make assessments about whether the person making the mistake actually has any business being in the profession in the first place.[8] Mistakes got implicitly classified in these assessments, with different repertoires of action appended to them. The more such normative errors a person was seen to make, the less likely it would be that he or she would retain employment within that surgical service.[8] Infallibility could be preserved here, too, because it was a matter of particular individuals not belonging in the profession or in that particular specialty or service (the person may have lacked the "calling"). To the extent that errors are the result of inexperience and lack of exposure, the solution is simply more training and more exposure. But if close calls are judged to result from the individual's fundamental unsuitability for the profession, then there is nothing systemic or deeper about the error that is interesting to probe. The source of failure lies with the individual, and the solution is not to have the individual practice in that specialty or service.[8]

The other way in which the inevitability of mistakes can be reconciled with infallibility as a working hypothesis is to blame bad luck—arising from a particular set of circumstances: "People don't start off to harm a patient, it just happens."[7(p. 192)] In this case, the close call can be said to be something external, something accidentally imported through happenstance or bad luck. If a close call is ascribed to a highly unusual set of circumstances, then there is not much reason to reflect and probe and learn, either. The rationalization is that this particular set of circumstances (anatomical, physiological, operational, team-composition, organizational, and so forth) will not likely repeat itself in exactly this way, so there is little value in trying to predict and prevent it from creating trouble again. Indeed, it is not very useful to share any lessons from that particular encounter with those circumstances with colleagues, either, because they will not likely meet those circumstances, and in the end errors are inevitable anyway: "If mistakes are seen as inevitable and a matter of bad luck arising from a particular set of circumstances, then this implies that attempting to learn from other people's mistakes (and by implication, reporting those mistakes) is not regarded as a valuable exercise."[7(p. 194)]

These various repertoires of reconciliation have a consequence for the ability of the medical profession to reflect seriously on mistakes and learn from them. Critical reflection on safety and

error is not a taken-for-granted feature of the professional identity of people working in health care. This makes it hard to legitimize the reporting and discussion of error. It is even harder to deal meaningfully with the personal consequences of having made an error. Leape called this a paradox:

> The paradox is that although the standard of medical practice is perfection—error-free patient care—all physicians recognize that mistakes are inevitable. Most would like to examine their mistakes and learn from them. From an emotional standpoint, they need the support and understanding of their colleagues and patients when they make mistakes. Yet, they are denied both insight and support by misguided concepts of infallibility and by fear: fear of embarrassment by colleagues, fear of patient reaction, and fear of litigation. Although the notion of infallibility fails the reality test, the fears are well grounded.[4(p. 1852)]

REPORTING SYSTEMS: VOLUNTARY, NONPUNITIVE, AND PROTECTED

So how do other fields do it? Reporting systems are alive and well in aviation, in nuclear power generation, in many military applications, in petrochemical processing, and in steel production. Let's discuss just two of them here. Safety is very much a part of the professional identity of airline pilots and nuclear power plant engineers. It may have something to do with the subtle fact that they will be the first at the site of an accident. And that any accident may take their lives too. This tends to focus the mind. The potential for reflection is present. The cultural, professional, and practical dispositions to do so are present as well. But more is necessary. Close-call reporting systems that actually work do a couple of things really well. They are nonpunitive. They are protected. And they are voluntary.[9]

Let's start with the last one, having a voluntary system. Why is that any good, leaving it to people's own judgment to report or not? There is a very simple reason: Having a mandatory system makes no sense. If reporting a close call is mandatory, then practitioners will smoothly engage in various kinds of rhetoric or interpretive work to decide that the event they were involved in was not a close call. Having a mandatory system would probably increase the putative underreporting rate in medicine even more. And making reporting mandatory implies some kind of sanction if something is not reported. Which destroys the first ingredient for success: having a nonpunitive system.

Nonpunitive means that the reporter is not punished for revealing his or her own violations or other breaches or problems of conduct that might be construed as culpable. This is normally seen as hugely problematic, particularly in medicine. As Leape pointed out, "this kind of thinking lies behind a common reaction by physicians: 'How can there be an error without negligence?'"[4(p. 1851)] The infallibility hypothesis indeed leaves few alternatives. Close calls that cannot be constructed or rationalized away as remediable or irredeemable incompetence or bad luck (and thus might actually be reported) have to be due to some potentially culpable omission or act. However, not punishing that which is reported makes great sense, because otherwise it would not be reported. This creates a dilemma, of course, for those receiving the report (even if via some other party, such as a quality or safety staff member). They want to hear everything that goes on—but cannot accept what goes on. Yet if they make very clear that they will not stand for some of the things that get reported, these things will quickly cease to be reported. This is a delicate balance. One voluntary report about an adverse medication event, for example, ended up in the media. The nurse who had reported it was identified, found, charged with a crime, and convicted.[10] The willingness to report anything by any other nurse would have taken a severe beating. From the position of a manager or an administrator, the best way to manage this balance is to involve the practitioners who would potentially report (not necessarily the one who did report, because if it is a good reporting system, that might not be known to the manager). What is their assessment of the "error" that was reported? How would they want to deal with a colleague who *did* such a thing? In the end, whether an "error" is culpable is not about the crossing of some clear line that was there before the error. Whether an act or omission is reckless or negligent is a judgment, and often a difficult one, that somebody will have to make. Perceived justness often lies less in the decision than in who is involved in making that decision. For a manager, keeping the dialogue open with his or her practitioner constituency must be the most important aim. If dialogue is killed by rapid punitive action, then a version of the dialogue will surely continue elsewhere (behind the back of the manager). That leaves the system none the wiser about what goes on and what should be learned. I will say more about the effects and difficulties of a nonpunitive system at the end of the chapter.

Finally, successful reporting systems are *protected*. This means that reports are confidential rather than anonymous. What is the difference? *Anonymity* typically means that the reporter is never known, not to anybody. No name or affiliation has to be documented anywhere. *Confidentiality* means that the reporter fills in name and affiliation and is thus known to whomever gets the report. But from there on, the identity is protected, under any variety of industrial or organizational or legal arrangements. If reporting is anonymous, two things might happen quickly. The first is that the reporting system becomes the garbage can for any kind of vitriol that practitioners may accumulate about their job, their colleagues, or their hospital during a workday, workweek, or career. The risk for this, of course, is larger when there are few meaningful or effective line management structures in place that could take care of such concerns and complaints. However, senseless and useless bickering could clog the pipeline of safety-critical information. Signals of potential danger would get lost in the noise of potent grumble. That's why confidentiality makes more sense. The reporter may feel some visibility, some accountability even, for reporting things that can help the organization learn and grow. The second problem with an anonymous reporting system is that the reporter cannot be contacted if the need arises for any clarifications. The reporter is also out of reach for any direct feedback about actions taken in response to the report. The NASA Aviation Safety Reporting System (ASRS) recognized this quickly after finding reports that were incomplete or could have been much more potent in revealing possible danger if only this or that detail could be cleared up. As soon as a report is received, the narrative is separated from any identifying information (about the reporter and the place and time of the incident) so that the story can start to live its own life without the liability of recognition and sanction appended to it. This recipe has been hugely successful. ASRS receives more than 1,000 reports a week.[11]

CLOSE-CALL REPORTING IN AVIATION IN PRACTICE

Months after the proficiency check in the simulator I meet Jack, the safety manager of another airline. Jack is going to tell me about close-call reporting and how it helps safety in his organization.

We sit in a small office in a single-story building. The office is in a corner, with windows on one side looking straight into one of the airport's ramp areas. Airliners are pulling in just outside, almost nudging their nose into the roof of the little building as they slide into their parking spot. Diesel trucks and electric buggies and lifts and stairs of all sizes and shapes start milling around the fuselage and wings and engine pods, jostling for space like worker bees tending to

their queen. The windows of Jack's little office are powerless to stop the noise and the smells from jet engines and auxiliary power units and from coming through. The airport, aviation, movement, people, hazard, risk—they all make their presence known continuously in this little office, thundering through the glass panes, wafting and seeping through the cracks. This is way beyond immersion in the field. Here, the operational world is simply inescapable. The point of why a safety man is sitting here is firmly within any observer's grasp.

"What about the unknown unknowns?" I ask. I explain the accident sequence involving the indication failure of the altimeter system to him. Jack knows it, of course. Then he shrugs and shakes his head. "If our pilots or other operators don't recognize something as bad news, it's not going to make it into the system," he acknowledges.

We are silent for a little bit. Then Jack inhales audibly. "Here's our system, let me show you," he says, swiveling toward a computer terminal on a narrow black table. A few mouse clicks later, he has taken me to the outer layer of the close-call reporting system: the first screen on which you, me, anybody from the company or any of its suppliers or subcontractors can make a selection about what kind of report to file. There's a bewildering list. Flight safety reports, cabin safety reports, hazardous materials reports, bird strike reports, maintenance safety reports, and more, all indicated in acronyms and abbreviations bubbling from top to bottom on the screen.

"Which would you like to see?" Jack asks. We choose a flight safety report (FSR). More clicks. A new window opens; fields appear, beckoning my fingers to go to the keyboard to start typing. Some fields are mandatory, such as where was the flight going? What is the aircraft type?

Then there are optional fields. What phase of flight? What was the weather like? We type, make things up. Just to see how this works.

Then we come to the ultimate display in the system—the space for the narrative about the close call. From this display, a large white field is staring blankly back at me, daring me with its invitation for free text. I can imagine that people who have never learned to tell stories, or to type, for that matter, may feel a bit intimidated. Where to start? Should you follow the chronology? Begin with a presumed cause of trouble, or conclude with that? There is no filter between what is typed here and what gets seen at the other end of the system (which, really, is Jack). So what goes in comes out. The whole narrative may even make it to a safety review meeting or to management.

CLOSE CALLS AS NARRATIVES OR NUMBERS?

In a sense, it is good that Jack gets the "garbage" that his pilots type in directly, because a lot of other close-call reporting systems use indexing systems. These are not automatic but rather are tools used by staff (like Jack) to chop the narrative up into categories. They allow information from the close-call database to be presented numerically and graphically and to be compared across space or time (as in "we have so many of these so-and-so incidents with this or that technology compared with only so many last month or compared with only so many in our sister hospital across town"). Often, managers get to see nothing *but* such bar charts or pie charts or number tables in the hope that it would present them with some actionable information.

It probably does not. At least not often. The whole point of the narrative is the narrative. Outside of the story, there is no close call, there is no incident. There is no build-up, no context, no resolution, only dead remnants arbitrated by somebody who was not there when it happened, classified remains that have been lobotomized out of the living story from which they came. This limitation, and the finding that classification should not be confused with analysis, was

noted, as follows, in 1998—when initial enthusiasm for reporting was building in health care[3]:

> Classification does involve a type of analysis but a type that greatly constrains the insights that can be obtained from the data. Typically, when classification systems are used as the analysis, a report of an incident is assigned, through a procedure or set of criteria, into one or another fixed category. The category set is thought to capture or exhaust all of the relevant aspects of failures. Once the report is classified the narrative is lost or downplayed. Instead, tabulations are built up and put into statistical comparisons. Put simply, once assigned to a single category, one event is precisely, and indistinguishably like all the others in that category. Yet research on human performance in incidents and accidents emphasizes the diversity of issues and interconnections. . . . Capturing a rich narrative of the sequence and factors involved in the case has proven essential. Often, new knowledge or changing conditions leads investigators to ask new questions of the database of narratives. The analyst often goes back to the narrative level to look for new patterns or connections.[12(p. 41)]

Categories force analysts to make decisions, to draw lines, to decide that an action or a circumstance is *this* but not *that*. What if it is both? Or neither? Attempts to map human capabilities such as decision making, proficiency, or deliberation onto discrete categories are doomed to be misleading, for they cannot cope with the complexity of actual practice without serious degeneration.[13] Classification disembodies data. It removes the context that helped produce the close call in its particular manifestation. This disables understanding because by excising performance fragments away from their context, classification destroys the local rationality principle. This has been the fundamental concept for understanding—not judging—human performance for the past 50 years: People's behavior is rational, if possibly erroneous, when viewed from inside their situations, not from the outside and from hindsight.

The local rationality principle also reminds us that the consequences of actions are not necessarily well correlated with intentions, yet this evaporates in the wake of close-call classification. It is important to note that the point in learning about close calls is not to find out where people went wrong. It is to find out why their assessments and actions made sense to them at the time, given their knowledge, goals, tools, and resources. For we have to assume that if it made sense to someone (given the background and circumstances), it will make sense to someone else, too, and the close call will not only repeat itself but perhaps not remain a close call the next time. Controversial behavior can be made to make sense (be understood) once resituated in the context that brought it forth.

After the observation of a close call is tidily locked away into some category, it has been objectified, formalized away from its context. Without context, there is no way to reestablish local rationality. And without local rationality, there is no way to understand human error. Classification probably presents managers and administrators, and possibly even practitioners, with an illusion of understanding. It disconnects human agents' performance from the context that brought it forth and from the circumstances that accompanied it, that gave it meaning, and that hold the keys to its explanation.

There is another organizational side effect of collecting close-call reports: It may feed the illusion that safety management is really "unsafety" management, that effective intervention consists of getting rid of the "bad stuff." But safety is more than the measurement and management of negatives (close calls), if it is that at all. There is little or no evidence that "safety" as such actually exists, independent of workers' minds or their

surrounding culture. Research has shown instead that safety is more a "constructed human concept"[14(p. 1550)] and has begun to probe how individual practitioners construct safety by assessing what they understand risk to be and how they perceive the difficulty of managing challenging situations.[15] Interestingly, Orasanu discovered a mismatch between risk salience (how critical a particular threat to safety was perceived to be by the practitioner) and frequency of encounters (how often these threats to safety are in fact met in practice).[15] The safety threats deemed most salient were the ones least frequently dealt with.

Given these results, it is no wonder that good empirical indicators of social and organizational definitions of safety are difficult to obtain. According to Rochlin, the description of what safety means to an individual is a part of that very safety, and is dynamic and subjective: "Safety is in some sense a story a group or organization tells about itself and its relation to its task environment."[14(p. 1555)] Clearly, such aspects of safety can only be captured by a less categorical, numerical approach. An approach is required which probes the interpretative aspect of human assessments and actions. For that, what we need are narratives about close calls, which can be as much stories of how things went wrong as stories about how things (which could have gone wrong) went right after all. They can be stories of resilience, in other words. They can be stories of how a system of people and technologies was able to recognize, absorb, and adapt to changes and challenges that perhaps fell outside what the team was trained or designed to handle.[16]

This aspect of close-call reporting is instructive even for the managers or administrators who may see themselves at the consuming end of the system. Resilience is created when people engineer extra margin into their operations, the kind of slack that allows them to adapt under pressure and accommodate surprise and that allows them to extemporize and accommodate the fluctuating pressures and tasks of actual work. Resilience is created when (1) people keep a discussion about risk alive even when everything looks safe; (2) teams and organizations have institutionalized the courage to show dissent independent of rank or status, to say "no" or "stop" even in the face of acute production pressures; and (3) past successes are no longer seen as an automatic guarantee of future safety. Such creation of resilience applies across scales and levels; resilience can and must be created throughout hierarchies—not just at the sharp end.

Nonetheless, the idea that close-call reporting is simply about counting negatives, presented to management and administrations in the form of various graphics, may be compelling to the health care industry for the same reasons that any numerical performance measurement is.

"Why not find a story of the month?" I asked Jack. Rather than presenting numerics, select a story to tell management. Human memory is made for stories, not numbers. Jack thinks this could be good idea. However, numbers are compelling to Jack's managers, too. "You see," he says, after another frenzy of mouse clicks and screens that flash open and close, "this is how we can generate statistics." He shows me a list of crude incident counts—so much of this kind, so much of that, a little table of categories with hit rates next to them. I begin to see how the quantification of close-call results helps assert the existence of an observer-independent reality. The quantified results are an objective window into this reality that can be offered to managers, with the illusion that here is a world that they can affect, influence, mold, shape, control, and understand without having to take some analyst's word for it:

> The use of figures and graphs not only embodies numbers, but gives the reader the sense of "seeing the phenomenon." By using figures and graphs the scientist implicitly says, "You don't have to take my word for it, look for yourself."[17(p. 56)]

What is finessed here is what the numbers stand for to begin with and how they were arrived at. Confidence about where to intervene is reduced to a kind of ranking or numerical strength, a sort of democracy of numbers. The problem, of course, is that managers in this case *do* take the analysts' word for it. It was an analyst, after all, who decided to put some things into some categories and others into other categories. This, however, as well as the rationale for it, has disappeared entirely by the time the numbers show up in the boardroom.

I don't say anything of the sort to Jack. He is now busy explaining to me how he is working with his programming colleague to force the user to enter his or her flight numbers in a particular way and to make sure that he or she uses an acceptable format for the time of the incident ("So you can't do, say, '6:00 P.M.' but have to write 18:00:00, and of course in UTC [Coordinated Universal Time], not local"). I nod dutifully but wonder who is doing the analysis while he is sitting there worrying about input values. Who's learning from failure now? There's nobody else in the office. I conclude that collection is easier than analysis. And that analysis is easier than taking meaningful action. And that taking meaningful action is still a bit removed from preventing an accident.

Gathering reports is only the beginning. The enthusiasm with which we encourage people to report is seldom matched by our ability to do anything meaningful *with* the reports—so that people will stay encouraged to report in the future. Close-call classifications easily become the stand-in for analysis, real understanding, and actionable intelligence. Classification alone can be seen as a sufficient quantitative basis for managerial interventions. Pieces of data from the operation that have been excised and formalized away from their origin can be converted into graphs and bar charts that are subsequently engineered into interventions. Never mind that the bar charts show comparisons between apples and oranges (for example, causes and consequences of a close call), which lead managers to believe they have learned something of value. It may not matter because managers can elaborate their idea of control over operational practice and its outcomes. The real world is not so easily fooled: Managerial "control" exists only in the sense of purposefully formulating and trying to influence workers' intentions and actions.[13] It is not at all the same as being in control of the consequences (by which safety ultimately gets measured health care–wide)—the real world is too complex and operational environments too stochastic.[18] Numbers that may seem managerially appealing are really quite sterile, inert. They do not reflect any of the nuances of what it is to "be there," doing the work, creating safety on the line. Yet, this is what ultimately determines safety (as outcome): People's local actions and assessments are shaped by their own perspectives—self-referential, embedded in histories, rituals, interactions, beliefs, and myths, both of their organization and themselves as individuals.

This is also a reminder that the collection of close-call reports is only the starting point. The number of reports collected, or the increase in such numbers, is often seen as a reason to celebrate the success of the system. But this is not the success. Close-call reporting is only a means to an end, not the end itself. One of the most important ways in which close-call narratives, in all their cultural, historical, and mythical richness, can contribute to learning by other people closely involved with the safety-critical processes is by integrating them into recurrent training. This is what happens in the aviation industry. Mandatory yearly crew resource management training that focuses on the soft skills (communication, interaction) for producing safe, successful outcomes can benefit hugely from the review of and critical reflection over cases from people's own operational environment. That is one place where the loop from close-call report to organizational learning can be closed—perhaps more effectively than with a pie chart beamed up on the wall during a management meeting.

Jack shows me other ways in which the learning loop gets closed. "I assign a risk factor to each incident," he says. Depending on the severity of the risk that he assesses it to be, the incident gets bumped up into the organization. The risk factor can also be renegotiated in such subsequent meetings. All risk control measures that are proposed after an incident has been bumped up have to be approved by the safety department. That would be Jack. Jack closes the loop.

I can't help but think of the normalization of deviance. The various manufacturers also are linked into the system, Jack explains. Not that they can see full reports, but they get numeric results about their equipment, so that they can see how well their stuff is doing and where the weak spots are. And again, I think about the unknown unknowns. No matter how well you are linked in, it won't matter much if the people who put the information in don't know what to look for, and if you don't either.

"What about the regulator?" I ask. "They get to see all reports," Jack adds, "with identifying information." The country out of which his airline operates clearly allows such openness: There is trust that the reports (and particularly the reporter) are not abused for what they (or the reporter) reveals.

WHO GETS TO KNOW ABOUT YOUR CLOSE CALL?

This is a particularly interesting question. How can people trust that their reports will not be used against them? What kinds of protections are fair? And will such protections not lead to the abuse of the close-call reporting system for accountability (rather than learning) purposes it was never intended to support? I think back to an incident in which I myself was a player.

The incident was minor: The landing-gear doors opened up on climb-out (in which the aircraft climbs to a predetermined cruising altitude after take-off) because of the ergonomics of the gear handle (which makes pulling it too far down very easy). However, we knew that this little event would show up on the automatic flight data recording system of the aircraft. Because gear doors are not supposed to open on climb-out, it would probably show up red or otherwise marked. Modern aircraft have an electronic store of astounding capacity that records up to hundreds of data points every second. The electronic footprint that each flight leaves as a result is huge, probably larger than the total electronic memory of the entire world during the closing days of World War II. We knew that if this little event showed up and we did not report it as a close call, then we might get questions—either from the equivalent of Jack or from the chief pilot, who oversees the operation of his fleet. It was close to midnight when we got back to our base airport. We decided to write a report.

My colleague went at it first. He opened the appropriate window on the computer terminal in the deserted crew room but was clearly not used to typing or to creating a narrative, or even to forming words or phrases that would carry what his meaning. After seeing him hunt and peck at some keys, only to repeatedly delete the painfully produced letters not much later, I gently nudged him out of the way and then we stood there. The soft buzz of fluorescent lights in the ceiling overhead was the only life left in the crew room besides us—two bleary-eyed guys trying to compose a text that would say enough but not too much, a text that would explain but not incriminate.

My fingers hovered over the grimy keyboard until they finally exploded into a feverish typing. When I stepped back and viewed the end result with my colleague, we saw that it had become a set of phrases and wordings that fulfilled the purpose of exculpating ourselves more than it would help the organization become stronger or smarter or better or safer. It wasn't our fault, you know, and we really thought we were being good

boys by volunteering our side of the story, thank you very much. My colleague thought it was a good narrative.

This, indeed, is the risk of close-call reporting. For some cases, the reporting system can become a liability management device more than an instrument for collective learning and organizational safety improvement. The system does not get a whole lot wiser, but at least we, the operators, get better protection against any consequences of our actions. I marvel at my own susceptibility to this inversion of intentions. On the way out of the crew room to the darkened parking lot, I tell myself that I should know better—that I should write reports that help the airline and everybody else, not me. Or at least not primarily me. But then, I have it easy. I have the chief pilot's ear any day. If I have a concern, I'll tell him. The incident with the gear doors I wouldn't even tell him about. It's because of the possible anomaly that would show up in the flight data recording that I felt compelled to send something in. But I could hardly call it a concern. The incident was so minor, after all . . . which, I realize, is what we all say until it contributes to something no longer so minor.

I later saw a medical colleague who lamented the lack of close-call reporting at his hospital. "People don't realize that they should be reporting this sort of stuff," he said. "That's the only way we can discover the weak spots before they become really dangerous." The way he talked about it, I started to understand that a close call in his hospital was considered much more a "miss" than anything "near." If it's a miss, it's a nonevent. And if it's a nonevent, there is nothing to report. Standard procedure at his hospital? Wipe the brow, say, "Whew, we got away with that one," then peel off the gloves and go home.

I now look back differently on my *non-mea-culpa* story, whipped into that grungy computer terminal the night of the gear-door event. Whatever our motive, whatever our motivation, the story at least made it into the system. The close call was on record now. Perhaps it was better to send in an exculpatory "don't-blame-me-I-was-only-behaving-like-a-boy-scout" story than not sending in anything.

We're back in Jack's little corner office. The row of windows that doesn't look out onto the ramp offers a view of something decidedly inglorious: a garbage dumpster. It says *FOD* on it, or Foreign Object Damage—stuff that can get sucked into jet engines and create all kinds of havoc. This can be anything from baggage labels to baby stroller parts to food cartons. The ramp must be clear of it, and a slew of garbage dumpsters is provided for anything found there by anybody. After an aircraft has taxied in and shut down close to the office, a man lumbers over to the dumpster, gray bags slung over each shoulder. Jack and I watch him as he hauls the bags into the Dumpster. Whatever he just threw in there, it is not FOD by any stretch. This is garbage from the aircraft that just taxied in. I suppose it had to go somewhere, that the airline got tired of paying for any other means.

The Dumpster lid bangs closed and the man walks back out onto the ramp. I see Jack looking after him and can't help but wonder if Jack sees the same analogy. Here, in his little corner of the airport, is a place where the dirty laundry of the airline, its garbage, its detritus can end up. Where all the bad news collects. Where it can get stored and taken care of, safely and securely. And where we can begin the process of recycling it into something productive.

WHAT ARE THE LESSONS FROM AVIATION?

The lessons from aviation for meaningful close-call reporting can be summarized as follows:

- Close-call reporting is critical for the creation of a safety culture. Incidents represent "free" lessons that can be used to discover and change unsafe conditions.

- Successful close-call reporting systems are confidential, nonpunitive, and protected. *Confidential* means that the reporter is known only to one or a few trusted people who have no say over possible sanctions. *Nonpunitive* means that the reporter cannot be blamed for something that becomes known only through the close-call report. *Protected* means that stored close-call data are not accessible by outsiders.

- Setting targets for close-call reports is useless. Measuring the number of reports as an indicator of greater or lesser safety is hugely unreliable, in part because the denominator will always be unknown (underreporting remains rife in health care).

- Reporting close calls is easier than analyzing close calls. And analyzing them is easier than changing processes or behaviors in the organization.

- A close-call reporting system is only a start. Considerable investments in analytic expertise and resources are necessary, as is the assurance of influence at relevant decision-making levels in the organization. Only then can an organization exploit the full potential of close-call reporting.

References

1. Rogers W.P., et al.: *Report of the Presidential Commission on the Space Shuttle* Challenger *Accident.* Washington, DC: Diane Publishing Company, 1986.
2. Vaughan D.: *The* Challenger *Launch Decision: Risky Technology, Culture, and Deviance at NASA.* Chicago: University of Chicago Press, 1996.
3. Institute of Medicine: *To Err Is Human: Building a Safer Health System.* Washington, DC: National Academy Press, 2000.
4. Leape L.L.: Error in medicine. *JAMA* 272:1851–1857, Dec. 21, 1994.
5. Vincent C.: *Patient Safety.* London: Elsevier Churchill Livingstone, 2006.
6. Karnieli-Miller O., et al.: Medical students' professionalism narratives: A window on the informal and hidden curriculum. *Acad Med* 85:124–133, Jan. 2010.
7. McDonald R., et al.: Rules, safety and the narrativisation of identity: A hospital operating theatre case study. *Sociol Health Illn* 28:178–202, Mar. 2006.
8. Bosk C.: *Forgive and Remember: Managing Medical Failure,* 2nd ed. Chicago: University of Chicago Press, 2003.

9. Barach P., Small S.D.: Reporting and preventing medical mishaps: Lessons from non-medical near miss reporting systems. *BMJ* 320:759–763, Mar. 18, 2000.

10. Dekker S.: Discontinuity and disaster: Gaps and the negotiation of culpability in medication delivery. *J Law Med Ethics* 35:463–470, Fall 2007.

11. Billings C.E.: *Aviation Automation: The Search for a Human-Centered Approach.* Mahwah, NJ: Lawrence Erlbaum Associates, 1996.

12. Cook R.I., Woods D.D., Miller C.: *A Tale of Two Stories: Contrasting Views of Patient Safety.* National Health Care Safety Council of the National Patient Safety Foundation at the American Medical Association, 1998. http://www.npsf.org/rc/tts/front.html (accessed Sep. 8, 2010).

13. Angell I.O., Straub B.: Rain-dancing with pseudo-science. *Cogn Technol Work* 1(3):179–196, 1999.

14. Rochlin G.I.: Safe operation as a social construct. *Ergonomics* 42:1549–1560, Nov. 1999.

15. Orasanu J.M.: *The Role of Risk Assessment in Flight Safety: Strategies for Enhancing Pilot Decision Making.* Paper presented at the 4th International Workshop on Human Error, Safety and Systems Development, Linköping, Sweden, 2001.

16. Hollnagel E., Woods D.D., Leveson N. (eds.): *Resilience Engineering: Concepts and Precepts.* Aldershot, UK: Ashgate, 2006.

17. Gergen K.J.: *An Invitation to Social Construction.* London: Sage, 1999.

18. Snook S.A.: *Friendly Fire: The Accidental Shootdown of U.S. Black Hawks over Northern Iraq.* Princeton, NJ: Princeton University Press, 2000.

CHAPTER 4

Human Factors Applications to Understanding and Using Close Calls to Improve Health Care

Tosha B. Wetterneck, M.D., M.S.; Ben-Tzion Karsh, Ph.D.

This chapter describes human factors ideas about close calls. It first defines the human factors (HF) discipline and its contribution to improving work safety. Next, the chapter discusses how HF methods and theories are (or are not) making their way into health care. The chapter then discusses systems thinking and HF views on errors and violations and their causes and accident investigation. Finally, the chapter discusses how HF researchers and professionals think about close calls and error management in organizations.

WHAT IS HUMAN FACTORS?

HF is a scientific discipline that discovers and applies information about human behavior, abilities, limitations, and other characteristics to the design of tools, machines, systems, tasks, jobs, and environments for productive, safe, comfortable, and effective human use. In practice, HF professionals design the fit between people and products, equipment, facilities, procedures, and environments. The goal of HF is to improve the productivity and performance of persons at work while also maintaining safety—that is, decreasing errors and work-related injuries. Human factors engineering (HFE) is considered the basic science of human performance—and therefore the basic science of safety and efficiency and the resulting quality outcomes. Quality and safety are emergent properties from the interaction between people and the system in which they work.[1,2] HF evaluates these interactions in the work system to design or redesign systems to improve quality and safety.

HF, as a scientific and applied discipline, emerged from different traditions around the world from the late 1800s through 1940s. Today, many leading companies employ HF professionals, and in academia, HF faculty are found in departments of industrial and systems engineering, psychology, and information science, and even a few schools of medicine. In the United States, for example, the federal Departments of Defense, Energy, and Transportation; the National Aeronautics and Space Administration (NASA); the Nuclear Regulatory Commission; and the Federal Aviation Administration embrace HF research and design and have developed design guidelines derived from decades of HF research. HF is also used extensively by government departments and associations outside the United States—for example, the European Organisation for the Safety of Air Navigation, the National Health Service in the United Kingdom, the National Aerospace Laboratory in the Netherlands, the Swedish Transport Administration, the European Agency for Safety and Health at Work, and the National Information and Communications Technology Australia.

HF professionals, who usually have master's degrees or doctorate-level training in industrial and systems engineering or psychology, are employed in the industries associated with the governmental agencies, as mentioned, as well as in other industries, including chemicals, medical devices, software, insurance, and agriculture. In contrast, clinical operations in health care delivery until recently have had little to no involvement with HF.

HF uses a systems approach to understanding and managing errors and close calls. This is very different from the traditional approach used for so long in health care, which focused on individuals. The systems approach involves focusing on the *conditions* under which individuals work. The system itself is composed of the people, the tasks to be done, the organization and the environment in which the work is being done, and the tools and technologies available to do the work. By creating better work systems, the people doing the work are optimally supported to be productive and defenses are built in to avert errors or poor productivity or to mitigate their effects. In health care, health care provider and system performance are optimized to help achieve safe, high-quality outcomes for patients, providers, and health care organizations.

HUMAN FACTORS AND THE HEALTH CARE DOMAIN

HF applications to health care can be traced back to the 1960s, with the publication of an analysis of medication errors in hospitals by Safren and Chapanis.[3] Anesthesiology was the first medical profession to embrace HFE (in the 1980s).[4] Through the application of HF principles and the implementation of multiple changes in care delivery, including teamwork training, use of simula-

tion for training, implementation of new technology (for example, pulse oximetry, improved patient monitors), and written procedures and guidelines for practice, mortality dropped significantly from the late 1970s to the late 1990s.[4]

Today, the Institute of Medicine (IOM), The Joint Commission, and patient safety experts recommend the application of HF to health care.[5-7] The Joint Commission's *Sentinel Event Alert* identifies specific sentinel events, describes their common underlying causes, and suggests steps to prevent occurrences in the future.[8] Many of the *Sentinel Event Alert*s concern safety risks and preventable adverse events associated with the use of technologies (such as infusion pumps, tubing connections, computerized physician order entry), which "typically stem from human–machine interfaces or organization/system design."[9] In addition, The Joint Commission encourages accredited organizations to voluntarily report "reviewable" sentinel events and the associated root cause analyses (RCAs); reporting is required when the Joint Commission has learned about the event from another source, such as complaints or the media.[10] The Joint Commission requires organizations to perform a proactive risk assessment (PRA) to analyze high-risk processes prospectively and determine ways to decrease or eliminate risk before harm occurs to patients from errors.[11*] Joint Commission International (JCI) also requires an RCA and PRA as part of its Sentinel Event Policy, as well as use of a proactive risk-reduction tool.[12†] The Joint Commission is reconsidering its Sentinel Event Policy, which may entail improved recognition, reporting, and analyses of not only adverse events but also hazards and close calls.[13]

---

*Standard LD.04.04.05: The hospital has an organization-wide, integrated patient safety program within its performance improvement activities. Element of Performance 10: At least every 18 months, the hospital selects one high-risk process and conducts a proactive risk assessment.

†Standard QPS.11: An ongoing program of risk management is used to identify and to reduce unanticipated adverse events and other safety risks to patients and staff. Measurable Element 2: The organization conducts and documents use of a proactive risk-reduction tool at least annually on one of the priority risk processes.

Note: Both LP04.04.05 and QPS.11 are effective as of the date of this publication. For current standards, please consult the current appropriate Joint Commission or Joint Commission International comprehensive accreditation manual.

However, the health care industry as a whole has not yet embraced HF as a means of improving safety. For this reason, the National Academy of Engineering and the IOM published a report outlining how health care and engineering can partner together to redesign health care delivery and achieve the improvements in safety that other industries have realized.[14] That partnership includes, but is not limited to, HF scientists and professionals working with clinicians to identify, analyze, and solve health care delivery performance and safety problems.

There are many reasons that HF theories and methods have not been taken up more readily in the health care setting. First, there is a general lack of awareness in health care of HF theories and methods and how they can be used to improve quality and safety.[14] Second, there are few incentives, financial or other, in health care to adopt HF principles to improve quality and safety.[14] The initial and ongoing investment in systems tools, information technologies, and personnel expertise is prohibitive for many organizations, and care providers will not invest unless there is a direct and immediate impact on revenue. Third, HF and health care apply different paradigms for adopting new practices.[2] Health care uses an evidence-based medicine approach to changing existing practice or incorporating new practices in care provision, with the gold standard being randomized controlled trials (RCTs). The HF discipline has developed many of its design guidelines for supporting physical and cognitive work from RCTs. However, most of these trials have not been performed in health care settings, and most are published outside the health care literature. Knowing whether and when the knowledge gained from these studies can be directly translated to the health care setting or whether more studies are needed requires HF expertise. For example, it is known how loud an auditory tone needs to be above the masking threshold for most people to hear it—and it is also known how the threshold varies by whether one is doing simple or complex cognitive work. That research was not done in health care, but health care providers' ears are not different from those of others. On the other hand, an auditory tone in a health care environment such as the operating room or intensive care unit, which contains dozens of other tones, may need to be more complex and louder to be discriminable. In other words, although the basic science of HF applies in general to the health care professionals who all share human capabilities and limitations, specific applications to health care's many and varied environments still need to be tested. In addition, some interventions may not require RCTs because *stronger* evidence is available from physics or geometry. For example, if enteral feeding tubes are made geometrically incompatible with intravenous (IV) tubes, an RCT is not needed to determine that the risk of wrong route errors decreased. Finally, health care providers and staff do not commonly receive education in HFE or systems thinking. Likewise, few universities have courses for engineers in health care delivery. This creates a gap in knowledge for both professions and the lack of a shared vocabulary to discuss patient safety problems.

HUMAN FACTORS AND SYSTEMS THINKING

HF theories about humans and work performance embrace *systems thinking*. A *system* is defined as "an aggregation of elements organized in some structure to accomplish system goals and objectives."[15(p. 36)] Humans at work perform within a "work system"; the system around them influences their performance and therefore the quality and safety of the outcomes of the work. The Systems Engineering Initiative for Patient Safety (SEIPS) model, developed in 2001, is an HF model that assists evaluation of system factors in relation to quality and patient safety[16] (*see* Figure 4-1, page 42). The work system is made up of five elements, as follows, which interact with one another to produce the processes of care, which in turn lead to patient and organizational outcomes:

Figure 4-1. The Systems Engineering Initiative for Patient Safety (SEIPS) Model for Patient Safety

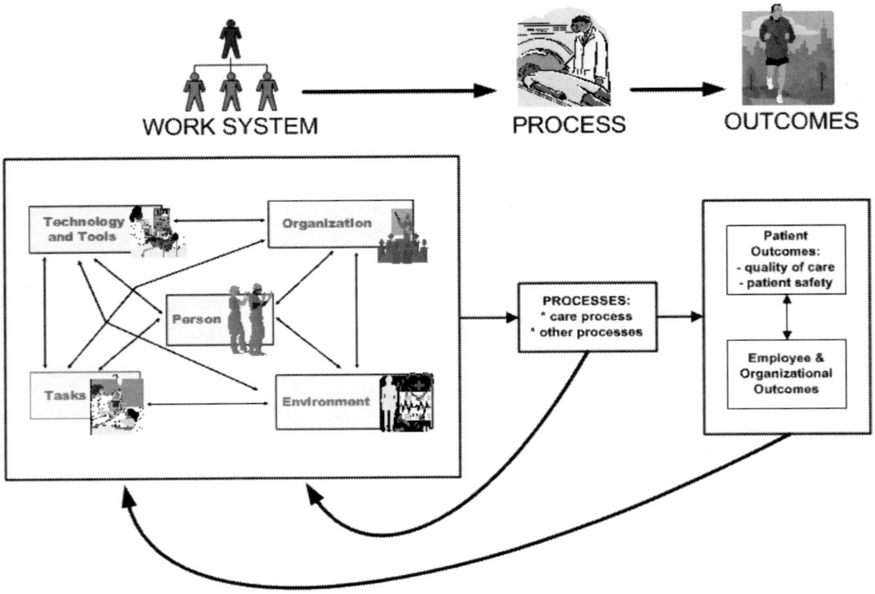

Source: Carayon P., et al.: Work system design for patient safety: The SEIPS model. *Qual Saf Health Care* 15(Suppl. 1):i50–i58, Dec. 2006. Used with permission.

1. *Tasks* are activities performed at work. Task characteristics include the variety and content of tasks, job demands such as time pressure and work load, and job control.

2. *Tools and technology* are used to perform the tasks; examples are the electronic health record (EHR) or patient-lifting and patient-transfer devices. Technology design characteristics include the equipment design, the display and interface design, and the level of automation.

3. Tasks are performed in a *physical environment* with characteristics such as the layout of a patient examination room, noise levels (for example, multiple loud alarms in an intensive care unit), lighting, and temperature.

4. The *organizational* conditions that the work is performed under include the policies and procedures in place, the safety culture, the

training that staff receive, finances, external regulations and accreditation requirements for the organization to follow, and the resources available to complete tasks.

5. The *people* involved are the final element. A *person* represents the health care provider(s) and staff, the patient, and anyone else involved in the work to be done. Person characteristics include personality traits, level of alertness and fatigue, physical limitations, risk aversion, experience level, and other human physical or psychological characteristics. The person is the center of the work system and interacts with all elements of the work system.

To produce quality outcomes, the work system should be designed to facilitate and enhance human performance. In addition, the SEIPS model recognizes that any change to an element of a work system will affect all parts of the system and the processes of care they produce. Therefore, change must be managed carefully so that the changes to the interactions between the elements are anticipated and redesigned to facilitate optimal human performance. There are many examples in health care where change has not been managed from a systems viewpoint and where unintended consequences were consequently realized (for example, reductions in physician–patient communication after implementation of EHRs).[17] If the desired outcomes are not being achieved, the goal is to reevaluate and redesign the work system.

The SEIPS model has been expanded by Karsh et al. to further describe the mechanisms through which system design affects health care outcomes[1] (*see* Figure 4-2, page 44). In this model, *human performance* is the transformation process that results in health care outcomes. The inputs into the human performance are the system elements: The patient and provider factors are the center of the system, nested within the work system and work-unit factors, which nest within the organization factors, which in turn nest within the industry (external environment) factors that influence health care. The transformation processes outline the three major influences on human performance:

1. Physical performance characteristics (for example, ability to see, walk, carry, manipulate, type)

2. Cognitive performance characteristics (for example, sensing, memory, communicating, problem solving)

3. Social/behavioral performance characteristics (for example, decision making, motivation, social learning)

These processes then lead to outputs or outcomes in physical and mental state for the health care provider and/or patient and impact the state of the work system.

HF scientists and professionals use system approaches to design or redesign work systems to meet the needs of the people working in them. This means focusing on and optimizing the conditions under which people work to improve human performance. As James Reason stated, "We cannot change the human condition but we can change the conditions under which humans work."[18(p. 769)] Translating this for health care, the road to high quality and safe patient outcomes runs through the health care professional. Therefore, if the physical and cognitive performance of health care professionals is not supported, patient care will inevitably suffer.

From an HF perspective of inpatient and outpatient health care delivery, the typical "client" is the health care professional. The goal of system redesign is to support the work of health care providers and staff, with the goal of producing better worker outcomes, such as safety, quality, productivity, and quality of working life. This is not to say that the HF perspective is not patient centered. On the contrary, according to the HF perspective, the high-quality patient outcomes are considered the work product of the health care providers and staff. The partnership of HF professionals, health care providers, organizations, and patients should ensure positive outcomes for all.

HOW DO HUMAN FACTORS PROFESSIONALS THINK ABOUT ERRORS AND WHAT CAUSES ERRORS?

What is the human condition? Humans by nature are fallible—that is, they are predisposed to make errors because of the motor, sensory, and cognitive limitations of being human. Human limitations that predispose people to make errors have long been studied by HF scientists and have been the subject of recent discussions and changes in health care. Examples include sleep deprivation and fatigue from long work hours, as experienced by residents,[19] and as addressed, in part, by the Accreditation Council for Graduate Medical Education's newly released duty-hours standards[20]; working-memory constraints and

Figure 4-2. Input–Transformation–Output Model of Health Care Professional Performance

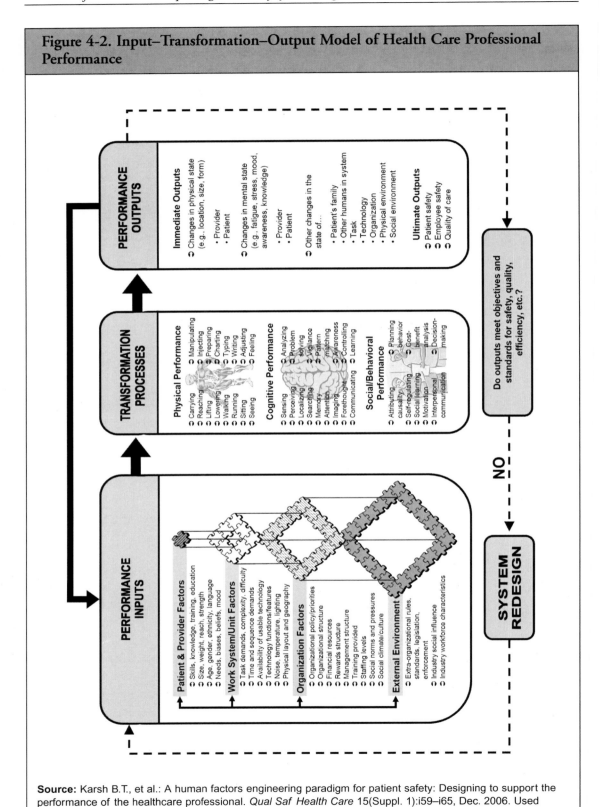

Source: Karsh B.T., et al.: A human factors engineering paradigm for patient safety: Designing to support the performance of the healthcare professional. *Qual Saf Health Care* 15(Suppl. 1):i59–i65, Dec. 2006. Used with permission.

the move to EHRs for easy access to information[21]; and attention and concentration limits and research showing how interruptions can result in medical errors and omitted tasks.[22] HF scientists focus on how to create systems to overcome these limitations and improve the reliability of humans to consistently perform. The context in which humans work—the work system—can also predispose people to error by exacerbating known human limitations. These context factors include work load, information flow/access to needed information, time constraints, teamwork, and organizational culture. Table 4-1 (*see* page 46) provides a comprehensive list of human limitations and work-context factors that predispose to errors. All these work-context issues apply in health care and have been found to be related to medical errors and poor patient outcomes. The work context can also promote errors solely by poor design. For example, poor infusion-pump interface design permitting "key bounce"—that is, double digits appearing when a number button is pushed once—leads to errors in pump programming.

Thus, it is the interplay between humans and the systems in which they work that results in errors.[15] Humans are not perfect, and well-intentioned people make errors when working with poorly designed systems. The flip side is that humans spend a lot of time overcoming bad design to keep the system working well and allow them to perform well in spite of bad design. Human adaptability and creativity are also part of the human condition.[23] Humans are attentive to changes in the working environment and can adapt in response to changes in the environment. These characteristics make humans very different from machines, which are rigid and insensitive to change. As such, one can think of design to reduce error but also to support and promote what humans do well.

The system's approach is very different from the traditional person approach, or the "blame and train" approach in health care. The person approach blames humans for their errors and focuses on (re)training, writing procedures, or taking disciplinary measures to deal with errors that occur. The focus is on humans "trying harder" not to commit errors rather than recognizing that there are systems factors affecting human performance that should be fixed. The systems approach, then, focuses on the pathways that lead to errors occurring.

Several HF accident-causation models, including Reason's Swiss cheese model,[18] (*see* Chapter 1, page 4) and Vincent's Organisational Accident Model,[24] outline the pathways that lead to adverse events. The Human Factors Analysis and Classification System (HFACS) model was developed and validated as a model for aviation which defines the holes in Reason's Swiss cheese model to better determine the contributing factors to errors.[25] This model, which is readily adaptable to the health care setting for analyzing close calls and accidents, has four main layers of failure matching the layers of cheese in Reason's model: (1) organizational factors, (2) unsafe supervision, (3) preconditions for unsafe acts, and (4) the unsafe acts themselves, such as errors and violations. Like the other models, the model suggests that if unsafe acts breach the system defenses, then there is a potential for an adverse outcome.

Both errors and violations are unsafe acts that lead to accidents, which in turn can result in harm to patients or others. HF and health care share Reason's definition of *error* as "a planned sequence of mental or physical activities [that] fail[s] to achieve its intended outcome,"[26(p. 9)] due to either a mistake in planning or execution. Errors are symptoms of underlying problems in the work system, just as a fever is a symptom of an infection and pain may be related to a broken bone in a person's body. Less attention has been focused on violations as unsafe acts; *violations* can be defined as "deliberate—but not necessarily reprehensible—deviations from those practices deemed necessary (by designers, managers, and regulatory agencies) to

Table 4-1. Human Characteristics and Work-Context Factors That Affect Human Performance

Human Characteristics

- Sensory capabilities and limitations
- Perceptual powers and perceptual confusion
- Top-down and bottom-up processing
- Working memory capacity and constraints
- Anthropometric dimensions
- Strength
- Endurance/systemic fatigue
- Local muscle fatigue
- Emotion
- Personality
- Motivation
- Learning
- Planning and forecasting
- Risk perception and risk attitude
- Heuristics and biases
- Sleep deprivation
- Attention/concentration
- Knowledge level
- Skill level
- Education level
- Experience
- Gender
- Ethnicity
- Culture
- Long-term memory organization (e.g., mental models, rules)
- Psychological consequences as the result of prior errors
- Adaptability
- Flexibility
- Creativity
- Context sensitivity

Work Context

- Time constraints
- Task complexity
- Task demands
- Sequence of work
- Linearity/nonlinearity of work
- Coupling
- Mental and physical work load
- Noise, lighting, and temperature
- Physical space
- Organizational structure
- Organizational culture
- Reward system
- Staffing
- Information presentation and access
- Information flow
- Training
- Work schedule/shift work
- Communication
- Interruptions and distractions
- Novel and unanticipated events
- Knowledge demands
- Workgroup culture
- Teamwork
- Automation
- Procedures
- Multiple and shifting objectives

Source: Adapted from Salvendy G. (ed.): *Handbook of Human Factors and Ergonomics*, 3rd ed. Hoboken, NJ: John Wiley & Sons, Inc., 2006; Norman D.A.: *Things That Make Us Smart: Defending Human Attributes in the Age of the Machine.* Cambridge, MA: Perseus Books, 1993; Karsh B.T., et al.: A human factors engineering paradigm for patient safety: Designing to support the performance of the healthcare professional. *Qual Saf Health Care* 15(Suppl. 1):i59–i65, Dec. 2006; Carayon P., et al.: Work system design for patient safety: The SEIPS model. *Qual Saf Health Care* 15(Suppl. 1):i50–i58, Dec. 2006; Eastman Kodak Company: *Kodak's Ergonomic Design for People at Work*, 2nd ed. Hoboken, NJ: John Wiley and Sons, 2004; and Wickens C.D., et al.: *An Introduction to Human Factors Engineering*, 2nd ed. Upper Saddle River, NJ: Prentice Hall, 2004.

maintain the safe operation of a potentially hazardous system."[26(p. 195)]

In health care, violations are characterized by actions that deviate from the standard policies and procedures of the organization. Often a means to perform a task more easily or quickly, they have been reported with the use of patient safety technologies such as bar-coding technology and smart intravenous pumps.[27]

The term *work-around*,[27] which is frequently used in health care, should be differentiated from the term *violation*. Violation includes both malevolent (that is, sabotage) and nonmalevolent acts, whereas *work-around* refers to non-malevolent acts.[28] What is important to know is that violations, like errors, usually have multiple causal factors from a systems point of view and result from a combination of active failures and latent conditions.[28,29] Unlike errors, when outcomes are good, violations are tacitly or explicitly approved acts; however, when adverse outcomes occur, those who violate are punished. For example, in an emergency situation, a nurse may forgo scanning the medication and patient bar code during medication administration as required by policy. If the patient does well, this will be overlooked or lauded. If the patient does poorly, this act will be scrutinized, and if it is found to be related to the poor outcome, it will be punished. However, in the same way that errors indicate a problem with underlying system design, so does the occurrence of violations.

HOW DO HUMAN FACTORS PROFESSIONALS THINK ABOUT CLOSE CALLS?

The term *close call* implies that nothing bad happened, but from an HF point of view, something bad already did happen—just no person or thing (for example, the patient, the operator, the equipment, the system) was harmed. From a safety and risk perspective, error(s) or violation(s) did occur, which may indicate that

something bad was happening. The factors that contribute to the errors and violations, and the breakdown in the system defenses that allow errors and violations to occur and reach the patient, are all important to understand. The fact that chance or quick thinking by a clinician or patient prevented an error or a violation from causing harm does not change the significance of the occurrence or the error or violation or the need to further evaluate it. System defenses are designed to make unsafe acts visible and correctable, so as to prevent errors from causing harm—that is, to create error-tolerant systems that allow for error detection and correction before harm occurs.[25] HF professionals use the term *incident* to imply that harm occurred as the result of an event and *close call* to imply that an event occurred but did not result in harm. Recent research suggests that there is indeed a difference in error-recovery efforts between (1) events that reach the patient and do not cause harm and (2) events that do not reach the patient, so differentiating between these two types of events could be useful.[30]

ERROR MANAGEMENT AND ERROR RECOVERY

HF engineers approach error management from two angles: error prevention and error recovery. The IOM report *To Err Is Human* focused on preventing errors in health care to prevent patient harm.[5] However, designing systems and processes to prevent error is only part of the error-management strategy. HF engineers recognize that errors will never be completely designed out of work systems. Ironically, skill-based errors actually increase as a person's expertise increases, but so does a person's ability to detect errors, both his or her own and those of others.[31] Therefore, the focus is on designing "error-tolerant" systems—systems in which errors can occur but without resulting in irreversible effects.[29,31] Error management involves putting into place strategies to prevent errors from occurring and defenses to prevent errors from reaching patients when they do occur—or recovery systems. Error

---

Table 4-2. System Defenses That Promote Error Recovery and Health Care Examples

- ■ Warnings and alarms
  - — Patient monitoring equipment in intensive care units and operating rooms
- ■ Physical barriers
  - — Universal precautions: Use of eye shields, gloves and gowns, etc., to prevent disease transmission
  - — Intravenous and phlebotomy needles with shields
- ■ Procedures
  - — Time-out protocols before surgical procedures
  - — Checklist for central line insertion
- ■ Hardware and software lockouts
  - — Designing electronic health records to allow only one patient record to be open at a time (to avoid wrong-patient errors)
- ■ Reminders
  - — Clinical decision support in electronic health records to promote needed preventive screening
- ■ Human–machine redundancy
  - — Use of bar-coding technology redundant to required visual check
- ■ Self-detection and correction of errors
  - — Double calculation of all chemotherapy doses
- ■ Forcing functions
  - — Hard-stop limits on "smart" IV pump programming

Source: Adapted from Salvendy G. (ed.): *Handbook of Human Factors and Ergonomics,* 3rd ed. Hoboken, NJ: John Wiley & Sons, Inc., 2006, p. 711.

---

recovery, the ability to detect an error that has occurred and subsequently correct it, turns potential harmful events into true close calls. Table 4-2 (above) outlines eight different mechanisms for system defenses and examples as seen in health care.

When designing system defenses, three essential features aid the success of recovery:[32]

1. *Observability* means that the occurrence of an error or a violation is detectable by someone who can take action. This involves providing feedback about the system state to the user or colleague. For example, computerized physician order entry can send a warning message to the user when a medication is ordered to which the patient is allergic. Thus, the system must support the ability to observe that errors are happening and the reversibility of the effects of errors—that is, before irreversible harm occurs.

2. *Traceability* refers to the ability to determine the actions that led to the error or violation and how to proceed differently. For example, if there is an error in a medication order, the ordering provider's name is present so the pharmacist can call him or her to discuss the order.

3. *Reversibility* allows a cancellation of the effects of the error to prevent harm that could occur until actions can be taken to correct the error.

Other strategies can be used to promote error recovery in systems.[32,33] On an individual level, people can be trained to self-detect their own errors through self-monitoring. Self-checking involves performing a task in incremental steps and checking the work along the way rather than only at the end. Standard checking involves a consistent double check of work, such as what is done with chemotherapy dosing calculations. Contingency plans can be developed for potential problems that could occur. For example, when performing a patient handoff at the end of the day, the care provider handing off could discuss with the recipient of the handoff the potential issues that could arise on the basis of the patient's current state—for example, fever and shortness of breath—and discuss how he or she would assess and treat the situation, given that he or she has more knowledge about the patient than the person covering overnight.

Sometimes, it is difficult for a person to detect his or her own errors; this is especially true when an error was based on inadequate knowledge of the situation or the disease process, as is the case with many misdiagnoses. In this situation, double-checking by other people is helpful. This may be in the form of supervision or auditing of tasks, or consultation with someone with expertise in the area. Finally, system error cueing can be developed, in which interfaces give feedback to users about errors. Examples of this are provided in Table 4-2. It is important when designing warning or reminder messages that the message is clear to allow the user to detect that an error is occurring and that the message be presented to the user at a time in the work flow where he or she is likely to take positive action. When possible, it is also helpful to provide enough information for the user to understand why the error occurred or to help him or her access this information, as well as to provide information about how to correct the error and the mechanism to do so.

Analysis of Errors

In health care, two common error-management strategies—RCA and PRA, as cited earlier in the chapter—can be used to evaluate close calls further. RCA is one of many methods of accident investigation and is intended to help systematically identify the root causes of error by collecting data about the accident, determining causal factors and the underlying reason for each causal factor, and then generating a list of basic causes that an organization could fix.[15] RCA usually focuses on one event, but multiple similar events can be grouped together for a larger RCA to generate more data about systems problems.

There are several requirements of the RCA/accident analysis process. First, it is important to have a systematic means of collecting data about the accident to ensure collection of all relevant information, even information that does not appear relevant at the time. The U.S. Department of Veterans Affairs (VA) National Center for Patient Safety has developed a list, "Triage and Trigger Questions," which incorporates HFE knowledge about human limitations and work-context issues.[34] The HFACS model, cited earlier,[25] and Dekker's *The Field Guide to Human Error Investigations*[35] can also serve as guides to focusing on these issues in the accident investigation.

Second, it is important to recognize several biases that obscure the true causes of the error when investigating accidents and that are well known in HFE.[35] Hindsight bias results from knowing the outcome of events and what could have been done differently to prevent the error or bad outcome. This knowledge can lead to a narrowing of the investigation into the causes of why the error occurred or why people acted in the manner that caused the error. Confirmation bias is related to the human tendency to entertain hypotheses about why errors occur early on in accident investigation. The bias exists when evidence confirming the hypothesis seems more relevant than evidence not confirming the hypothesis and thus the nonconfirming evidence is not fully considered. Attribution bias is the tendency to blame accidents and errors on personal inadequacies rather than to attribute them to system factors beyond a person's control.[35]

Processes involved in close-call events are good candidates for PRA to analyze where in the process errors or violations are likely to occur, determine their causes, and take actions to reduce error risk and improve system defenses. Yet, there are many issues with using and adapting PRA methods in health care. First, there are more than 50 known risk assessment methods, with new methods or changes to previously established methods occurring on a regular basis. Many of the PRA methods require significant expertise and resources to perform, which are not commonly available in health care organizations. (Lyons et al. has published a compendium of known PRA methods specifically directed at the health care audience to help guide health care organizations in choosing a method to meet their needs.[36]) The most commonly used PRA method in health care is failure mode and effects analysis (FMEA); the VA has also created a modified version of FMEA—Healthcare Failure Mode and Effects Analysis (HFMEA)—designed to better fit health care processes.[37] However, significant problems have been reported with the performance of FMEA in health care,[38,39] such as the amount of time it takes to complete the FMEA, the human resources—that is, frontline staff and FMEA facilitators—needed, and poorly defined scope leading to scope creep, which have led to guidelines for organizations when performing FMEA[40] and further modifications of the PRA and FMEA process in health care to preserve the integrity of the process while managing organizational constraints.[41]

Analysis of close-call events can also be used to further understand how system defenses are recovering from errors. For example, Kanse et al.

analyzed 31 close calls in the hospital medication use process, which has many "planned" error-recovery opportunities, reflecting checks by nurses and pharmacists and technology throughout the process.[42] Kanse et al. were able to identify episodes where error-recovery opportunities were missed (for example, not completed or the error breached the defense), episodes of "unplanned" recovery (recovery occurring ad hoc), and episodes in which systems factors positively and negatively influenced the recovery process. Such analysis of close calls and error-recovery pathways can lead to further improvements in system defenses by improving recovery processes and formalizing unplanned recovery acts. Table 4-3 (*see* page 51) outlines examples of how human factors analysis has been used to redesign technologies and systems to decrease the likelihood of error occurrence or to improve error detection and recovery.

CONCLUSION

For too long in health care, the focus has been only on fighting fires related to patient safety. Efforts have focused on serious adverse events and the active failures that led to patient harm. Health care has much to learn from the HFE discipline about systems thinking, error analysis, error management, and systems redesign. The evaluation of close calls provides the opportunity to understand human error and violations as symptoms to problems that exist in the work system. HFE principles and models guide error and violation analysis to explore the human performance and work-context issues that exist and contribute to close calls. Error-management strategies that focus both on error prevention and the creation of error-tolerant systems by promoting error recovery will improve the safety of health care delivery.

Table 4-3. Examples of Human Factors Analysis and Subsequent Interventions Performed to Reduce the Likelihood of Errors or to Improve Error Detection

Article	Close-Call Incident	Results of Human Factors Analysis	Interventions Undertaken
1. Lin, Vicente, and Doyle, 2001	Patient-controlled analgesia IV pump programming errors	IV pump did not meet the information-requirement needs of end users. IV pump interface did not conform to basic HF design principles.	Redesign pump interface to improve feedback to end user, decrease number of programming steps, provide clearer message wording
2. Koppel et al., 2008	Medication administration without scanning patient ID band or medication bar code when using bar-coded medication administration technology	There are multiple systems factors related to end users not scanning patient ID bands and medication bar codes, including technology design and patient, organizational, environmental, and task-related factors.	Technology redesign, improvement in patient ID band and medication bar code placement and durability, change in organizational policies to promote safe processes
3. Bonnabry et al., 2008	Drug–drug interactions not considered when prescribing a medication using CPOE	Risk assessment revealed that the current CPOE system presented the drug–drug interaction alert to users too late in the prescribing process.	Technology redesign to present the drug interaction to the user at the time of the medication being ordered versus during the order validation process
4. Peute and Jaspers, 2007	Errors in laboratory ordering using a computerized ordering system, e.g., omitted orders and canceling orders	Usability assessment revealed multiple interface design flaws and computer work flows that did not match the institution work flows for laboratory ordering.	Technology redesign needs identified; system was not implemented beyond pilot stage; institution incorporated usability testing before future technology purchases
5. Michels et al., 1997	Critical events visible on patient monitors occurring during anesthesia administration	Simulation testing of detection of critical events using the traditional cardiovascular digital and waveform monitors versus a graphical monitor display using shapes and colors found that the shape and color display improved detection times.	Technology redesign of anesthesia monitors
6. Thursky and Mahemoff, 2007	Incorrect antibiotic prescribing based on culture results	End users required the ability to see microbiology results and point-of-care education regarding appropriate antibiotic selection.	Design and implementation of a computerized antibiotic decision support tool and real-time microbiology browser
7. Baxter et al., 2005	Incorrect decisions about manipulating ventilator settings in neonates with respiratory distress syndrome	Cognitive task analysis determined the importance of the hierarchical communication structure in the ICU and the need for manual verification of data reads by the computer.	Redesign of computerized decision support to minimize false alarms, present the user with the data to supports the computer's recommended actions; redesign of the processes of care to ensure that computer-generated alarms are addressed

Note: IV, intravenous; HF, human factors; ID, identification; CPOE, computerized provider order entry; ICU, intensive care unit.

References:

1. Lin L., Vicente K.J., Doyle D.J.: Patient safety, potential adverse drug events, and medical device design: A human factors engineering approach. *J Biomed Inform* 34:274–284, Aug. 2001.

2. Koppel R., et al.: Workarounds to barcode medication administration systems: Their occurrences, causes, and threats to patient safety. *J Am Med Inform Assoc* 15:408–423, Jul.–Aug. 2008. Epub Apr. 24, 2008.

3. Bonnabry P., et al.: A risk analysis method to evaluate the impact of a computerized provider order entry system on patient safety. *J Am Med Inform Assoc* 15:453–460, Jul.–Aug. 2008. Epub Apr. 24, 2008.

4. Peute L.W., Jaspers M.W.: The significance of a usability evaluation of an emerging laboratory order entry system. *Int J Med Inform* 76:157–168, Feb.–Mar. 2007. Epub Jul. 18, 2006.

5. Michels P., Gravenstein D., Westenskow D.R.: An integrated graphic data display improves detection and identification of critical events during anesthesia. *J Clin Monit* 13:249–259, Jul. 1997.

6. Thursky K.A., Mahemoff M.: User-centered design techniques for a computerised antibiotic decision support system in an intensive care unit. *Int J Med Inform* 76:760–768, Oct. 2007. Epub Sep. 6, 2006.

7. Baxter G.D., et al.: Using cognitive task analysis to facilitate the integration of decision support systems into the neonatal intensive care unit. *Artif Intell Med* 35:243–257, Nov. 2005. Epub Jul. 1, 2005.

References

1. Karsh B.T., et al.: A human factors engineering paradigm for patient safety: Designing to support the performance of the healthcare professional. *Qual Saf Health Care* 15(Suppl. 1):i59–i65, Dec. 2006.

2. Henriksen K.: Human factors and patient safety: Continuing challenges. In Carayon P. (ed.): *Handbook of Human Factors and Ergonomics in Health Care and Patient Safety.* Mahwah, NJ: Lawrence Erlbaum Associates, 2007, pp. 921–935.

3. Safren M.A., Chapanis A.: A critical incident study of hospital medication errors. *Hospitals* 34:32–34, May 1, 1960.

4. Spath P.L. (ed.): *Error Reduction in Health Care. A Systems Approach to Improving Patient Safety.* New York City: John Wiley & Sons, Inc., 2000.

5. Institute of Medicine: *To Err Is Human: Building a Safer Heath System.* Washington, DC: National Academies Press, 1999.

6. Aspen P., et al. (eds.): *Preventing Medication Errors: Quality Chasm Series.* Washington DC: National Academies Press, 2007.

7. Gosbee J.W., Gosbee L.L. (eds.): *Using Human Factors Engineering to Improve Patient Safety: Problem Solving on the Front Line,* 2nd ed. Oak Brook, IL: Joint Commission Resources, 2010.

8. The Joint Commission: *Sentinel Event Alert.* http://www.jointcommission.org/SentinelEvents/Sentinel EventAlert/ (accessed Sep. 14, 2010).

9. The Joint Commission: Safely implementing health information and converging technologies. *Sentinel Event Alert* Issue 42, Dec. 11, 2008. http://www.jointcommission.org/SentinelEvents/Sentinel EventAlert/sea_42.htm (accessed Sep. 14, 2010).

10. The Joint Commission: *Sentinel Event Policy and Procedures.* Jul. 2007. http://www. jointcommission.org/ SentinelEvents/PolicyandProcedures/ (accessed Jul. 30, 2010).

11. The Joint Commission: *2010 Comprehensive Accreditation Manual for Hospitals: The Official Handbook.* Oak Brook, IL: Joint Commission Resources, 2009.

12. Joint Commission International: *Joint Commission International Accreditation Standards for Hospitals,* 4th ed. Oak Brook, IL: Joint Commission Resources, 2010.

13. Looking at sentinel events along the continuum of patient safety. *Jt Comm Perspect* 30:3–5, Aug. 2010.

14. Institute of Medicine and National Academy of Engineering: *Building a Better Delivery System: A New Engineering/Health Care Partnership.* Washington, DC: National Academies Press, 2005.

15. Salvendy G. (ed.): *Handbook of Human Factors and Ergonomics,* 3rd ed. Hoboken, NJ: John Wiley & Sons, Inc., 2006.

16. Carayon P., et al.: Work system design for patient safety: The SEIPS model. *Qual Saf Health Care* 15(Suppl. 1):i50–i58, Dec. 2006.

17. Ash J.S., et al.: The unintended consequences of computerized provider order entry: Findings from a mixed methods exploration. *Int J Med Inform* 78(Suppl. 1):S69–S76, Apr. 2009. Epub Sep. 12, 2008.

18. Reason J.: Human error: Models and management. *BMJ* 320:768–770, Mar. 18, 2000.

19. Institute of Medicine: *Resident Duty Hours: Enhancing Sleep, Supervision, and Safety.* Washington, DC: National Academies Press, 2009.

20. Accreditation Council for Graduate Medical Education: *Duty Hours Proposed Standards.* http://acgme-2010 standards.org/pdf/Proposed_Standards.pdf (accessed Sep. 21, 2010).

21. Bates D.W., Bitton A.: The future of health information technology in the patient-centered medical home. *Health Aff (Millwood)* 29:614–621, Apr. 2010.

22. Rivera-Rodriguez A.J., Karsh B.T.: Interruptions and distractions in healthcare: Review and reappraisal. *Qual Saf Health Care* 19:304–312, Aug. 2010. Epub Apr. 8, 2010.

23. Norman D.A.: *Things That Make Us Smart: Defending Human Attributes in the Age of the Machine.* Cambridge, MA: Perseus Books, 1993.

24. Vincent C., Taylor-Adams S., Stanhope N.: Framework for analysing risk and safety in clinical medicine. *BMJ* 316, Apr. 11, 1998. http://www.bmj.com/cgi/content/ full/316/7138/1154 (accessed Jul. 30, 2010; password required).

25. Wiegmann D.A., Shappell S.A.: *A Human Error Approach to Aviation Accident Analysis: The Human Factors Analysis and Classification System.* Burlington, VT: Ashgate Publishing Company, 2003.

26. Reason J.: *Human Error.* Cambridge: Cambridge University Press, 1990.

27. Koppel R., et al.: Workarounds to barcode medication administration systems: Their occurrences, causes, and threats to patient safety. *J Am Med Inform Assoc* 15:408–423, Jul.–Aug. 2008. Epub Apr. 24, 2008.

28. Alper S.J., Karsh B.T.: A systematic review of safety violations in industry. *Accid Anal Prev* 41:739–754, Jul. 2009. Epub Apr. 18, 2009.

29. Bogner M.S. (ed.): *Human Error in Medicine.* Hillsdale, NJ: Lawrence Erlbaum Associates, Inc., 1994.

30. Kessels-Habraken M., et al.: Defining near misses: Towards a sharpened definition based on empirical data about error handling processes. *Soc Sci Med* 70:1301–1308, May 2010. Epub Feb. 12, 2010.

31. Amalberti R., Hourlier S.: Human error reduction strategies in health care. In Carayon P. (ed.): *Handbook of Human Factors and Ergonomics in Health Care and Patient Safety.* Mahwah, NJ: Lawrence Erlbaum Associates, 2007, pp. 921–935.

32. Kontogiannis T.: User strategies in recovering from errors in man–machine systems. *Saf Sci* 32:49–68, Apr. 1999.

33. Kontogiannis T.: A framework for the analysis of cognitive reliability in complex systems: A recovery centered approach. *Reliability Engineering & System Safety* 58:233–248, Dec. 1997.

34. National Center for Patient Safety, U.S. Department of Veterans Affairs: *Triage and Triggering Questions.* http://www.patientsafety.gov/CogAids/Triage/index.html# page=page-1 (accessed May 4, 2010).

35. Dekker S.: *The Field Guide to Human Error Investigations.* Burlington, VT: Ashgate Publishing, 2002.

36. Lyons M.: Towards a framework to select techniques for error prediction: Supporting novice users in the healthcare sector. *Appl Ergon* 40:379–395, May 2009. Epub Dec. 16, 2008.

37. DeRosier J., et al.: Using Health Care Failure Mode and Effect Analysis: The VA National Center for Patient Safety's prospective risk analysis system. *Jt Comm J Qual Improv* 28:248–267, May 2002.

38. Wetterneck T.B., et al.: Challenges with the performance of failure modes and effects analysis in healthcare organizations. In Human Factors and Ergonomics Society (ed.): *Proceedings of the 48th Annual Meeting of the Human Factors and Ergonomics Society.* Santa Monica, CA: Human Factors and Ergonomics Society, 2004, pp. 1708–1712.

39. Wetterneck T.B., et al.: Using failure mode and effects analysis to plan implementation of smart I.V. pump technology. *Am J Health Syst Pharm* 63:1528–1538, Aug. 15, 2006.

40. Wetterneck T.B., Hundt A.S., Carayon P.: FMEA team performance in health care: A qualitative analysis of team member perceptions. *J Patient Saf* 5:102–108, Jun. 2009.

41. Carayon P., et al.: Patient safety and proactive risk assessment. In Yih Y. (ed.): *Handbook of Healthcare Delivery Systems.* Boca Raton, FL: CRC Press, forthcoming.

42. Kanse L., et al.: Error recovery in a hospital pharmacy. *Ergonomics* 49:503–516, Apr. 15–May 15, 2006.

CHAPTER 5

Disclosing Close Calls to Patients and Their Families

Albert W. Wu, M.D., M.P.H.; Thomas H. Gallagher, M.D.; Rick Iedema, Ph.D.

When a patient is harmed by health care, the incident needs to be handled appropriately by the physician and other health care workers involved and by the health care organization. There is clear professional and social consensus that physicians and health care organizations are obligated to disclose harmful incidents to the patient or to the family in cases where the patient lacks decision-making capacity.[1-6] It is less clear, however, what the obligations are regarding the handling of close calls. Individual clinicians may differ in their enthusiasm for disclosure of close calls.[7-9] Should close calls be disclosed to patients and families? If so, should this be done always or only sometimes, and if only sometimes, under what circumstances? This chapter discusses some of the arguments posed by stakeholders with different perspectives on this question and offers suggestions for how these incidents might be handled, both with regard to patients and families, as well as within organizations.

DEFINITIONS

In keeping with the definitions applied elsewhere in this book, an *adverse event* is an injury caused by medical care. Identifying something as an adverse event does not imply error, negligence, or poor-quality care. It simply indicates that an undesirable clinical outcome resulted from some aspect of diagnosis or treatment rather than from the underlying disease process. Some adverse events are preventable, in which case they are caused by errors, including latent and/or active errors.

As noted in the Introduction, a *close call*, synonymous with a *near miss*, is defined as an event or situation that did not produce patient injury, because it did not reach the patient due to chance or to capture before reaching the patient, or if it did reach the patient, it did not harm the patient due to robustness of the patient or to timely intervention.

Although the epidemiology of close calls is not well described, it is evident that close calls are more frequent than adverse events.[10-13]

POLICY REGARDING DISCLOSURE

There is an extensive body of policy statements from individual organizations, professional societies, regulatory bodies, and health authorities establishing the duty to disclose harmful errors to patients.[1-4,14] For example, since 2002 The Joint Commission has required health care organizations to have policies for disclosing unanticipated outcomes to patients.[*]

---

* Standard RI.01.02.01: The hospital respects the patient's right to participate in decisions about his or her care, treatment, and services. Element of Performance 21: The hospital informs the patient or surrogate decision-maker about unanticipated outcomes of care, treatment, and services that relate to sentinel events considered reviewable by The Joint Commission.

Joint Commission International requirements call for patients to be told of unanticipated medical outcomes.[15] However, there is little guidance on disclosing errors that do not cause harm (but *see* Introduction (pages xi–xxi) for discussion of The Joint Commission's evolving Sentinel Event Policy).

In the United States, where self-regulation plays a prominent role in assuring the quality of health care services, national professional societies have long maintained the importance of disclosing harmful events to patients.[1,2] For example, the American Medical Association (AMA)'s Code of Medical Ethics Opinion 8.12—Patient Information, states the following:

> It is a fundamental ethical requirement that a physician should at all times deal honestly and openly with patients. Patients have a right to know their past and present medical status and to be free of any mistaken beliefs concerning their conditions. Situations occasionally occur in which a patient suffers significant medical complications that may have resulted from the physician's mistake or judgment. In these situations, the physician is ethically required to inform the patient of all the facts necessary to ensure understanding of what has occurred. Only through full disclosure is a patient able to make informed decisions regarding future medical care.[2]

Similar codes exist in other countries, including Australia, the United Kingdom, and Canada. Individual states now mandate disclosure of serious unanticipated outcome (9 states as of 2010: Nevada, Florida, New Jersey, Pennsylvania, Oregon, Vermont, California, Tennessee, and Washington).[16] For example, Pennsylvania requires institutions to report to the patient, in writing, within seven days of discovery, any "event, occurrence, or situation involving the clinical care of a patient in a medical facility that results in death or compromises patient safety

and results in unanticipated injury."[17] In addition, at least 34 states and the District of Columbia have enacted laws that preclude some or all information contained in a practitioner's apology from being used in a malpractice lawsuit.

Policy on Close Calls

Despite clear direction regarding the disclosure of harmful incidents, there is little explicit discussion of close calls in any of the existing policies on adverse events. For example, the disclosure policy at Sunnybrook and Women's Hospital (Toronto) states that for "non-significant medical events," which are defined as "minor incidents that do not have a negative impact on patient outcomes now or in the foreseeable future" and for which there are no procedures "required to prevent negative patient outcomes," "disclosure to the patient and/or substitute decision maker or family is discretionary" on the part of health care workers.[18] The disclosure policy at the Johns Hopkins Hospital includes a similar clause.[19,20]

The Australian Standard, enacted in 2003, also excludes close calls from disclosure. However, a report, *Indicators for Effective Open Disclosure*, which was presented to the Australian Commission on Safety and Quality on HealthCare in 2010, recommends that the disclosure of close calls be contingent on careful dialogue with the patients (and family members) involved.[21]

Large-Scale Close-Call Events

Special care needs to be taken with decisions regarding close-call incidents that affect a cohort of individuals. Although a clinically negligible impact of an inappropriate treatment regimen may justify nondisclosure to an individual patient, erring on the side of openness assumes special importance in the case of a cohort-based close call. For example, in Adelaide, Australia, a technology was mistakenly set to provide a radiation dose 5% less than what it should have been for approximately 900 patients. This was not revealed at the time of discovery and led to a great outcry in the media four years after the fact, despite the fact that the hospital fixed the machine as soon as the problem came to light.[22] With this kind of situation in mind, the new Australian Open Disclosure Fundamentals recommend that a distinction be made between close calls that pertain to individuals and those that pertain to cohorts of patients. Recommendations are also emerging in the United States that encourage health care organizations to disclose these events even when the risk of harm to patients is extremely low and stress the importance of developing institutional policies in this area.[23,24]

PATIENT EXPECTATIONS ABOUT DISCLOSURE OF CLOSE CALLS

There is abundant evidence that patients expect to be told of virtually all harmful errors that occur in their care. There have been fewer studies of patient expectations about the disclosure of close calls. Witman and colleagues surveyed 149 patients from an ambulatory general medicine clinic; virtually all (98%) wanted at least some acknowledgement of even minor errors.[25] Hingorani et al. found that 92% of patients wanted to be informed of adverse events.[26] In a focus group study, Gallagher and colleagues found that patients wanted to be informed of all harmful errors but that patients were mixed on disclosure of close calls—some were in favor, but others thought it would just make them nervous.[8]

Several recent studies suggest that many patients are aware that close calls occur in their care. Weingart et al. found that hospitalized patients were aware of both adverse events and close calls, which occurred in their care at a rate of 5.7 per 100 admissions.[27] Weissman and colleagues also found that hospitalized patients were aware of and could report about adverse events and close calls.[28] In a Toronto hospital, Friedman and colleagues similarly found that patients interviewed after discharge reported close calls with a 4%

incident rate (95% confidence interval [CI], 1.73%–7.69%).[29] The implication of this research is that clinicians may need to discuss close calls with patients and families to confirm assumptions about what happened and its severity.

ETHICAL CONSIDERATIONS

The following is a brief review of arguments for and against disclosure of close calls. First presented are arguments based on an examination of the likely harms and benefits of disclosure versus nondisclosure—the consequentialist arguments. The harms and benefits to the patient and to the physician or health care organization are provided separately. Then presented is a brief discussion of arguments based on the physician's and organization's duties to the patient—the fiduciary arguments.

Consequentialist Arguments
Benefits of Disclosing Close Calls to the Patient
There are ways in which a patient could benefit from learning that a close-call incident has occurred. In the event that the patient suspects something has gone wrong, an explanation of what happened, with reassurance that there are no adverse consequences, might be comforting. Having this information could promote the patient's ability to act (autonomy). On one hand, it might persuade some patients to seek second opinions or to switch providers. On the other hand, discussions about close calls could strengthen the patient–physician relationship. Ideally, these discussions would occur in the context of an ongoing dialogue about care that takes an approach of being open with patients. Discussions about and appreciation of the uncertainties surrounding decision making and which course of action is right versus wrong could benefit all parties involved.

In addition, such discussion is important because what the clinician assumes to be a close call may well turn out to be an adverse event for the patient. A recent Australian study involving

100 patients and family members telling stories about incidents and disclosure indicates the importance of matching clinical decisions about the (non)impact on a patient of what happened with patients' and family members' knowledge about what happened.[21] The following is an example of such a dissonance:

> A middle-aged female patient was sent on for eye surgery by a doctor-in-training. The surgery was deemed not to be necessary and is cancelled by a senior consultant who saw her just before going into theatre. The doctor-in-training nevertheless was unapologetic and continued to dismiss the patient's concerns. The patient remains upset at the response of the doctor-in-training, but is full of praise of the senior consultant spotting and discussing the error.[21]

The study describes cases of detrimental (physical and psychological) impact having occurred for patients without this impact having been evident to the treating clinicians. In these cases, patients (or their loved ones) tended to seek recourse through other clinicians (their primary care physicians, clinicians at other hospitals) or even the complaints mechanism in order to get clarification about why their original care appeared unsatisfactory or even harmful.

Discussion about close calls could therefore improve not just patients' but also clinicians' understanding and appreciation of the potential for errors and adverse events in health care. Further, such discussion could help to modulate everyone's perceptions and expectations. In some cases, this could also encourage patients and families to participate more actively as members of the health care team and could drive improvements.

Harms of Disclosing Close Calls to the Patient

There are ways in which the disclosure of a close call could harm a patient. Patients may become upset to learn of errors and close calls in their care, reacting with disappointment, anxiety, and anger. For example, in one hospital, a patient was given an anticoagulant medication before surgery for a coronary bypass operation. Because of this error, the surgery was delayed by three days. The patient was very upset by the delay. Some patients might lose confidence or trust in the providers or organizations where they receive care. As a consequence, they might be less likely to adhere to beneficial advice or treatment. All of these could lead to diminished health outcomes. Studies of patient preferences, however, suggest that openness is increasingly expected by all patients. For patients, then, the potential and actual harms associated with disclosure are not taken to outweigh its moral and practical benefits.

Benefits of Disclosing Close Calls to the Physician/Health Care Organization

Physicians could benefit from discussing close calls with patients in other ways as well. Patients may appreciate the physician's candor, with a resulting increase in trust and strengthening of the relationship. Dialogue with patients (or even relatives) can reveal the full complexity of errors and close-call events and enable clinicians to improve their practice as a result. Clinicians may also realize that their understanding of an incident as a close call is inaccurate, given what the patient tells them. For example, the team may gain a greater appreciation of the nonmedical impact of a close call, such as missed work required to complete additional testing, which may be important to a patient. An increased appreciation of the inevitability and uncertain impact of errors could help clinicians be more aware of the potential for error and follow more safety practices. Clinicians may also feel relieved at being able to unburden themselves of knowledge or personal experiences they have of hazardous practices.

Health care organizations could also benefit from the increased transparency that accompanies discussing close calls with patients. Close calls should be easier to discuss than full-blown incidents given the absence of harm. Close calls therefore constitute a critical training ground for the discussions that clinicians must have when things go seriously wrong and that patients expect when (almost) harmed.

Harms of Disclosing Close Calls to the Physician/Health Care Organization

On the other hand, physicians and health care organizations could also be harmed by the disclosure of close calls. There is relatively little risk of successful litigation related to disclosure of a close call because by definition there is no physical injury; there is no valid personal injury claim without an injury.[30] However, in specific cases, individual patients may lose confidence in their physicians and seek care elsewhere. In some situations, this could damage the reputations and/or incomes of the physicians, particularly with the capacity of the Internet to amplify negative opinion. Physicians' self-confidence or self-esteem could also suffer, especially if their mental model of medical errors focuses on blaming individuals rather than on continual professional and organizational learning.

On a practical level, a tremendous amount of time and energy could be required for the disclosure of all close calls. Particularly for some types of practices (for example, critical care medicine) and depending on the operational definition of *close call*, a physician might be responsible for discussing multiple incidents per day, for even a single patient. For example, direct observation studies of hospital care suggest that seriously ill hospitalized patients may be subjected to 200 decisions and interventions per day, with an average of 2 errors per patient per day.[31] A requirement to disclose all incidents would place a heavy burden on a clinician. There is no consensus on which close-call events are more desirable to be disclosed and which less so. For example, should physicians disclose diagnostic errors that were resolved before the physician took action on them? Furthermore, in not all cases is the time spent on disclosing close calls

balanced by improvements in staff learning, resilience building, and patient confidence.

Fiduciary Arguments

Health care workers and health care organizations have a fiduciary responsibility to act in the best interests of patients, which includes disclosing to patients incidents that could benefit their health or welfare. This fiduciary duty clearly supports a general obligation to disclose harmful errors to patients. In addition, as patients may derive some direct benefits from the disclosure of close calls in some circumstances, there may be similar justification on fiduciary grounds for an obligation to disclose close calls to patients.

WHEN SHOULD A CLOSE CALL BE DISCLOSED?

There are potential benefits to both patients and providers for disclosing close calls. There are also some modest harms, particularly if such disclosure occurs in the setting of the "blame and shame" culture that still exists in many organizations and jurisdictions. Adding a further counterweight is the potential burden on some physicians of having to disclose every close call to patients. A requirement to disclose all close calls would seem to place an undue burden on some physicians, particularly those whose patients are the sickest. Practically speaking, the latter argument mitigates against a blanket rule requiring disclosure of all close-call events. If disclosure of close calls is to be discretionary in some cases, what circumstances should dictate when a close call should be disclosed?

Several criteria could be applied in deciding whether to tell a patient about a specific close-call event. Perhaps the most important criterion for disclosing a close call is if it is evident that the patient could benefit in some way from the information or has knowledge to add to the existing information. In some cases, this opportunity may represent a "teachable moment" in which the disclosure could be used to reinforce a point for both the patient and the clinician. For example, a close call involving a drug to which the patient is allergic could be used to highlight the importance of the patient always telling every provider about all allergies and medications and playing a more active role as a member of the health care team. It could also highlight the importance for the clinician in charge of handoff to specify such information more systematically and carefully.[32]

A second and obvious criterion for disclosure would be if the patient witnessed the close call. In this circumstance, the patient is likely to be "waiting for the other shoe to drop." The patient would be comforted to learn from the provider what happened and would feel more respected if the physician were candid in acknowledging the incident and open to learning about the patient's experience of the care being provided. In addition, the patient who observed the close call would be more likely to be suspicious and distrusting if the physician said nothing. The patient might also feel entitled to an apology and might be dissatisfied if it is not forthcoming.

A third criterion might be represented in a situation in which additional monitoring or testing is necessary to ensure that the error did not lead to harm or in which a change in the treatment plan is required to keep the error from harming the patient. Information about the error might be required in this situation to allow and motivate the patient to make an informed decision. For example, a patient would likely be more amenable to additional laboratory tests to ensure that an overdose of an anticoagulant did not cause any adverse effects.

A final and less specific criterion might be whether there is sufficient time for discussion. Thoughtfully conducted, such a discussion can almost always provide the opportunity to benefit the patient–physician/nurse relationship. A physician or nurse can explain the usual process of care, how the system works, and the uncertainty

and risks that are inherent to that system. The discussion can be used to invite the patient to provide information that might help improve his or her own care or to help clinicians do their work.

Overall, these arguments suggest that disclosure of close calls is desirable but that there are trade-offs, primarily in terms of time, so that disclosure should occur when it is feasible.

HOW TO DISCLOSE A CLOSE CALL

Disclosure of close calls should occur within a comprehensive institutional system of handling incidents. Organizations should have a policy regarding the disclosure of errors and adverse events and should have standard operating procedures in place indicating how these discussions should be conducted. The policy should include a focus on improving systems rather than blaming individuals and an assurance that disclosing physicians will never be punished for disclosing. Parenthetically, it must acknowledge that a just culture requires organizations to reserve the option of taking disciplinary actions in response to acts that are reckless or violate specific rules.

Organizations should provide educational materials to providers to increase awareness of patient safety as an issue and should increase the capacity for and confidence of individual providers to conduct disclosure discussions with patients and families. At the same time, organizations should provide just-in-time support for conducting live disclosures, including assistance from risk managers or other experts in the process. They should also acknowledge the emotional burden that accompanies adverse events and disclosure of these incidents[33–39] and make support services available to staff.

The initial disclosure discussion can be difficult, even when it is a close call that is being disclosed (*see* Sidebar 5-1, page 61). Disclosure is eased substantially if the discussion takes place as part

Sidebar 5-1. Things to Say and Not to Say in Disclosing a Close Call	
Things to Say in Disclosing a Close Call	**Things Not to Say in Disclosing a Close Call**
That was a close call. I'm very sorry that this happened.	Oh well. No harm, no foul!
I will try to get to the bottom of this. We want to make sure this sort of thing doesn't happen again and harm someone the next time.	Oops. Good thing nothing happened.
Things do go wrong sometimes. In the future, if you have any questions, don't be afraid to speak up.	

of an ongoing dialogue about the patient's health, health care decisions, treatments, and course of care. In this regard, descriptions of uncertainties and things that go wrong are a more natural part of the discussion than would be an isolated disclosure. In the disclosure of adverse events, people universally want and expect to know what happened, an apology, and an assurance that steps are being taken to prevent similar events from happening in the future. This framework applies equally well to close-call events. For example, in the case of a close call involving prescribing and then intercepting an antibiotic to which the patient has an allergy, the physician might say the following:

> That was a close call. I didn't notice that you are allergic to this medication, even though you mentioned it to me in the past. Fortunately, the pharmacist also has this information and caught it before the medicine was dispensed. You could have had a bad reaction to it, and I am very sorry that I made this error. This will remind me to always double-check about allergies before I write a prescription. You can also help to prevent this kind of thing from happening: Whenever you see any kind of nurse or physician, make sure to tell them that you are allergic to this medicine.

REPORTING TO INCIDENT REPORTING SYSTEMS

Regardless of whether a close call is disclosed to the patient, its discovery virtually always exposes flaws in the system of care. For this reason, providers should nearly always report the incident to their institution's incident reporting system. This allows the organization to gain a better understanding of its epidemiology of incidents and failure points, contributing factors, and recovery mechanisms. In some cases, it can help by alerting objective analysts to failures latent in processes at different points in the system. More importantly, reporting of close calls is critical to the health service and the team itself for gaining insight into its alertness to risk. In some sites, such reports are discussed at practice improvement meetings, enabling clinicians to better understand colleagues' perceptions of risk and variations in their levels of process knowledge and clinical-medical confidence.[7] In addition, disclosing to a reporting system may also allow for an investigation and could supply additional perspectives, including potentially a consumer perspective, to be brought to bear in determining if an incident should be disclosed to the patient after all.

It is worth noting that physician enthusiasm for reporting close calls to institutions may be lower than for minor or serious errors,[40] which high-lights the importance of educating providers about the benefits of reporting close calls. Wachter has suggested, as have others, that expending additional energy to get health care workers to report close calls may not be a good use of patient safety resources.[41] In particular, health care workers require feedback to maintain the habit of adverse event reporting.[42] Therefore, before encouraging more reporting of close calls, institutions should be certain they have the capacity to analyze and act on these reports.

CONCLUSION

Although there is consensus that physicians and health care organization are obligated to disclose harmful errors, there is no preponderance of opinion regarding disclosure of close calls. In some circumstances, there could be net benefits to patients or physicians that result from disclosing a close call. In other cases, there are potential modest harms that could occur. In practical terms, a requirement to disclose all close calls could be onerous to some physicians, especially for patients receiving the most intensive treatment. We conclude that the disclosure of close calls should be determined on a case-by-case basis, ideally following discussion with the patient (and or relatives) to establish his or her knowledge and assessment of what happened and his or her sense of its severity.

Close calls should usually be disclosed if it was apparent to the patient that an error occurred or if the patient could benefit from having the information. When providers become aware of close calls, they should be reported to institutional incident reporting systems to allow systemic learning to occur. The discussion of close calls is the most beneficial for both patients and providers if it occurs in the setting of an ongoing open discussion of the patient's health and course of care. In this context, close calls have the potential to strengthen the patient–physician relationship. Disclosure should include a state-ment that there was a close call, with a description of what happened, and include any errors or failures within the system of care, an apology, and a statement of what steps will be taken to ensure that providers will learn from the event. There are unanswered questions, including whether there are differing obligations to disclose different types of close calls and the role of patients in judging whether there is an adverse outcome. Further work is needed on how to turn the commitment to the principle of transparency into the practice of maximizing learning from medical errors.

References

1. American College of Physicians Ethics Manual, Third Edition. *Ann Intern Med* 117:947–960, Dec. 1, 1992.
2. American Medical Association: *Code of Medical Ethics: Opinion 8.12—Patient Information.* http://www.ama-assn.org/ama/pub/physician-resources/medical-ethics/ code-medical-ethics/opinion812.shtml (accessed Oct. 1, 2010).
3. National Quality Forum (NQF): *Serious Reportable Events in Healthcare—2006 Update: A Consensus Report.* Washington, DC: NQF, 2007.
4. The Joint Commission: *2010 Comprehensive Accreditation Manual for Hospitals: The Official Handbook.* Oak Brook, IL: Joint Commission Resources, 2010.
5. Australian Commission on Safety and Quality in Health Care: *Open Disclosure Standard: A National Standard for Open Communication in Public and Private Hospitals Following an Adverse Event in Health Care,* 2003. http://www.safetyandquality.gov.au/internet/safety/publishing.nsf/Content/OD-Standard (accessed Sep. 22, 2010).
6. National Patient Safety Agency, National Health Service: *Being Open: Communicating with Patients, Their Families and Careers Following a Patient Safety Incident.* http://www.nrls.npsa.nhs.uk/resources/?entryid45=65077 (accessed Oct. 4, 2010).
7. Hor S.Y., et al.: Multiple accountabilities in incident reporting and management. *Qual Health Res* 20:1091–1100, Aug. 2010.
8. Gallagher T.H., et al.: Patients' and physicians' attitudes regarding the disclosure of medical errors. *JAMA* 289:1001–1007, Feb. 26, 2003.
9. Gallagher T.H., et al.: U.S. and Canadian physicians' attitudes and experiences regarding disclosing errors to patients. *Arch Intern Med* 166:1605–1611, Aug. 14–28, 2006.
10. Callum J.L., et al.: Reporting of near-miss events for transfusion medicine: Improving transfusion safety. *Transfusion* 41:1204–1211, Oct. 2001.
11. Bates D.W., et al.: Incidence of adverse drug events and potential adverse drug events. Implications for prevention. ADE Prevention Study Group. *JAMA* 274:29–34, Jul. 5, 1995.

12. Bates D.W., et al.: The costs of adverse drug events in hospitalized patients. Adverse Drug Events Prevention Study Group. *JAMA* 277:307–311, Jan. 22–29, 1997.

13. Lundy D., et al.: Seven hundred and fifty-nine (759) chances to learn: A 3-year pilot project to analyse transfusion-related near-miss events in the Republic of Ireland. *Vox Sang* 92:233–241, Apr. 2007.

14. Massachusetts Coalition for the Prevention of Medical Errors: *When Things Go Wrong: Responding to Adverse Events.* Mar. 2006. http://www.macoalition.org/ publications.shtml (accessed Oct. 1, 2010).

15. Joint Commission International: *Joint Commission International Accreditation Standards for Hospitals,* 4th ed. Oak Brook, IL: Joint Commission Resources, 2010.

16. Mastroianni A.C., et al.: The flaws in state "apology" and "disclosure" laws dilute their intended impact on malpractice suits. *Health Aff (Millwood)* 29:1611–1619, Sep. 2010.

17. Patient Safety Authority: *Act 13-Medical Care Availability and Reduction of Error (MCARE) Act.* http://patientsafetyauthority.org/PatientSafetyAuthority/ Governance/Pages/Act13.aspx (accessed Oct. 5, 2010).

18. Sunnybrook & Women's College Health Sciences Center: *Sunnybrook Policy: Disclosure of Adverse Medical Events and Unanticipated Outcomes of Care.* http://www.jointcentrefor bioethics.ca/research/documents/sunnybrook_policy.pdf (accessed Sep. 23, 2010).

19. Johns Hopkins Hospital: Medical Error Disclosure. PAT026 in *The Johns Hopkins Hospital Interdisciplinary Clinical Practice Manual: Patient Care.* Baltimore: Johns Hopkins Hospital, 2009.

20. Sexton J.D., et al.: Care for the caregiver: Benefits of expressive writing for nurses in the United States. *Progress in Palliative Care* 7:307–312, 2009.

21. The Open Disclosure Indicator Development and 100 Patient Stories Project Consortium: *The Open Disclosure Indicator Development and 100 Patient Stories Project— Final Report to the Australian Commission on Safety and Quality in Health Care.* Sydney, Australia: Australian Commission on Safety and Quality in Health Care & UTS Centre for Health Communication, 2010.

22. Delaney G., Oliver L., Coleman R.: *Review of the Radiation Incident at Royal Adelaide Hospital Report 15/8/08.* Adelaide, Australia: South Australia Department of Health, 2009.

23. Veterans Health Administration (VHA): *Disclosure of Adverse Events to Patients.* VHA Directive 2008-002, Jan. 18, 2008. http://www1.va.gov/vhapublications/ viewpublication.asp?pub_id=1637 (accessed Sep. 23, 2010).

24. Dudzinski D., et al.: The disclosure dilemma; Large-scale adverse events. *N Engl J Med* 363:978–986, Sep. 2, 2010.

25. Witman A.B., Park D.M., Hardin S.B.: How do patients want physicians to handle mistakes? A survey of internal medicine patients in an academic setting. *Arch Intern Med* 156:2565–2269, Dec. 9, 1996.

26. Hingorani M., Wong T., Vafidis G.: Attitudes after unintended injury during treatment: A survey of doctors and patients. *West J Med* 171:81–82, Aug. 1999.

27. Weingart S.N., et al.: What can hospitalized patients tell us about adverse events? Learning from patient-reported incidents. *J Gen Intern Med* 20:830–836, Sep. 2005.

28. Weissman J.S., et al.: Comparing patient-reported hospital adverse events with medical record review: Do patients know something that hospitals do not? *Ann Intern Med* 149:100–108, Jul. 15, 2008.

29. Friedman S.M., et al.: Errors, near misses and adverse events in the emergency department: What can patients tell us? *CJEM* 10:421–427, Sep. 2008.

30. Prosser W.L., et al. (eds.): *Prosser and Keeton on Torts,* 5th ed. Eagon, MN: West Group, 1984.

31. Donchin Y., et al.: A look into the nature and causes of human errors in the intensive care unit. *Crit Care Med* 23:294–300, Feb. 1995.

32. Millman A., et al.: Patient-assisted incident reporting (PAIR): Including the patient in patient safety. *J Patient Safety,* in press.

33. Wu A.W.: Medical error: The second victim. The doctor who makes the mistake needs help too. *BMJ* 320:726–727, Mar. 18, 2000.

34. Wu A.W., et al.: How house officers cope with their mistakes. *West J Med* 159:565–569, Nov. 1993.

35. Bell S.K., Moorman D.W., Delbanco T.: Improving the patient, family, and clinician experience after harmful events: The "when things go wrong" curriculum. *Acad Med* 85:1010–1017, Jun. 2010.

36. Scott S.D., et al.: The natural history of recovery for the healthcare provider "second victim" after adverse patient events. *Qual Saf Health Care* 18:325–330, Oct. 2009.

37. Scott S.D. , et al.: Caring for our own: Deploying a systemwide second victim rapid response team. *Jt Comm J Qual Patient Saf* 36:233–240, May 2010.

38. Sirriyeh R., et al.: Coping with medical error: A systematic review of papers to assess the effects of involvement in medical errors on healthcare professionals' psychological well-being. *Qual Saf Health Care,* in press. May 31, 2010 [Epub ahead of print].

39. Iedema R., et al.: Patients' and family members' experiences of open disclosure following adverse events. *Int J Qual Health Care* 20:421–432, Dec. 2008. Epub Sep. 17, 2008.

40. Garbutt J., et al.: Lost opportunities: How physicians communicate about medical errors. *Health Aff (Millwood)* 27:246–255, Jan.–Feb. 2008.

41. Wachter R.M.: The end of the beginning: Patient safety five years after "To Err Is Human." *Health Aff (Millwood)* 2004(Suppl. Web exclusives), Nov. 30, 2004. http://content.healthaffairs.org/cgi/reprint/hlthaff. w4.534v1 (accessed Oct. 1, 2010).

42. Leape L.L.: Reporting of adverse events. *N Engl J Med* 347:1633–1638, Nov. 14, 2002.

PART II

Case Studies of Close Calls

Event Prevented Before Reaching the Patient

CHAPTER 6

Outpatient Endoscopy: Closing the Loop on Colonoscopy Orders

Lydia C. Siegel, M.D., M.P.H.; Tejal K. Gandhi, M.D., M.P.H.

CASES

Case 1

Ms. P arrived for her colonoscopy as scheduled at 2:00 P.M. (14:00) but already felt slightly nervous about having fasted for so long and was unsure whom to ask for information. She had taken half of her morning insulin as suggested, but she had never gone this long without eating. After spending an hour in the waiting room, she felt some warning sweats and checked her blood sugar: It was 46. She ate her emergency package of cheese and crackers in the waiting room, but then a nurse explained to her that her procedure would need to be rescheduled because she no longer had an empty stomach.

Case 2

Ms. B was preparing for her first screening colonoscopy and generally preferred to triple-check all medical instructions. She had filled the prescription for the oral sodium phosphate preparation the week before. She called the phone number from the instruction sheet and was connected with the triage nurse, who asked her several questions about her health. After reviewing Ms. B's chart and learning about her renal problems, the triage nurse asked her not to use the preparation and indeed to throw it away, and instead faxed a prescription to Ms. B's pharmacy for a different preparation, with a separate set of instructions to follow.

Case 3

Mr. R walked out of his primary care physician's office with colonoscopy literature in hand. He was considering his physician's recommendation for his first screening, which he had thus far avoided. Now he had a prescription for the preparation to take, but he still had to schedule the appointment, along with a physical therapy evaluation for his back pain and audiology. He waited while the front desk staff called the endoscopy department to schedule the appointment, but the assistant was put on hold while the schedulers looked up available time slots. Mr. R said he would call later to find out when his appointment would be and went home. However, it slipped his mind to call back, so he missed his appointment. The next year, at his physical, the process was started over.

BACKGROUND

There is broad consensus on recommendations to initiate colon cancer screening at 50 years of age in the general population,[1] and colonoscopy is a cost-effective intervention to screen for this third-most common cause of cancer and third-leading cause of cancer death in the United States.[2,3] However, rates of screening are low throughout the United States, ranging from 25% to 48%.[4] In addition, missed colorectal cancer is a leading cause of outpatient malpractice cases.[5] Minimizing opportunities for errors in the colonoscopy process, from scheduling to procedure completion, is therefore a high priority. Research shows that quality improvement approaches to improving patient safety can be applied in the area of endoscopy.[6]

INVESTIGATION

On the basis of the identification of three close-call cases, as well as overall physician dissatisfaction with the endoscopy process, an investigation was begun at the medical center to determine the factors contributing to failures in successful completion of scheduled colonoscopy. To begin the investigation, a multidisciplinary team was convened, co-led by the director of endoscopy and the lead administrator. The team's creation and activities were facilitated by a performance improvement consultant from the hospital quality department. The other team members were as follows: the nurse manager of endoscopy, the clinic practice manager, the director of endoscopy, the triage nurse, and an endoscopy physician. The impetus for process improvement came from primary care. However, given the complex set of issues involved in the colonoscopy process, including scheduling, triage, and preparations, the endoscopy department led the improvement project.

The group's aim was as follows: "The staff will work to create a simple, timely, and efficient endoscopy referral process for referring physicians and patients which reliably provides the information patients and clinicians want and need in order to ensure an adequately prepared patient."

The team explicitly defined the scope of the investigation, with the starting point being when the patient learns from the primary care physician or gastroenterologist that he or she needs to have an endoscopy procedure and the endpoint being when the patient checks in for the procedure and is deemed to be medically ready for the procedure. The scope was further narrowed to

include patients referred for general screening colonoscopies and upper endoscopies. Patients beyond this definition, including those needing urgent or advanced studies such as motility studies, and those from other referral sites were to be dealt with in later phases.

To begin the investigation, the team first undertook a series of interviews. Team members met with primary care physicians, endoscopists, endoscopy staff, endoscopy schedulers, and others involved with the process in order to understand the process thoroughly before they conceived of any type of process redesign. The team gathered input from the triage team because patient contacts with frontline staff had revealed the need for a more systematic and widespread educational effort, and it conducted a survey of primary care physicians regarding the existing order process to identify other gaps. The team spent several weeks outlining each step of the process in an effort to understand and map the flow of the current order process, identify weaknesses and opportunities for redesign, and then start to develop core concepts and sample ideas for system improvement. The results of this analysis are summarized in Table 6-1 (*see* page 71).

Triage and Preparation Issues

At the time of Cases 1 through 3, the triage system had no systematic outreach approach and aimed to reach all patients. However, only 60% of patients were contacted successfully before their procedures. There was no system for prioritizing patients with medical problems requiring special attention, such as chronic kidney disease, diabetes, or anesthesia risk. The three cases outline some of the higher-risk close calls, such as hypoglycemia in diabetic patients with afternoon appointments, and prescription of a contraindicated preparation, such as sodium phosphate preparation for a patient with renal failure.

Other close calls included a lack of instructions on stopping anticoagulation medication, including

Table 6-1. Identified Problems, Types of Close Calls, and Solutions

Problem Identified	Type of Close Call	Solution
Scheduling		
Too little clinical information for appropriate triage	Cancellations for lack of pre-procedure anesthesia consults and misallocated resources, or procedure scheduled at site not equipped for medical complexity	Indications and relevant history entered by referring physician; appointment scheduled by endoscopy department with improved triage
Scheduling delays	Callers on hold, scheduling opportunities lost, and a backlog of orders	Initiation of call by patient, with closer and prompt follow-up of each order
Following up on missed appointments	Missed/delayed opportunities; dropped appointments	Creation of established follow-up calls and letters recorded in chart with feedback loop to referring physician
No trackable order	Frequent loss to follow-up; no feedback mechanism when procedures were not scheduled or missed	Creation of an electronic order system
Appointment Readiness		
Multiple preparations in use	Risk of medical adverse event; confusion over instructions	Only two preparations now in use; set of instructions mailed according to prescription sent to patient
Incomplete preparation	Rescheduled, dropped appointments, potentially missed polyps	Clear, uniform instructions mailed to patient ahead of time
More complex needs among speakers of other languages	Language barriers/lack of access	Coordination of interpreter scheduling
Escort for ride home	Rescheduled and risk of missed appointments	Escort now emphasized in instructions and required at check-in
Risk for Medical Complications		
Patients on insulin with afternoon appointments	Potential for hypoglycemic complications	Patients on insulin scheduled for morning procedures
Screening for patients on warfarin and clopidogrel	Rescheduled or dropped appointments	Triage nurse contacts referring physician or prescribing cardiologist for management plan
Variable preparations, some contraindicated	High-risk patients with contraindicated preps	Indications entered by referring physician; endoscopy orders the prep on the basis of order form and chart review
Airway issues	Inconsistent anesthesia referrals	Order flagged for anesthesia appointments and presence during procedure

Source: Brigham and Women's Hospital, Boston. Used with permission.

warfarin or clopidogrel, which required either rescheduling or a repeat study if biopsy was needed. Some patients were too sick from the preparation to come to the endoscopy appointment as scheduled and did not know whom to call. There was no formal patient education system in place, so for other patients the obstacles were more basic, such as misunderstanding the preparation, having recently eaten, and lacking an escort home. Although there were some last-minute attempts to arrange for anesthesia for patients with difficult airways, most of these patients needed to be rescheduled, creating inefficiencies and delays in testing.

The process placed the entire responsibility on the primary care physician to educate the patient, prescribe the colon preparation, and schedule the appointment. This led to a large gap for the patients to bridge alone in order to show up at endoscopy at the appointed time and be prepared and ready for the procedure. Primary care physicians were also frustrated about needing to help prepare patients for another department's procedures.

Scheduling Issues

Primary care and endoscopy worked independently and in parallel to ensure that screening colonoscopies were completed, leading to inefficiencies. The main dissatisfaction on the primary care side was that primary care physicians could not get patients scheduled when necessary. On the endoscopy side, schedulers spent time answering calls from primary care offices and also calling patients to schedule studies and reschedule studies when patients missed the initial appointment. As a result, patients were falling through the cracks. Primary care physicians and endoscopists were both concerned about the high rate of missed appointments and cancellations; patients whose appointments had to be rescheduled were dissatisfied.

REDESIGNING THE ENDOSCOPY REFERRAL PROCESS

Refining the Order System

The team ultimately chose and gained approval for an electronic order entry system with a set of features built in that were designed to refine the order entry process and minimize the chances for the type of close call that had occurred under the previous system (Case 3). The ordering physician selects the study and enters the indications that will dictate the initial triage step, distinguishing between a routine screening colonoscopy and a patient at higher risk for whom a diagnostic study is ordered. To continue ordering the routine screening colonoscopy, a second screen enables identification of patients on insulin, warfarin, or clopidogrel; those with body mass index (BMI) > 40 kg/m^2 or known sleep apnea; those with a pacemaker or an implantable cardioverter defibrillator (ICD); and those with the absence of all higher-risk features. Any study required within 48 hours would be arranged directly by telephone with the triage nurse.

Standardizing the Preparations and Enhancing Patient Education

There were problems with the multiple different colon preparations prescribed under the old process. The team gave the responsibility for prescribing the preparation to endoscopy, which chose two sets based on the two most common insurance coverage patterns. With a standardized preparation identified, the team created a set of uniform instructions, written at a sixth-grade reading level, for mailing to patients with their prescriptions. These instructions provided answers to most patients' questions, including timing of the preparation, fasting, how to handle medications, and the importance of an escort. This process change freed the triage staff to focus on communicating with all of the higher-risk patients.

ADVANTAGES OF THE NEW PROCESS

This new process has several advantages. The triage nurse already has access to patient information from the electronic order form, so that she or other triage staff can contact the high-risk patients first. Low-risk patients can be called by scheduling staff. Theoretically, only high-risk orders would require personal review by a triage nurse, but 100% of orders are still double-checked against each patient's medical record as a redundant step for safety.

Another improvement is the clarification of responsibility between referring physicians and endoscopy. The referring physicians now discuss with patients the need for screening; place the order, complete with triage information; and then generate a printable paper requisition for the patient with instructions on how to call endoscopy to arrange the appointment. From there, the responsibility passes to endoscopy. The electronic order is immediately received by endoscopy, and from there the order is tracked in a systematic way with programmed reminders, as outlined in Sidebar 6-1 (right). Instead of multiple phone calls coming in to multiple individual schedulers, there is now a single request queue for triage and schedulers.

For low-risk patients, after chart review–based verification by the triage team, the procedures are scheduled; patients are assessed the same day as the procedure. For high-risk patients, a triage nurse conducts the preprocedure assessment by telephone to determine the safest way to complete the procedure. For example, patients on insulin are now scheduled for morning appointments to avoid long waits while NPO (nothing by mouth). Rather than giving blanket instructions such as "take ½ your morning insulin," the nurse will discuss the regimen with each patient to come up with a safe, individualized plan.

Sidebar 6-1. Backup System for Missed Appointments

The multidisciplinary team identified the need to create a backup system to capture those patients who missed their appointments for any reason. This backup system also falls within the responsibility area of endoscopy and consists of the following:

1. At 3 days, if the patient has not called endoscopy to schedule the initial appointment, the patient will receive a phone call.
2. If contact is made and a procedure is scheduled, the patient will receive a packet in the mail with a prescription and the preparation instructions.
3. Patients who schedule an appointment will receive a reminder phone call within 5–7 days of the appointment.
4. At 14 days, if no contact has been made, endoscopy will attempt a second phone call to remind the patient of the need to schedule an appointment.
5. At 30 days, if no contact has been made, endoscopy will send another reminder letter, with a copy sent to the primary care physician and recorded in the patient's chart.
6. At 60 days, if there is still no contact, endoscopy will send a reminder letter, with a copy again sent to the primary care physician and recorded in the patient's chart.

Source: Brigham and Women's Hospital, Boston. Used with permission.

DISCUSSION

Perspectives on Results

From the perspective of the endoscopists, the system is safer and improved. The ordering physician, who knows the patient best, can designate him or her as high or low risk in a more reliable way. The triage nurses also feel that their time is better spent planning with and educating the higher-risk patients to avoid close calls and adverse events, as well as catching additional triage errors. Endoscopy triage staff are able to focus more on upstream management of medical issues than on time-consuming clerical issues and can spend time managing the high-risk patient pool and getting those patients through the procedure safely.

The higher-risk preparations, including sodium phosphate have been eliminated for all patients, not just those with chronic kidney disease. Most patients, having received the standardized information packet in English (or Spanish, as appropriate), arrive with more knowledge about their procedure. Patients who otherwise might have been overlooked are followed for a full 75 days after the initial order was placed, after which time they are referred back to the primary care physicians' offices for further follow-up, with a written handoff given to the primary care physician and a letter added to the electronic chart.

Primary care physicians and their office staff have also been overwhelmingly positive about the changes, which fit well into their existing work flow. Most like the ease of electronic order entry and the new process, particularly the fact that patients who do not schedule or who miss their appointments receive reminders. They appreciate the ability to screen for potential anesthesia problems and to flag safety concerns and medical complications without having to order a separate consult, as well as the time saved from not having to review instructions for the colon preparation with patients. Patients are less frustrated about wait times when calling and have fewer questions about preparation. Endoscopy staff members who schedule the appointments with patients feel similarly positive; they feel much better equipped to meet patients' needs and to answer questions for patients scheduled for screening colonoscopies.

Factors Contributing to Success

The composition of the multidisciplinary team for this initiative was a factor contributing to the success of the process redesign. The team had strong sponsorship from the highest levels and had the clinical, quality, and administrative expertise to complete the project. The involvement of managers and administrators, as well as of those who worked in the process, was an invaluable asset, and the full involvement of all stakeholders ensured buy-in.

Ongoing Challenges

There are still opportunities for error by the ordering physician. Because the redesigned endoscopy referral process relies on the test orderer to enter all fields accurately, some high-risk comorbidities are missed. As a backup, the triage team continues to review the electronic medical record for relevant medications and problems and to check BMI for high-risk patients in particular. In addition, the nurse will often review the most recent notes entered by the primary care physician and cardiologist in order to catch additional issues that could pose a problem. Patients initially stratified as low risk according to physician orders are then categorized by endoscopy as high risk after review by triage.

Many primary care physicians want the system to go a step further, with added capacity to track all patients who miss their studies and the ability to schedule appointments for straightforward screening appointments before patients leave the primary care office. Because a high no-show rate still exists, as many of the physicians have noted, some physicians have adapted by trying to set up high-risk tests before patients leave the office.

CONCLUSIONS

Although there is still progress to be made, the enhanced endoscopy process created a safer, trackable pathway that enabled endoscopy to address the needs of both complex and healthy patients well in advance of their appointments and to accommodate all requests in a more timely and safe manner, while also creating a process that fits into the work flow of the ordering physicians. Identifying and learning from close calls, such as those represented in the three cases, is essential for redesigning safer care processes and, ideally, for preventing serious adverse events.

The authors gratefully acknowledge Kristen Almechatt; Rebecca Cunningham, M.D.; David Faling, M.D.; Irina Filina, R.N., C.G.R.N.; Anthony Komaroff, M.D.; Armin Lilienfeld, M.D.; Diana Mero; Jose Paredes; Diana Post, M.D.; John Saltzman, M.D.; Julie Santiago; Louise Schneider, M.D.; and Lori Tishler, M.D.

References

1. U.S. Preventive Services Task Force: *Screening for Colorectal Cancer: U.S. Preventive Services Task Force Recommendation Statement*, Oct. 2008. http://www.uspreventiveservicestaskforce.org/uspstf08/colocancer/colors.htm (accessed October 1, 2010).
2. Jemal A., et al.: Cancer statistics, 2009. *CA Cancer J Clin* 59:225–249, Jul.–Aug. 2009. Epub May 27, 2009.
3. Maciosek M.V., et al.: Colorectal cancer screening: Health impact and cost effectiveness. *Am J Prev Med* 31:80–89, Jul. 2006.
4. Ata A., et al.: Colorectal cancer prevention: Adherence patterns and correlates of tests done for screening purposes within United States populations. *Cancer Detect Prev* 30(2):134–143, 2006. Epub Apr. 25, 2006.
5. Gandhi T.K., et al.: Missed and delayed diagnoses in the ambulatory setting: A study of closed malpractice claims. *Ann Intern Med* 145:488–496, Oct. 3, 2006.
6. Lieberman D., et al.: Standardized colonoscopy reporting and data system: Report of the Quality Assurance Task Group of the National Colorectal Cancer Roundtable. *Gastrointest Endosc* 65:757–766, May 2007.

CHAPTER 7

Medication Safety: Neuromuscular Blocking Agents

David U, M.Sc.(Pharm.); Bonnie Salsman, B.Sc.(Pharm.)

The risks of harmful errors with neuromuscular blocking agents (NMBAs) have been well recognized for more than a decade. Harmful errors with these agents have been reported as occurring worldwide. In addition to dozens of documented incidents in the United States and Canada, errors with these agents have been reported in other countries, including Kenya, Mexico, and Saudi Arabia.[1–4] The following case demonstrates how a close-call incident in a Canadian hospital acted as a catalyst to support the implementation of labeling and packaging improvements in Canada.[5]

CASE

During the process of preparing a medication in an operating room (OR), a 10-mL vial of the NMBA succinylcholine was inadvertently substituted for sodium chloride 0.9% and used as the reconstitution agent. Fortunately, an anesthesiologist noticed the error before the medication was administered, and a potential tragedy was averted. Recognizing that this serious substitution error could recur and lead to a harmful patient event, the anesthesiologist reported the incident to the pharmacy, asking that the underlying causes of the incident be investigated and addressed. On investigation, it was determined that a key factor in the incident was a recent change in the succinylcholine and sodium chloride products purchased by the hospital.

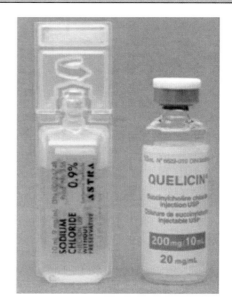

Figure 7-1. Sodium Chloride 0.9% (left) and Vial of Succinylcholine (right)

Source: Institute for Safe Medication Practices Canada. Used with permission.

Previously, succinylcholine had been supplied in a uniquely shaped long, slim vial that was readily distinguishable from other products; sodium chloride 0.9% had been provided in a "polyamp" format that also had a distinctive appearance (*see* Figure 7-1, above).

During the months before the close-call event, the sole Canadian supplier of succinylcholine had changed the format of the vials to a size and shape that was similar to other commonly used vials. In addition, the polyamp format of sodium chloride 0.9% (supplied by a different manufacturer) had been discontinued. For many facilities, these simultaneous changes created a "look-alike" product hazard with the sodium chloride 0.9% and succinylcholine 10-mL vials (*see* Figure 7-2, right).

Recognizing that the risk associated with the simultaneous changes in these two products could also exist in other facilities and that this could lead to harmful events, the hospital reported the close-call incident to the Institute for Safe Medication Practices Canada (ISMP Canada).

In response to the incident report, ISMP Canada published a safety bulletin that alerted hospitals of the hazard and provided recommendations for safe storage and handling of NMBAs.[5] In addition, the manufacturer of the succinylcholine and sodium chloride products was advised of the problem, and a meeting was held to discuss potential improvements in packaging and labeling. The manufacturer responded very favorably to the suggestions and subsequently made changes to the product packaging and labeling (*see* Figure 7-3, page 79; **online extras** Figures 7-1, 7-2, and 7-3 are available in color online at http://www.jcrinc.com/VNM10/Extras).

Perhaps more importantly, the close call involving the sodium chloride 0.9% and succinylcholine acted as a catalyst for the pursuit of a broader opportunity to improve medication safety by implementing packaging changes for all NMBAs in Canada.

BACKGROUND

NMBAs are muscle-paralyzing agents that cause respiratory paralysis and therefore must be used in concert with patient intubation and mechani-

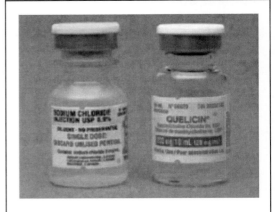

Figure 7-2. Look-Alike Product Hazard: Sodium Chloride 0.9% (left) and Vial of Succinylcholine (right)

Source: Institute for Safe Medication Practices Canada. Used with permission.

cal ventilation. They have been identified as high-alert medications because errors with these agents are more likely to result in harm than are errors with other agents.[6]

The incident described in our case report had similarities to an earlier close-call incident reported to ISMP Canada, in which a pharmacy technician had mistakenly provided two 10-mL vials of the NMBA vecuronium bromide to the emergency department instead of two 10-mL vials of acyclovir 500 mg, as prescribed.[7] The nurse initially assumed that vecuronium was an alternative name for acyclovir and used the vecuronium to prepare a minibag for administration. Fortunately, an adverse drug event was averted when the nurse had second thoughts and called the pharmacy for verification. The similarity in packaging between the vecuronium and acyclovir products was also identified as a possible contributing factor in this incident. Both products were packaged in similar 10-mL vials, and both had red flip-top caps, creating a look-alike product hazard.

In September 2005, an *ISMP Medication Safety Alert!* reported that the U.S. Pharmacopeia

Figure 7-3. Succinylcholine Vials with a Red Cap and Red Ferrule with the Words "WARNING: PARALYZING AGENT"

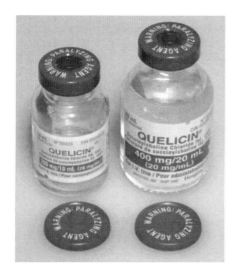

Source: Institute for Safe Medication Practices Canada. Used with permission.

(USP)–ISMP Medication Errors Reporting Program had received more than 50 reports involving misuse of NMBAs and noted, "The true incidence of injuries from accidental administration of neuromuscular blocking agents is likely much higher than reflected by error reports."[8] Although this safety alert noted that most of the errors had taken place outside the OR setting, errors involving the administration of NMBAs inside the OR to patients who were not intubated also pose a risk of harm.[9]

Information from the USP's MEDMARX program indicates that 651 errors with NMBAs were reported between January 1, 2000, and December 2005, of which 332 (51%) reached the patient and 61 (9.4%) resulted in harm.[10] In its 2009 *Patient Safety Advisory,* the Pennsylvanias Patient Safety Authority noted that it had received 154 event reports involving errors with NMBAs between June 2004 and June 8, 2009, and that of those:

77.9% (*n* = 120) of the events reached the patient and 9.1% (*n* = 14) of the events were indicated by the facility as resulting in harm to the patient, which is nearly 13 times greater when compared to all medication errors reported to the authority (0.7%) in that time period.[11]

The ISMP, ISMP Canada, the U.S. Food and Drug Administration,[12] USP,[13] and other patient safety organizations have published a multitude of recommendations on safe labeling and handling of NMBAs. Examples of recommendations that have the potential to prevent substitution errors with these products include the following:

■ When purchasing NMBAs, review the packaging and labeling of the available marketed products and choose products with distinctive labeling and packaging. Avoid purchasing NMBA products with an appearance similar to other medications.[13]

■ Limit NMBAs to areas that routinely provide care for ventilated patients.[13] Ideally, NMBAs should not be stored in patient care units.[7,14]

■ Segregate all NMBAs in storage areas (for example, use separate locked storage or secured boxes in refrigerators).[13,14] Within the pharmacy, include a sign on NMBA storage locations that states, "Supply with a Warning Label."[7]

■ Where NMBAs must be stored in patient care areas, place the vials in plastic bags and apply auxiliary warning labels on both sides of the bag. The pharmacy should dispense NMBA doses with a bright auxiliary warning label, for example, "WARNING: Paralyzing Agent. Causes Respiratory Arrest. For Use in Intubated Patients Only."[7,14]

■ Provide NMBAs only in sealed intubation or anesthesia kits to ensure that these agents are not available until an intubation procedure has begun.[13]

■ Provide point-of-care communication when there is a change to a product.[5]

■ Do not store NMBAs in multiproduct drawers of automated dispensing cabinets. (Use single-item access drawers and display electronic alerts when NMBAs are withdrawn.)[13]

■ Use bar-code readers to verify product and patient identity before administration.[13]

In 2003, the USP's *Pharmacopeial Forum* published a recommendation that the ferrules and overseals of products containing NMBAs should contain the alert "Warning—Paralyzing Agent" if room permits, or at least "Paralyzing Agent."[15] This proposal became an official requirement in the United States on October 1, 2005.

In March 2005, when the incident described in our case report occurred, the majority of Canadian manufacturers had not yet implemented the packaging improvements for NMBAs that were already being put in place in the United States. The close-call report provided an impetus for action. ISMP Canada's bulletin stated the following:

> The dangers associated with current packaging and labelling of neuromuscular blocking agents and the opportunity for standardization need to be addressed. It is time to formulate a requirement that all Canadian pharmaceutical manufacturers package neuromuscular blocking agents in vials such that the cap, . . . metal ferrule, and overseal state "**Warning: Paralyzing Agent**" or "**Paralyzing Agent**."[5(p. 2)]

In September 2005, the labeling of NMBAs was identified as a high-priority item during a stakeholder meeting on labeling and packaging of pharmaceuticals, co-convened by ISMP Canada and the Canadian Patient Safety Institute and with support from Health Canada. In February 2006, ISMP Canada convened a collaborative meeting with Canadian manufacturers of NMBAs to discuss safe packaging and labeling of NMBAs. The attending stakeholders reached

---

Sidebar 7-1. Recommended Features for Packaging and Labeling of Neuromuscular Blocking Agents

1. Red cap with white lettering: "Paralyzing agent" or "Warning: Paralyzing Agent"
2. Red ferrule with white lettering: "Paralyzing agent"
3. Red lettering on the product label: "Paralyzing agent" or "Warning: Paralyzing Agent"
4. Peel-off label, using the color scheme and content information recognized by the ASA/CAS recommended standards, for application to a prepared syringe (ASA = American Society of Anesthesiologists [http://www.asahq.org]; CAS = Canadian Anesthesiologists' Society [http://www.cas.ca])
5. Space on the product label for bar code application
6. Development of a universal symbol for neuromuscular blocking agents and proposal for global use: placement of this symbol (e.g., on the label), to be determined
7. Review of potential benefit of using tall man lettering for generic names of neuromuscular blocking agents

Source: Neuromuscular blocking agent labelling and packaging initiative. *ISMP Canada Safety Bulletin* 6:2, Apr. 25, 2006. Used by permission of Institute for Safe Medication Practices Canada.

---

agreement on the ideal features of NMBA packaging and labeling. The recommended features are shown in Sidebar 7-1 (above). Manufacturers responded favorably and began incorporating the recommended features into the packaging and labeling of their products.

In 2007, ISMP Canada received yet another report of a close call with an NMBA. A nurse chose a vial of succinylcholine (Quelicin) instead of the heparin that she intended to administer:

> As she was walking back to the patient's bedside, she noticed white lettering on the red cap that read "WARNING: PARALYZ-ING AGENT" [*see* Figure 7-3]. This prompted her to realize that she had selected the wrong vial. Incorrect administration and serious patient harm were thus averted.[16]

The recovery from the substitution error and avoidance of a potentially harmful event were attributed to the actions taken in response to earlier close-call reports and to the manufacturer's decision to change the labeling and packaging of the succinylcholine product.

As of May 2010, the manufacturers of all NMBA products distributed within Canada had implemented ISMP Canada's recommendation to place a warning on the closure system.

REMAINING BARRIERS AND NEXT STEPS

This case report and subsequent discussion are not intended to provide a full review of safety measures related to the handling of NMBAs. Although addressing look-alike product issues through changes to the packaging of Canadian NMBA products appear to have reduced the opportunity for harmful events with these agents, the possibility of substitution errors and other types of errors still exists. To reduce opportunities for harmful errors with NMBAs, a multifaceted approach incorporating system and practice changes, use of technology, ongoing vigilance, and monitoring of close-call and actual events is required. Moving toward widespread implementation of bar code verification for preparation, dispensing, and administration of all medications has the potential to reduce significantly substitution errors with NMBAs and other agents. ISMP Canada and the Canadian Patient Safety Institute have endorsed the adoption of the GS1 (GS1 US; http://www.gs1us.org/about_us) global standard for automated identi-

fication of pharmaceuticals in Canada and issued the *Joint Technical Statement on Pharmaceutical Automated Identification and Product Database Requirements*, in collaboration with pharmacy supply-chain stakeholders.[17]

The successful response to a close-call incident described in our case report clearly illustrates the potential advantages of sharing incident reports with an external organization for analysis. It is particularly important that close-call incident reports involving labeling, packaging, and naming problems be filed with an external body because these issues can clearly have an impact on other health care facilities and providers. In addition, although learning from events can inform safety solutions across jurisdictions, the packaging and labeling of products can be unique within the borders of countries. Therefore, it is important that information on the unique products within each country be collected and shared with the appropriate organization or agency. ISMP Canada is a collaborating partner in the Canadian Medication Incident Reporting and Prevention system, which provides a defined mechanism and tools for Canadian facilities and practitioners to report medication incidents, including close calls.

This case report provides an example of how information from close-call reports can reveal underlying causes that have the potential to lead to harmful events and how such reports can provide the impetus for significant changes designed to prevent potentially harmful adverse drug events.

References

1 Cohen M.R., Proule S. (eds.): Safety briefs. *ISMP Medication Safety Alert! Acute Care* 1, Oct. 23, 1996.
2. Ansari M.M., Magaji G.K., Abraham A.: Apnea after reversal of neuromuscular blockade. A case of rare mix-up. *Saudi Med J* 28:641–642, Apr. 2007.
3. Smetzer J., Cohen M. (eds.): Safety briefs. *ISMP Medication Safety Alert! Acute Care* 3, May 20, 1998.
4. Smetzer J., Cohen M. (eds.): A caution about Narcan–Norcuron confusion. *ISMP Medication Safety Alert! Acute Care* 3, Oct. 7, 1998.
5. Report of near miss with succinylcholine warrants action. *ISMP Canada Safety Bulletin* 5:1–2, Apr. 2005.

6. Institute for Safe Medication Practices (ISMP): *ISMP's List of High-Alert Medications.* 2008. http://www.ismp.org/tools/highalertmedications.pdf (accessed Jul. 5, 2010).

7. Neuromuscular blocking agents—Time for action. *ISMP Canada Safety Bulletin* 2:1–2, Dec. 2002.

8. Paralyzed by mistakes: Preventing errors with neuromuscular blocking agents. *ISMP Medication Safety Alert! Acute Care* 10, Sep. 22, 2005.http://www.ismp.org/newsletters/acutecare/articles/20050922.asp (accessed Oct. 1, 2010).

9. "Paralyzing" mix-ups in the operating room: Opportunity to improve safety with neuromuscular blockers. *ISMP Canada Safety Bulletin* 4:1–2, Jul. 2004.

10. U.S. Pharmacopeia: USP medication error analysis: Medication errors involving neuromuscular blocking agents. *USP Patient Safety CAPSLink*, Apr. 2006. http://www.usp.org/pdf/EN/patientSafety/capsLink2006-04-01.pdf (accessed Sep. 21, 2010).

11. Pennsylvania Patient Safety Authority: Neuromuscular blocking agents: Reducing associated wrong-drug errors. *Pennsylvania Patient Safety Advisory* 6, Dec. 2009. http://patientsafetyauthority.org/ADVISORIES/Advisory Library/2009/Dec6(4)/Pages/109.aspx (accessed May 21, 2010).

12. Preventing medical errors: USP statement on preventing errors with neuromuscular blockers. *FDA Patient Safety News*, Aug. 2006. http://www.accessdata.fda.gov/scripts/cdrh/cfdocs/psn/transcript.cfm?show=54#6 (accessed May 24, 2010).

13. Phillips M.S., Williams R.L.: Improving the safety of neuromuscular blocking agents: A statement from the USP Safe Medication Use Expert Committee. *Am J Health Syst Pharm* 63:139–142, Jan. 15, 2006.

14. Near-fatal pediatric accident should force reassessment of a common cost-cutting measure. *ISMP Medication Safety Alert! Acute Care* 4, Aug. 25, 1999.

15. The journal of standards development and official compendia revision. *Pharmacopeial Forum* 29(3):709, 2003; as cited in Phillips M.S., Williams R.L.: Improving the safety of neuromuscular blocking agents: A statement from the USP Safe Medication Use Expert Committee. *Am J Health Syst Pharm* 63:139–142, Jan. 15, 2006.

16. Enhanced labelling of neuromuscular blockers makes a difference. *ISMP Canada Safety Bulletin* 7:3, Nov. 13, 2007.

17. Canadian Pharmaceutical Bar Coding Project: *Joint Technical Statement on Pharmaceutical Automated Identification and Product Database Requirements.* Jan. 15, 2010. http://www.ismp-canada.org/barcoding/download/CanPharmBarcode_JointTechnicalStatement.pdf (accessed Jul. 14, 2010).

CHAPTER 8

Oncology: The Patient's Family Speaks Up

Saul N. Weingart, M.D., Ph.D.; Audrea Szabatura, Pharm.D., B.C.O.P.; Deborah Duncombe, M.H.P.; Sarah Kadish, M.S.; Amy Billett, M.D.; Sylvia Bartel, R.Ph., M.P.H.

Until the 1960s, the diagnosis of acute lymphoblastic leukemia (ALL) was a virtual death sentence. With a survival rate close to zero, the diagnosis of ALL was a particularly poignant tragedy, given that ALL is overwhelmingly a disease of children.

With the development of multi-agent chemotherapy, the prognosis for ALL changed dramatically for the better. The life expectancy of a patient diagnosed with ALL improved from weeks to months to years. In 2010, about 85% of children are cured of the disease. Nevertheless, the treatment of ALL is neither simple nor benign, requiring multiple cycles of treatment over about two years of therapy. ALL therapy remains one of the most complex treatments in all of oncology. And, occasionally, something goes awry.

CASE

The patient was a 3-year-old boy who lived with his family near Boston. He developed fatigue, malaise, and fever that did not go away. He saw the family pediatrician, where routine blood work showed something terribly wrong. He was referred to the children's hospital where additional testing confirmed ALL, and he was immediately started on treatment. He did reasonably well through the first months of treatment, progressing from induction through consolidation therapy. He was now in the maintenance phase, receiving 3-week cycles of chemotherapy, including vincristine on the first day by vein, dexamethasone by mouth on the first 5 days, 6-mercaptopurine (6-MP) by mouth on the first 14 days, and weekly methotrexate by vein.

Although there were ups and down in treatment, the pattern of clinic visits every 3-weeks had become more routine over the weeks and months of care. After a clinic visit and review of the patient's laboratory reports, the oncologist provided the family with a prescription for 6-MP. The clinician also faxed a copy to the on-site outpatient pharmacy to save the family some waiting time. The family picked up the filled prescription for 6-MP and left for home. This was the third time that this patient had received a prescription for 6-MP. The medication was provided as 30 cc of yellow-colored liquid in a plastic bottle. The pharmacy also provided a 3 cc oral syringe.

As the patient's family prepared to administer the dose of 6-MP, they noticed that the instructions on the bottle differed from last time. The label said to take "18 mL/day for 14 days"—a daily dose of 18 mL. This seemed peculiar, given that the previous instruction had said to give *1.8* mL (not 18 mL) daily. The family contacted the clinician on call. He said that 1.8 mL per day was the usual dosage and that they should continue with this. The on-call doctor then notified the pharmacy.

ERROR DISCLOSURE AND INITIAL INVESTIGATION

The patient's oncologist contacted the family the following day to apologize for the error and to let them know that an investigation was under way. To investigate the incident, the pharmacy staff retrieved the oncologist's original prescription and the pharmacy's prescription label. In reconstructing the event, they discovered that the prescription that had been faxed from the clinic to the outpatient pharmacy was quite difficult to read. The pharmacy technician transcribed the faxed prescription into the pharmacy computer system and generated a label for the bottle. She then prepared the suspension. A pharmacist verified the preparation, the data in the pharmacy computer system, and the label before placing the medication in the pick-up area. The patient arrived with a copy of the original prescription, received the medication, and was given an opportunity to ask questions of the pharmacist.

ROOT CAUSE ANALYSIS

An interdisciplinary team was assembled to review the incident in detail and to identify contributing factors that should be addressed in order to prevent future errors. Participants included the members of the pharmacy staff who were involved in the incident, the pharmacy manager and director, the hospital medication safety officer, and the patient's oncologist. The hospital risk manager facilitated the analysis.

The analysis proceeded in the usual fashion: first, by outlining a detailed map of the steps involved in the process of prescribing, preparing, and dispensing—including transcribing—6-MP **online extras** (*see* http://www.jcrinc.com/VNM10/Extras).

In this case, the prescription was handwritten on a tamper-proof prescription form (because of a new federal regulation) as follows:

6-mercaptopurine (10mg/mL)
18mg (1.8mL) po QHS
for 14 days, start today/daily.
Dispense 30mL.

The technician incorrectly transcribed this information as "Take 18mg (18mL) by mouth every day at bedtime for 14 days." The instructions containing this decimal point error were printed on the medication label. The pharmacist who reviewed the faxed prescription against the label noted that the faxed prescription had the word *VOID* in several places, making it difficult to read the dosage, directions, and volume instructions. When the original prescription was compared side by side with the faxed prescription, it became clear that the shaded background in the prescription details section on the original was an unevenly shaded background on the faxed copy. This decreased the contrast between the handwriting and the background.

The team next identified a variety of human factors that contributed to the incident, as follows:

1. Handwritten prescriptions are generally less legible than typed electronic prescriptions.

2. The providers were unaware that the new, tamper-proof prescription blanks, when faxed, produced the word *VOID* across the paper and created a hard-to-read background (*see* Figure 8-1, page 85).

3. Manual transcription of prescriptions into the pharmacy computer introduced opportunities for transcription errors.

4. Because 18mL is a commonly dispensed volume of 6-MP, the pharmacist and pharmacy technician expected to see this instruction. Interpreting "1.8mL" as "18mL" suggests a case of confirmation bias, in which the pharmacy staff erroneously saw what they expected to see.

5. The outpatient clinic was a busy and noisy environment, with many distractions and interruptions.

Figure 8-1. Tamper-Proof Prescription Blank, When Faxed

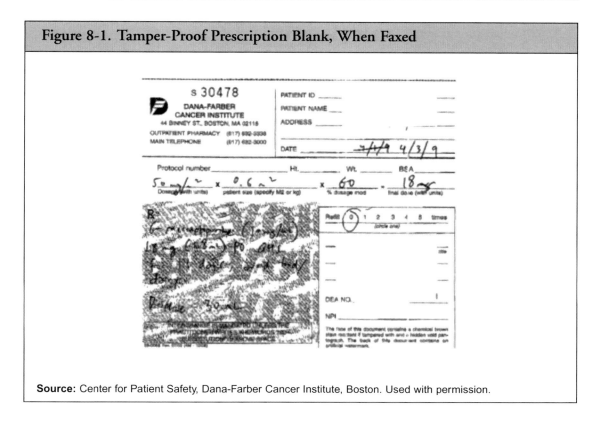

Source: Center for Patient Safety, Dana-Farber Cancer Institute, Boston. Used with permission.

The team examined other factors, as well. For example, the pediatric clinic had not yet implemented electronic prescribing of take-home medications. The materials were poorly designed, as the *VOID* markings obscured the section of the prescription blank where medication name, dosage, and instructions are written. The outpatient pharmacy was understaffed at the time of the event, which occurred during lunch hour. In addition, two pharmacy positions were vacant at the time.

ACTION PLAN

On the basis of its findings, the team recommended a series of improvements to reduce the risk of similar events in the future, as follows:

1. The stock of tamper-proof prescription paper was replaced with a form that did not obscure the drug information on the prescription when faxed. Staff also notified the vendor, requesting that it redesign the form.

2. Pharmacy staff created a checklist as an aid during medication preparation to help reduce the risk of errors due to interruptions.

3. A longer-term project to generate electronic prescriptions and allow for direct interface with the outpatient pharmacy was already in development. About two months after this incident, electronic prescriptions replaced paper prescriptions in the clinic.

4. An industrial engineer from the quality department worked with outpatient pharmacy staff to perform an analysis of transcription errors and to conduct an improvement project.

In the improvement project (recommendation 4), staff collected baseline data on transcription errors, comparing prescription type, error type, and peak/off-peak time of day. Transcription errors were common, especially in free-text "Directions" fields and when the computer provided default values. The error rate was more

Table 8-1. Pharmacy Transcription Improvements

Category	Total transcription errors observed	Rate	Total transcription errors observed	Rate	Total transcription errors observed	Rate
	Baseline		Self-Check		Independent Double-Check	
DIRECTIONS	16	5.0%	16	6.8%	2	0.7%
NATIONAL DRUG CODE	8	2.5%	8	3.4%	1	0.3%
REFILLS	6	1.9%	1	0.4%	0	0.0%
DATE	4	1.3%	1	0.4%	0	0.0%
DAYS SUPPLY	3	0.9%	4	1.7%	2	0.7%
PHYSICIAN NAME	3	0.9%	1	0.4%	0	0.0%
QUANTITY	2	0.6%	4	1.7%	0	0.0%
DOSE	2	0.6%	2	0.8%	0	0.0%
BRAND VS. GENERIC	1	0.3%	1	0.4%	0	0.0%
KEYSTROKE	1	0.3%	0	0.0%	0	0.0%
Total Errors Observed	46		38		5	
Total Transcriptions Observed	320		237		303	
Errors per transcription that reached checking pharmacist		14.4%		16.0%		1.7%

Source: Center for Patient Safety, Dana-Farber Cancer Institute, Boston. Used with permission.

than 10% at times, although these errors were detected consistently and were corrected by the pharmacist. The pharmacy staff introduced several innovations, using rapid-cycle improvement techniques. For example, pharmacy technicians checked their own transcriptions before completing the order. However, this self-check intervention did not appreciably affect the error rate (likely caused by confirmation bias). An independent double check, however, resulted in an 88% reduction in the number of transcription errors compared with baseline (Table 8-1, above).

At the patient's next clinic appointment, the pharmacy manager met with the family to apologize for the error. He shared the findings from the investigation and the action plan. The family was very understanding and supportive of the staff.

DISCUSSION

A close call is a gift, providing an opportunity to examine latent conditions that allow errors and injuries to occur. Because no one is hurt, staff are often willing to discuss the mistake and to learn from their experience.

In this case, the incorrect prescription label resulted from a technician's transcription error. But there was more to the story than that. The root cause analysis exposed a more complicated scenario. The error was caused in part by a new kind of paper that made it hard to read a handwritten instruction. A good general rule is that no "innovation" is entirely benign. The risk of transcription errors was probably exacerbated by the hectic environment in the outpatient pharmacy, production pressure, staffing issues, and confirmation bias. These kinds of problems are common in the inpatient setting and may be even more prevalent in ambulatory specialty care. This case also illustrates unintended consequences of a change. Before the introduction of the federal regulation requiring tamper-proof paper for prescriptions, there was little loss of clarity between the paper original and the faxed copy. The intended change to tamper-proof paper created the unintended consequence of hard-to-read faxed copies.

This case highlights several hot-button issues in patient safety. Medication errors in ambulatory care are a topic of increasing interest, with error rates exceeding those of the inpatient setting.[1] Children are at high risk of medication errors, in large part because of calculation errors. Children's medications are calculated as weight-based doses, whereas adults usually receive a fixed dose.[2,3] Electronic prescribing is a very promising strategy for reducing errors, but it has not yet been fully implemented in health care in the United States.[4] This case demonstrates the role that patients and families can play as vigilant partners in patient safety,[5] identifying and intercepting errors before they become injuries. An alert, active family is an often-unrecognized source of resilience in the health system.

This case also highlights several under-studied areas of significant risk. Little is known about medication errors in ambulatory pharmacies. Several small studies have reported error rates from 0.08% to 24% in U.S. community pharmacies.[6–10] A national observational study of prescription dispensing in 50 pharmacies in the United States identified about 4 errors per day in a pharmacy that filled 250 prescriptions daily. This translates into an estimated 51.5 million dispensing errors each year.[6] The most frequent transcription errors involved label instructions, label information, drug quantity, strength, drug, and dosage form. Transcription errors were also common in a study of 40 Danish community pharmacies, in which about 60% of errors occurred during transcription.[11]

Oral chemotherapy, such as 6-MP, is also an under-studied area but one that is attracting increased attention. Although many patients prefer the convenience of taking their treatment by mouth at home rather than by intravenous infusion at a cancer clinic, few of the safety features that are in routine use for infusion chemotherapy have been developed for oral agents. In a survey of 42 comprehensive cancer centers, most had no required elements for prescribing oral chemotherapy, such as dosage calculating, diagnosis, protocol, or cycle number.[12] Only one-third required written informed consent. One-quarter had no formal process for monitoring adherence. The present case

notwithstanding, many patients have difficulty with medication adherence and with handling and safe administration of oral chemotherapy in the home.[13–16]

CONCLUSIONS

Close calls can teach us a lot about the anatomy of error. But they should also lead us to make real improvements in the delivery of care. Simple things—such as replacing error-producing prescription blanks—can make an immediate difference in one organization. Notification of the paper vendor takes this lesson beyond the walls of a single clinic to other vulnerable practices. Close calls can also bring resources, such as the skills of an industrial engineer, to the front lines, enabling clinical staff members to improve the safety and effectiveness of their own work.

References

1. Gandhi T.K., Lee T.H.: Patient safety beyond the hospital. *N Engl J Med* 363:1001–1003, Sep. 9, 2010.
2. McPhillips H.A., et al.: Potential medication dosing errors in outpatient pediatrics. *J Pediatr* 147:761–767, Dec. 2005.
3. Fortescue E.B., et al.: Prioritizing strategies for preventing medication errors and adverse drug events in pediatric inpatients. *Pediatrics* 111:722–729, Apr. 2003.
4. Jha A.K., et al.: Use of electronic health records in U.S. hospitals. *N Engl J Med* 360:1628–1638, Apr. 16, 2009. Epub Mar. 25, 2009.
5. Hibbard J.H., et al.: Can patients be part of the solution? Views on their role in preventing medical errors. *Med Care Res Rev* 62:601–616, Oct. 2005.
6. McGhan W.F., Smith W.E., Adams D.W.: A randomized trial comparing pharmacists and technicians as dispensers of prescriptions for ambulatory patients. *Med Care* 21:445–453, Apr. 1983.
7. Flynn E.A., Barker K.N., Carnahan B.J.: National observational study of prescription dispensing accuracy and safety in 50 pharmacies. *J Am Pharm Assoc (Wash)* 43:191–200, Mar.–Apr. 2003.
8. Knudsen P., et al.: Preventing medication errors in community pharmacy: Frequency and seriousness of medication errors. *Qual Saf Health Care* 16:291–296, Aug. 2007.
9. Szeinbach S., et al.: Dispensing errors in community pharmacy: Perceived influence of sociotechnical factors. *Int J Qual Health Care* 19:203–209, Aug. 2007. Epub Jun. 12, 2007.
10. James K.L., et al.: Incidence, type and causes of dispensing errors: A review of the literature. *Int J Pharm Pract* 17:9–30, Feb. 2009.

11. Knudsen P., et al.: Preventing medication errors in community pharmacy: Root-cause analysis of transcription errors. *Qual Saf Health Care* 16:285–290, Aug. 2007.

12. Weingart S.N., et al.: Oral chemotherapy safety practices at US cancer centres: Questionnaire survey. *BMJ* 334:407, Feb. 24, 2007. Epub Jan. 12, 2007.

13. Partridge A.H., et al.: Adherence to therapy with oral antineoplastic agents. *J Natl Cancer Inst* 94:652–661, May 1, 2002.

14. Weingart S.N., et al.: Medication errors involving oral chemotherapy. *Cancer* 116:2455–2464, May 15, 2010.

15. Simchowitz B., et al.: Perceptions and experiences of patients receiving oral chemotherapy. *Clin J Oncol Nurs* 14:447–453, Aug. 2010.

16. Walsh K.E., et al.: Medication errors among adults and children with cancer in the outpatient setting. *J Clin Oncol* 27:891–896, Feb. 20, 2009. Epub Dec. 29, 2009.

CHAPTER 9

Surgery: Safety Culture, Site Marking, Checklists, and Teamwork

Andrew M. Ibrahim; Martin A. Makary, M.D., M.P.H.

CASE

A 68-year-old overweight man arrived at the hospital for a planned right-knee replacement surgery. On the morning of surgery, he was seen by the attending surgeon, who accurately marked the right knee with his initials. However, when the patient was taken to the operating room (OR) with the resident and anesthesia staff, he was positioned for a left-knee surgery. When the attending surgeon arrived, the left knee had already been prepped and draped. Immediately before making incision, the attending physician paused and looked for his initials. Unable to find them, he asked that the sterile draping be taken down, and it was revealed that the wrong knee had been prepped for surgery. The patient was then repositioned and re-prepped, and a right-knee replacement was carried out successfully.

BACKGROUND

Errors in surgery can be catastrophic to the patient, surgeon, and hospital. An adverse event such as wrong-site surgery, for example, can result in permanent disability, destruction of a physician's career, millions of dollars in malpractice-related costs, and perhaps long-lasting damage to the community's trust in the hospital.

More common than adverse events are close calls, in which patient harm can be averted or mitigated through mere chance or established safety systems. Safety systems are best established when frontline personnel nominate areas of potential patient harm which need to be improved. The safety literature is providing increasing insight into the anatomy of errors. For example, we now know that a retained surgical sponge is more likely to occur when the surgery is emergent, when unplanned changes in procedure occur (as when new diagnoses are encountered in the OR), when multiple surgical teams are involved, and/or when the patient is obese.[1,2] Adding appropriate safety checks can significantly reduce such risks.

Errors in surgery can occur during and between all stages of patient care. Most errors can be traced in part to overarching miscommunication among caregivers, as the patient progresses from one stage of care to the next, as represented by arrows in Figure 9-1 (*see* page 90).

IDENTIFYING THE CAUSE OF THE CLOSE CALL

The close call in this case raised particular concern because it happened just weeks after a wrong-site surgery in the same department. Thus, after the close call was reported, a task force, including nursing, surgical, and anesthesia members, was created. The team performed a root cause analysis, which revealed a number of

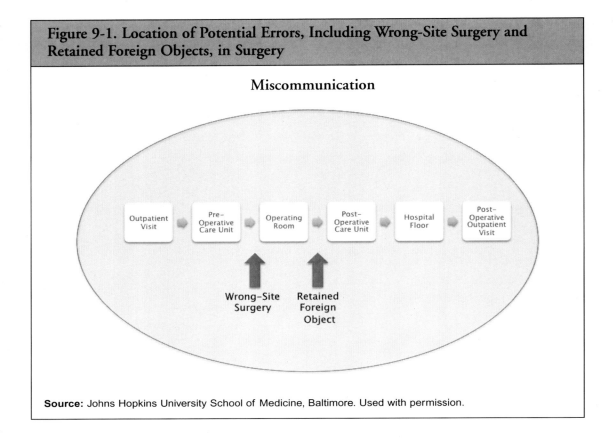

Figure 9-1. Location of Potential Errors, Including Wrong-Site Surgery and Retained Foreign Objects, in Surgery

Source: Johns Hopkins University School of Medicine, Baltimore. Used with permission.

important contributing factors, as follows:

- The patient operated on in the same OR just before the close call had a left-knee replacement. Although the room was cleaned, the equipment was kept in the same position, oriented for another left-knee operation.

- The surgeon who placed initials on the patient's knee was not present in the OR before draping the patient.

- No routine procedure for use of a preoperative checklist existed to confirm patient and procedure before incision.

- There was no mechanism in place for reporting errors or close calls.

- The nursing staff did not feel comfortable speaking up when they perceived that there might be a patient safety concern because they thought they would be ridiculed for doing so.

In addition to these findings, a hospitalwide survey carried out on close calls revealed that such close calls were happening relatively frequently and for similar systems-related reasons. The survey also revealed that most employees did not report close calls because (1) "no harm" was caused to the patient and (2) they were concerned that reporting would jeopardize their employment.

PREVENTING SURGICAL ERRORS

In 2003, the high rates of surgical errors prompted the development of the Universal Protocol for Preventing Wrong Site, Wrong Procedure, Wrong Person Surgery™ by The Joint Commission.[3] In 2006, Joint Commission International instituted a similar requirement with its International Patient Safety Goal 4, "Ensure correct-site, correct-procedure, correct-patient surgery."[4] The practice involves a preprocedural verification process, marking of the procedure site, and a pre-incision pause or "time-out."[3,4] Each of these processes has been further developed and is used along with other safety measures, such as surgical counts.

Site Marking

Before surgery, the patient is seen while awake and confirms the site of the surgery with the surgeon. Then the surgeon writes initials at the site, indicating acknowledgement of the appropriate place for incision. In the case provided, this proved to be the only mechanism through which a serious error was prevented. Yet not all cases are so fortunate. For example, during a 30-month period in Pennsylvania, correct site markings failed to prevent 16 wrong-site surgeries, of which 6 were not recognized until after the procedure had been completed.[5]

Routine Use of a Safety Checklist

The use of a preoperative checklist has been a landmark intervention to reduce errors in surgical patients. In a study of nearly 8,000 patients at eight major medical centers around the world, the implementation of a checklist was followed by significant reductions in morbidity and mortality.[6] The checklist enables all operating staff to confirm verbally the correct patient, correct operation, and correct equipment and to discuss anticipated concerns in the case. An example of a five-point checklist is as follows[7]:

1. State names and roles of team members.

2. Verify the correct patient, correct procedure, and correct site.

3. Confirm that appropriate antibiotics were given prior to incision.

4. Review critical steps.

5. Allow team members to express any potential problems or concerns they anticipate during the case.

Surgical Counts

This strategy involves routine counts toward the end of the procedure to ensure that all sponges, tools, and equipment can be located. In the event

that a count is incorrect, the missing item must be found to ensure that it is not left in the patient. Although helpful, this practice often occurs under time constraints when the case is finishing and there is pressure to "move on." "Falsely correct" counts have been observed, in which a count is performed and wrongly declared to be correct. For example, in a review of 191,000 cases at the Mayo Clinic, where 34 retained foreign objects were found, nearly half of cases with retained objects had a falsely correct count at the end of the case.[2] X-rays to screen for retained foreign bodies are generally reserved for high-risk cases or cases where there is a concern that the sponge or needle count may not be correct.

Tools that can be used to improve safety for surgical patients include the preoperative checklist, OR debriefings and counts, and the Safety Attitudes Questionnaire (SAQ; *see* Figure 9-2, page 92).

Although routine use of a safety checklist and site marking are evidence-based practices recognized to mitigate risk in the OR, no magic bullet exists to eliminate errors in surgery. Ultimately, we believe that improving the safety of the surgical patient is based on establishing a local culture of safety.

OPERATING ROOM CULTURE AND TEAM COMMUNICATION

Historically, open and clear communication in the OR has been distorted by the steep hierarchy inherent in the surgical culture. In the past, it was common for intimidation by surgeons to be rewarded. We now know that such behavior patterns worsen patient safety by preventing nurses and other surgical staff from pointing out potential errors or mistakes by surgeons.[8] In a review of errors reported to The Joint Commission in 2006, poor communication contributed to nearly 70% of sentinel events,[9] which made it apparent that improving team communication is paramount in preventing future errors.

Figure 9-2. Tools That Can Be Used to Improve Safety for Surgical Patients

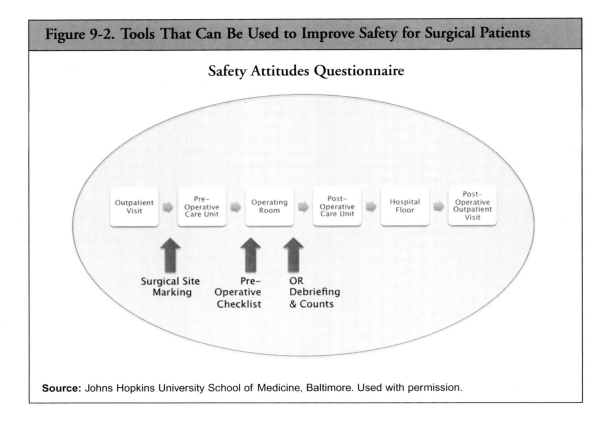

Source: Johns Hopkins University School of Medicine, Baltimore. Used with permission.

Effective communication reflects the culture of the OR and ultimately that of the hospital. An SAQ adapted for the surgical setting might ask for the participants' degree of agreement with statements such as the following[10]:

■ I am encouraged by my colleagues to report any patient safety concerns I may have.

■ The culture in this clinical area makes it easy to learn from the mistakes of others.

■ Medical errors are handled appropriately in this clinical area.

■ I know the proper channels to direct questions to regarding patient safety in this clinical area.

■ I receive appropriate feedback about my performance.

■ I would feel safe being treated here as a patient.

■ In this clinical area, it is difficult to discuss mistakes.

If we use these statements to measure the culture and safety climate, what are some of the tools that can be used to effectively improve both? The routine use of a surgical safety checklist, as discussed, plays a significant role in improving OR culture and building teamwork. In addition to addressing OR pragmatics, team members introduce themselves by name and role and are encouraged to express any concerns that they may have about the case. From the authors' experience, many surgical cases are completed without many staff in the room knowing one another's names. By conducting team introductions at the start of a case, team collaboration within the OR increases, as does the perceptions of safety.[7]

Postoperative debriefings are also helpful in promoting team communication and improving patient safety.[8] Most debriefings include counts of sponges, needles, and instruments, as well as

Figure 9-3. Opportunities to Identify Near Misses Exist at Every Stage of Patient Care

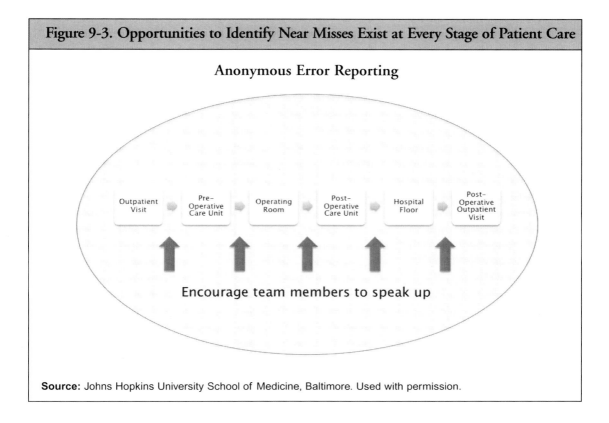

Source: Johns Hopkins University School of Medicine, Baltimore. Used with permission.

verifications of correct labeling of surgical specimens. The routine use of debriefings promotes a culture of learning from experience and treats any errors or critical incidents as learning opportunities rather than cause for blame and punishment.

Opportunities to identify close calls exist at every stage of patient care, which can be facilitated by developing a mechanism for anonymous error reporting (including near misses) and encouraging team members to speak up (*see* Figure 9-3, above).

PUTTING NEW STRATEGIES AND PRACTICES IN PLACE

As a result of the root cause analysis, several new strategies and practices were put into place. First, a preoperative checklist[7] was developed to be used with key members, including the attending surgeon, anesthesia, and nursing in the OR before the prepping and draping of the patient.

This checklist included the following items:

- Confirmation of the correct patient
- Confirmation of the surgical site, including identification of previously marked initials by the *same* individual who made them
- Confirmation that the appropriate equipment was in the room before surgery, with appropriate placement
- Invitations to nursing, anesthesia, and surgery staff members to share any safety concerns about the surgery prior to incision

This list was later revised to the five-point checklist now widely used by many institutions (*see* page 91).

In addition, an internal Web site was developed at which any employee of the hospital could anonymously report errors to be reviewed by hospital administrative staff. A cultural assessment was also carried out, using the SAQ[11] to identify areas of hospital safety culture that could be improved. (Adapted from the airline industry, the SAQ items have validated benchmark data against which institutions can compare their own scores.)

Since the initiation of the checklist and the institution of a reporting system, many more close calls have been reported. However, the number of adverse events has decreased. Future meetings have been planned to discuss ways to encourage staff to report errors without fear of losing employment, and anyone found to ridicule a person for expressing a safety concern is spoken to by the chair of surgery.

The system of care in the OR was reengineered so that the attending surgeon must be present during the draping process, and equipment must be placed into a neutral position after each case. To avoid "top-heavy" changes, ideas for changes to the routine flow of patient care were solicited from the frontline providers. This principle governed all quality improvement strategies in recognition of the fact that top-down decision making that does not use provider input can be counterproductive.

CONCLUSIONS

Reporting of close calls in surgery reflects open communication of care providers, which has been shown to improve outcomes,[12] and identifies errors that have the potential to cause harm if they recur. Such a practice demonstrates to patients and employees the hospital and organizational commitment toward patient safety.

In the case of the close call of a wrong-site surgery, the only mechanism in place that prevented the sentinel event was the diligent search for initials marking the surgical site. Although no harm ultimately was done to the patient in this case, the systematic review of the event led to important changes within the hospital. A preoperative checklist was developed to be used by

all OR teams in the hospital. Team members introduced themselves by name and role, allowing for greater ease of communication, including when there is concern that an error may occur. Attention was called to the wider hospital dynamics, which led to the creation of an anonymous reporting system to identify areas of patient safety concerns. Had this close call not been acted on, it may have taken a patient injury to bring about such valuable changes.

References

1. Gawande A.A., et al.: Risk factors for retained instruments and sponges after surgery. *N Engl J Med* 348:229–235, Jan. 16, 2003.
2. Clarke J.R., Johnston J., Finley E.D.: Getting surgery right. *Ann Surg* 246:395–403, discussion 403–405, Sep. 2007.
3. The Joint Commission: *Universal Protocol.* http://www.jointcommission.org/PatientSafety/Universal Protocol/ (accessed Aug. 4, 2010).
4. Joint Commission International: Joint Commission *International Accreditation Standards for Hospitals,* 4th ed. Oak Brook, IL: Joint Commission Resources, 2010.
5. Cima R.R., et al.: Incidence and characteristics of potential and actual retained foreign object events in surgical patients. *J Am Coll Surg* 207:80–87, Jul. 2008. Epub May 23, 2008.
6. Haynes A.B., et al.: A surgical safety checklist to reduce morbidity and mortality in a global population. *N Engl J Med* 360:491–499, Jan. 29, 2009. Epub Jan. 14, 2009.
7. Makary M.A., et al.: Operating room briefings and wrong-site surgery. *J Am Coll Surg* 204:236–243, Feb. 2007. Epub Dec. 8, 2006.
8. Chen C.L., et al.: Patient safety. Chapter 12 in Brunicardi F.C., et al. (eds.): *Schwartz's Principles of Surgery,* 9th ed. New York City: McGraw-Hill Professional, 2009, pp. 313–342.
9. The Joint Commission: *Sentinel Event Statistics.* http://www.jointcommission.org/SentinelEvents/Statistics (accessed Mar. 15, 2010).
10. Makary M.A., et al.: Patient safety in surgery. *Ann Surg* 243:628–635, May 2006.
11. Sexton J.B., et al.: The Safety Attitudes Questionnaire: Psychometric properties, benchmarking data, and emerging research. *BMC Health Serv Res* 6:44, Apr. 3, 2006.
12. Makary M.A., et al.: Surgical specimen identification errors: A new measure of quality in surgical care. *Surgery* 141:450–455, Apr. 2007. Epub Jan. 24, 2007.

CHAPTER 10

Transfusion Medicine: The Problem with Multitasking

Barbara Rabin Fastman, M.H.A., M.T.(A.S.C.P.)S.C., B.B.; Harold S. Kaplan, M.D.

CASE

A blood component pickup slip was dropped onto the control desk of a harried transfusion service technologist by one of several transporters waiting at the blood issue desk. The request was for one unit of packed red blood cells for Mr. QL, a 58-year-old severely anemic patient admitted to the hospital with multiple myeloma. The technologist was completing an emergency release of blood components for a bleeding patient in the operating room (OR). Also, with the telephone receiver tucked under her chin, she was assuring an obstetrical nurse that an expedited typing and cross-matching of blood for her patient was indeed under way. She took the pickup slip from the desk, and, anticipating a pickup for the next patient, she pulled another slip from a clattering printer and proceeded to the cross-matched blood refrigerator to retrieve the packed cell unit for Mr. QL. Approximately 10 minutes following the unit's issue by the technologist and pickup by transport personnel, an urgent telephone call from Mr. QL's nurse alerted the laboratory that the wrong unit had been sent to her patient's floor. Fortunately, the error had been detected through routine bedside verification procedures just before the unit was to be transfused. The unit's label and accompanying paperwork identified that it had been cross-matched for another patient, Mr. RC (whose pickup slip had just

been pulled from the printer). On initial laboratory investigation, it was recognized that the incorrectly issued unit was type A and that Mr. QL was blood type O. The correctly matched group O packed red cell units for Mr. QL were identified and were subsequently issued and administered without event.

CLOSE CALLS AND THE VULNERABILITY TO "SURPRISE"

The issuing of the wrong unit of blood—and almost transfusing type A blood to a type O recipient, as described in the case—exemplifies the kind of unexpected, or "surprise," event discussed by James Reason.[1] Such surprises typically occur at the human/system interface.

Reason's three questions for predicting where these unforeseen events are most likely to occur, also provided in Chapter 1 (page 6–7), are also listed here:

1. *The "hands-on" question:* Which activities involve the most direct human interaction with the system?

2. *The "criticality" question:* Which activities, if executed inadequately, have the greatest potential for harm?

3. *The "frequency" question:* How often are these activities performed in routine operations?

An activity such as blood unit issue, which scores high on all three questions, is considered vulnerable to surprise. In reports submitted to the Medical Event Reporting System for Transfusion Medicine (MERS-TM), which captures the details of close-call events and promotes their reporting, the vast majority of close-call events were detected and trapped before blood component issue.[2] However, as many as 25% of the close-call events were detected either at the time of issue from the laboratory or at the time of blood administration.[3] Because of the potential for "surprise" and because the planned barriers at these points of the process are so proximate to the patient, close calls caught at the time of issue or administration are of special concern. In this case, the safety check at the bedside saved the day, although it obviously would have been safer if a barrier further upstream had trapped the error before or at the point of issue[4] or had prevented its occurrence in the first place.

It is important to realize that the most frequent non–close-call "wrong blood event" is the administration of properly labeled blood to a patient other than the intended recipient. These events occur three times more frequently than wrong blood events caused by phlebotomy error (38% versus 13%).[5] Phlebotomy errors, although much more common overall than administration of blood to the wrong patient, are usually caught by a planned barrier when the sample first arrives and is checked in at the laboratory. Although wrong blood events are often associated with clinical urgency and with patients having similar names, the failure to adequately check the patient's identification at the bedside was the most common underlying factor[6]—as reported to the Serious Hazards of Transfusion (SHOT) hemovigilance system, which is focused on learning from adverse events and near misses.

ROOT CAUSE ANALYSIS

In the case of Mr. QL, a root cause analysis (RCA) was performed to determine the causes (as there is always more than one cause) of the incorrect selection of the unit and of the failure of the safety barrier at the point of blood unit issue. The individual who responded to the request for blood and who selected and issued the incorrect unit was a knowledgeable, licensed technologist with 12 years of blood transfusion laboratory experience, 5 of them in the laboratory in which the case occurred. Her 5 years of performance reviews were consistently good to excellent, with no previous instances of attitudinal or performance problems. The RCA revealed the multiple interacting causes, foremost being the recognition of "an underlying vulnerability due to excessive multitasking demands."

The term *multitasking* was first coined in 1966 but has only recently become common vernacular. (The Merriam-Webster Online Dictionary describes multitasking as "the performance of multiple tasks at one time."[7]) The technologist was dealing with an emergency, was on the telephone, and had two blood pickup requests in her hand at the same time: one slip that she had picked up from the control desk and one slip that she had pulled from the printer. Referring to the slip from the printer, she retrieved the unit of blood intended for Mr. RC, thinking that it was for Mr. QL, and issued it to the transporter waiting at the control desk for Mr. QL's blood unit. She had unknowingly defeated the computer-aided final issue check by scanning the medical record number (MRN) from Mr. RC's pickup slip (from the printer) instead of scanning the MRN from Mr. QL's pickup slip (from the control desk). The computer software responded appropriately within its limitations, matching the pickup slip to the unit. The system is not designed to go beyond this check in ensuring that the unit release matches the order for a particular patient.

The causal tree analysis shown in Figure 10-1 (*see* page 97) depicts the results of the RCA. In this analysis of a close call, both the failure side and the recovery side of the causal tree are identified.[8] The causal code key for this close-call event is provided in Table 10-1 (*see* page 98).

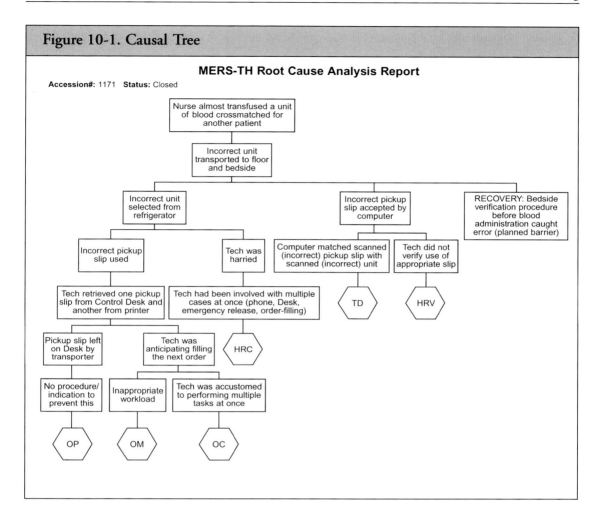

Figure 10-1. Causal Tree

MERS-TH Root Cause Analysis Report

Accession#: 1171   Status: Closed

Causes and Contributing Factors

What might have caused the failures in performance of an experienced individual executing such a vital but routine task? Langer has described *mindfulness* as "a state of alert and lively awareness, which is specifically manifested in typical ways. Generally, mindfulness is expressed in active information processing, characterized by cognitive differentiation: the creation of categories and distinctions."[9(p. 138)] A relative lack of mindfulness often accompanies well-practiced routines and may displace conscious mindful performance with more automated behavior. Could these slips, mistakes, and missed discrepant cues have resulted from a lack of mindfulness, amplified by hurry, overload, and multitasking?

In a survey of hospital transfusion-service staff, the leading reasons identified for mistakes in transfusion services were as follows[10]:

1. Interruptions

2. Others (outside the laboratory) not knowing the procedures

3. Pressure to deliver

4. Staff/work-load disparity

5. Individual slip or mistake

The task list for the transfusion control desk technologist, as represented in the case provided, included relatively straightforward individual routines: communicating by telephone and in person, processing orders/requests, logging in patient samples, prioritizing other

Table 10-1. Causal Code Key	
OP Organizational: Protocols/Procedures	Failure resulting from the quality or availability of hospital policies and procedures. They may be too complicated, inaccurate, unrealistic, absent, or poorly presented.
OM Organizational: Management Priorities	Internal management decisions in which safety is relegated to an inferior position when faced with conflicting demands or objectives. This may be a conflict between production needs and safety. An example of this is decisions made about staffing levels.
OC Organizational: Culture	A collective approach and its attendant modes to safety and risk rather than the behavior of just one individual. Groups might establish their own modes of function as opposed to following prescribed methods. An example of this is not paging a manager/physician on the weekend because that was not how the department operated; "It's just not done".
HRC Human Rule Based: Coordination	A lack of task coordination within a health care team in an organization. An example would be an essential task not being performed because everyone thought that someone else had completed the task.
TD Technical: Design	Inadequate design of equipment, software, or materials. Can include the design of workspace, software, forms, etc. An example is a form that requires a supervisory review that does not contain a field for signature.
HRV Human Rule Based: Verification	The correct and complete assessment of a situation including related conditions of the patient and materials to be used before beginning the task. An example would be failure to correctly identify a patient by checking the wristband.

Source: The causal codes are drawn from Kaplan H.S., et al.: Identification and classification of the causes of events in transfusion medicine. *Transfusion* 38:1071–1081, Nov.–Dec. 1998.

technologists' work loads, preparing components, issuing components, returning units to inventory, and performing daily refrigerator quality control. However, as the work load increased, the expectation for concurrent efforts and the burden of multitasking also increased, along with the potential for error.

Even though multitasking is often identified as a common underlying element in such mistakes, it is considered an essential competence for managing work flow. We pride ourselves on our ability to multitask, despite increasing evidence that multitasking not only makes us less efficient but also lessens our cerebral capacity to carry out the very tasks we are attempting to execute. Neuroimaging studies suggest an apparent limit on the overall amount of brain activation available in performing concurrent dual tasks, even if they draw on different cortical networks.[11] The

term *multitasking* is somewhat misleading because we typically do not actually perform more than one task at a time. To do task B, we must first turn off task A and then turn on task B, with a brief period of inhibition of our ability to return to task A.[12] The term *task-switching* has been used to emphasize this reality.[13]

In the case under discussion, the latent underlying conditions making the laboratory vulnerable to failure were its heavy work load and an associated excessive reliance on multitasking. In following the laboratory's multitasking mode of handling urgent demands and numerous interruptions, the control desk technologist made distinct errors in both selection and issue.

CORRECTIVE ACTIONS

As is typical in health care, the corrective actions that many hospitals would rely on for the type of event represented in this case would consist of retraining personnel, creating or refining procedures, and/or telling staff to be more careful. Yet on the basis of the output of the causal analysis in this event, the laboratory focused instead on limiting both the need for and the use of multitasking in order to prevent recurrence. For the short-term (immediate) intervention, only one pickup slip would be handled at a time, and no pickup slip left on the desk by a transporter would be accepted. For the longer-term intervention (within three months), the burden of intrusive phone calls was to be reduced and the information available to floors was to be enhanced by accelerating the completion of linkage of the new transfusion laboratory information system to the hospital information system.

The short- and long-term corrections of system vulnerability combined the use of inherent and procedural risk reduction strategies. Risk reduction or management strategies can be categorized by their order of probable diminishing efficacy: inherent, passive, active, and procedural.[14] Inherent strategies either do away with a risk or decrease its significance to acceptable limits. Passive strategies, such as "gates," reduce risk just by their physical presence. Active strategies make use of alarms and interlocks to prevent, detect, or mitigate unsafe conditions. Procedural strategies, which are built around people, standard operating procedures, checklists, and training, are the most often used in medicine.

CONCLUSION

The capture and analysis of close-call events provide an ongoing means of helping to identify and manage system vulnerabilities. In the close-call case under discussion, a follow-up audit verified that short- and long-term corrections were successfully implemented, preventing recurrence of this type of incorrect blood unit issue in the past few years. However, it must be borne in mind that "a design can only be described as inherently safer in the context of a particular hazard. The design may or may not be inher-

ently safer with respect to another hazard of the system."[14(p. 110)] This underscores the continuing value of the surveillance of close calls for potential hazards not yet identified.

References

1. Reason J.T.: *Managing the Risks of Organizational Accidents.* Burlington, VT: Ashgate Publishing Company, 1997.
2. Medical Event Reporting System–Transfusion Medicine (MERS-TM): *About MERS-TM.* http://www.mers-tem.org/about.html (accessed Sep. 22, 2010).
3. Callum J.L., et al.: Reporting of near-miss events for transfusion medicine: Improving transfusion safety. *Transfusion* 41:1204–1211, Oct. 2001.
4. Kaplan H.S.: Getting the right blood to the right patient: The contribution of near-miss event reporting and barrier analysis. *Transfus Clin Biol* 12:380–384, Nov. 2005. Epub Nov. 28, 2005.
5. Linden J.V., et al.: Transfusion errors in New York State: An analysis of 10 years' experience. *Transfusion* 40:1207–1213, Oct. 2000.
6. Stainsby D., et al.: Serious hazards of transfusion: A decade of hemovigilance in the UK. *Transfus Med Rev* 20:273–282, Oct. 2006.
7. *Merriam-Webster Online Dictionary,* s.v. "multitasking." http://www.merriam-webster.com/dictionary/multitasking (accessed Sep. 23, 2010).
8. Kaplan H.S., Rabin Fastman R.: Organization of event reporting data for sense making and system improvement. *Qual Saf Health Care* 12(Suppl. 2):ii68–ii72, Dec. 2003.
9. Langer E.J.: Minding matters: The consequences of mindlessness-mindfulness. *Advances Exp Soc Psychol* 22:137–173, 1989.
10. Sorra J., et al.: Staff attitudes about event reporting and patient safety culture in hospital transfusion services. *Transfusion* 48:1934–1942, Sep. 2008. Epub May 23, 2008.
11. Just M.A., Keller T.A., Cynkar J.: A decrease in brain activation associated with driving when listening to someone speak. *Brain Res* 1205:70–80, Apr. 18, 2008. Epub Feb. 19, 2008.
12. Dux P.E., et al.: Isolation of a central bottleneck of information processing with time-resolved FMRI. *Neuron* 52:1109–1120, Dec. 21, 2006.
13. Crenshaw D.: *The Myth of Multitasking: How "Doing It All" Gets Nothing Done.* San Francisco: Jossey-Bass, 2008.
14. Hendershott D.: Inherently safer design. In Phimster J., Bier V., Kunreuther H. (eds.): *Accident Precursor Analysis and Management: Reducing Technological Risk Through Diligence.* Washington, DC: National Academies Press, 2004, pp.103–117.

Event Reached the Patient but Did No Harm

CHAPTER 11

Radiotherapy: Using Risk Profiling to Identify Errors and Close Calls in the Process of Care

Michael B. Barton, M.B.B.S., M.D.; Geoffrey P. Delaney, M.B.B.S., M.D., Ph.D.; Douglas J. Noble, B.Sc., B.M., B.Ch., M.P.H.

PATIENT SAFETY IN RADIOTHERAPY

Radiotherapy, which uses x-ray or electron beams to kill cancer cells, is indicated in the treatment of approximately half of all cancer patients.[1] Treatment is usually given in multiple episodes to allow normal tissues to repair any damage. More than 80% of treatments are intended to cure the disease or to increase survival.[2] Despite the benefits of radiotherapy for patients with malignant and benign conditions, treatment errors can be severe, and even deadly, as described in a recent series of articles in the *New York Times.*[3] Many of these errors reflect unregulated, poorly thought-out procedures and lack of appropriate training. An event in the United Kingdom illustrates this point. One radiotherapy department introduced a new computer system; it was thought that the computer did not make an adjustment to the dose of radiotherapy to be delivered, when in fact it did. Consequently, staff made a manual adjustment, leading to 1,000 patients receiving the wrong dose of radiotherapy during a period of almost 10 years.[4] The process of radiotherapy is technically complex, as described in Sidebar 11-1 (*see* page 104). With the use of technology and devices of increasing complexity, users must be mindful of the associated safety risks and possible adverse events.[5]

The existence of an agreed-on process of care in radiotherapy is key to ensuring that appropriate safeguards against error are in place. This was first suggested by the chief medical officer for England in his 2006 *Annual Report on the State of Public Health in the United Kingdom.*[6] The report stated that although errors are comparatively rare in radiotherapy, the effects of delivering excessive radiation to an already ill individual could be so devastating that national action is required. This report set forward three types of frequently reported errors—ineffective training for using improved technology, suspect mechanisms for data transfer, and a deficient system to detect radiation-dosing errors—and proposed a seven-step process on which to base risk reduction endeavors.

In 2008, the World Health Organization (WHO) responded to this report and commissioned an important piece of background epidemiology to establish the frequency of error and the stage in the process of care at which errors were occurring. Between 1976 and 2007, some 7,741 errors in radiotherapy were reported, of which 4,616 were near misses (they did not reach the patient; *see* Figure 11-1, page 105) and 38 (1.2% of the remaining 3,125 errors) resulted in the patient's death; *see* Figure 11-1, page 105).[7]

The incidents depicted in Figure 11-1 were mapped to an internationally agreed-on process

Sidebar 11-1. Complexity of Radiotherapy

The process of radiotherapy is technically complex and involves many different staff members and different professional groups handing off work between each other during the process of deciding to treat, imaging the area needing treatment, planning the radiation, calculating the radiation dose, delivering the treatment, and following quality assurance processes to ensure correct delivery. Radiotherapy has come to rely on computer systems of progressively increasing sophistication, which is especially true as technology has genuinely improved and more complex treatments are possible. Precision (targeting only the tumor site for radiotherapy with minimal effects to normal tissue) and accuracy (hitting that target every time) are core tenets of modern practice. Advances in technology have facilitated the improvement of this process dramatically.

Yet, keeping up with technological advances has not been without challenges. Just as home computers regularly undergo upgrades of operating systems (for example, Windows XP to Windows 7) and software packages (for example, Word 2003 to Word 2010), so too do radiotherapy operations undergo similar changes, except of a more dramatic magnitude. Baseline levels of technician training are nonstandardized, leaving the task of quality assurance to individual departments. Training is invariably based on apprenticeship and experience. When new technology is introduced, systems that in other industries would immediately trigger organizationwide education and training programs are less prevalent (although not absent). In addition, reliance on computerization can lull workers into a false sense of security about the safety of treatment delivery.[1,2]

There is another layer of complexity. The physician responsible for delivery of radiotherapy in fact has little to do with many of the numerous steps in the process of care. Following initial clinical assessment and prescription of a treatment plan, a complex series of steps occurs, involving imaging specialists, physicists, and radiotherapists. The physician maintains an overview of the process, but a majority of physicians will not have a detailed understanding of the specific functions of the physicists and other ancillary workers involved. This in itself is not necessarily problematic, but it does create the need for systems and processes that assure the quality of the process and thereby help ensure patient safety. This is the context of ensuring patient safety in modern radiotherapy practice.

References:
1. Leunens G., et al.: Human errors in data transfer during the preparation and delivery of radiation treatment affecting the final result: "Garbage in, garbage out." *Radiother Oncol* 23:217–222, Apr. 1992.
2. Fraass B.A., et al.: The impact of treatment complexity and computer-control delivery technology on treatment delivery errors. *Int J Radiat Oncol Biol Phys* 42:651–659, Oct. 1, 1998.

of care devised and authorized by WHO[8] (*see* Figure 11-2, page 106).

WHO developed the process of care in radiotherapy to guide quality assurance and patient safety efforts in radiotherapy departments worldwide. Establishing the process provided a substantive backbone for mapping risk. Although many of the risks to patient safety vary from department to department, others are similar across departments. WHO grouped the major errors according to the stage of the process of

Figure 11-1. Adverse Events and Near Misses in Radiotherapy, According to the Position in the Process of Care

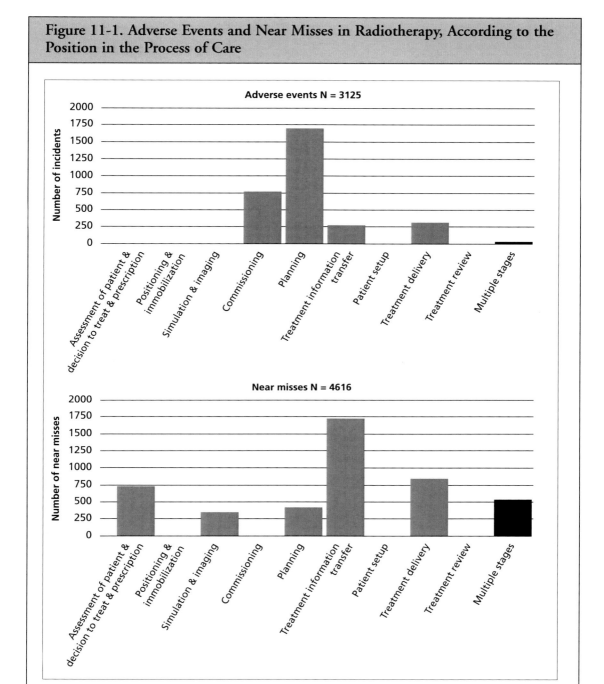

Source: World Health Organization: *Radiotherapy Risk Profile,* 2008.
http://www.who.int/patientsafety/activities/technical/radiotherapy/en/index.html (accessed Aug. 4, 2010). Used with permission.

care in a technique it termed *risk profiling*. This was a new way of thinking about radiotherapy systems. Table 11-1 (*see* page 107) provides an example in the simulation step in the process of radiotherapy, which shows the major risks to patient care, their relative impact, and potential

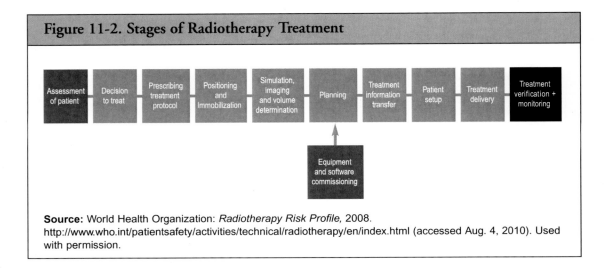

Figure 11-2. Stages of Radiotherapy Treatment

Source: World Health Organization: *Radiotherapy Risk Profile,* 2008. http://www.who.int/patientsafety/activities/technical/radiotherapy/en/index.html (accessed Aug. 4, 2010). Used with permission.

mitigating factors. Risk profiling in health care is now used more frequently to identify hidden dangers within processes of care.[9]

Simulation During the Process of Care

Simulation of treatment is a step in the process of radiotherapy that is used to determine the correct area to treat and to define normal tissue structures to be avoided. Simulation involves imaging the treatment site and creating and recording anatomical landmarks that can guide daily treatment. Plain-film imaging has recently been replaced with computerized tomography (CT) imaging, in a process known as "virtual simulation."

After simulation, beam directions and relative dose strengths are mapped out, and doses are calculated on specialized radiotherapy treatment planning systems (TPSs). The calculated doses and beam configurations are transferred to megavoltage linear accelerators (MLAs) for treatment delivery. Digitally reconstructed radiographs (DRRs) are produced by the TPS and used in the verification process. Treatment machines take images of the treatment fields to verify that the patient has been placed in the correct position. These images may be repeated during the course of the treatment to ensure that the patient remains in the intended treatment position.

CASES

Background

There was little local experience with virtual simulation when it was introduced in May 2003 into the radiotherapy department at a teaching hospital in New South Wales, Australia. Historically, simulation was a radiotherapy planning process whereby the patient was imaged using kilovoltage image intensifiers to "simulate" the directions of the proposed radiotherapy beams. During that appointment, the clinicians could evaluate the position of the tumor and aim the beams appropriately. However, with the increasing use of CT imaging in radiotherapy, the process of virtual simulation, whereby the patient's topographic data were obtained by CT scanning, was developed. Further planning and dose calculation is then performed, after the patient has left the department. Reference points are used to ensure that what is planned on the patient is based on the CT scan and is readily transferable to the treatment delivered to the patient. These reference marks—in most cases, measurements from laser lights that are present in the CT and treatment rooms—are generally marked by tattooing spots on the patient. Using computer simulation, the clinician and planning staff, as stated, could then plan the patient's treatment at a later point in time, without the

Table 11-1. Risks Inherent in Simulation, Their Potential Impact, and Solutions

Risks	Potential impact	Solutions
Incorrect identification of patient	High	ID check open questions, eliciting an active response as a minimum 3 points of ID Photo ID
Incorrect positioning of reference points and guides	High	Competency certification Appropriate education Independent checking
Defining wrong volume	High	
Incorrect margin applied around tumour volume	High	
Incorrect contouring of organs at risk	High	
Incorrect image fusion	Medium	
Light fields and cross-hairs could be misaligned	Medium	Equipment quality assurance Quality control checks with protocol for sign-off procedures
Inability to identify the isocentre consistently	High	
Poor image quality	Medium	
Incorrect imaging protocol	Medium	Planning protocol checklist Independent checks Signature protocols
Incorrect area imaged	Medium	
Wrong side/site imaged	High	
Altered patient position	High	
Incorrect orientation information	High	

Source: World Health Organization: *Radiotherapy Risk Profile,* 2008. http://www.who.int/patientsafety/activities/technical/radiotherapy/en/index.html (accessed Aug. 4, 2010). Used with permission.

patient being in attendance. The benefits of this approach are that more information can be obtained using CT (such as internal organs not seen on image intensification), and the process is more efficient for the patient. Radiotherapy begins only after the treatment plan is generated and checked. Images are regularly taken on the treatment machine of the radiation portals during a course of radiotherapy to verify that the radiation is directed to the correct area of the body. This process, known as "portal imaging," is the final verification step in the process of treatment delivery.

Errors

In February 2004, quality assurance checks detected errors in the geographic placement of the treatment field for the first few treatments in 3 patients, prompting a review of all 416 patients who had undergone virtual simulation

---

Sidebar 11-2. Contributing Factors

- Virtual simulation protocol lengthy and complex
- Short time frame for clinical implementation of the new virtual simulation process
- Insufficient staff to develop the protocol and educate new staff
- Insufficient planning for the change to virtual simulation
- Skill mix of senior/junior radiation therapy staff in the departments was insufficient to address the additional workload and process change implementation
- Inadequate "dummy runs" and audits of the process implementation for all treatment sites
- A number of quality assurance steps delegated inappropriately to junior staff

Source: Root Cause Analysis Findings, Liverpool Hospital, New South Wales, Australia. Used with permission.

up to that point. Errors were detected in this review for 6 patients, and a near miss was detected for 1 patient. In 3 of the 6 cases in which an error occurred, the error was detected during quality assurance imaging procedures on the first, second, and eighth treatments, respectively, and was corrected for the remaining treatments. For the remaining 3 cases, which were palliative single-fraction treatments, the incorrect placement was only identified after the treatment and hence was not correctable. However, the tumor was still within the treatment field, and thus an adequate dose was still delivered in 2 of the 3 single-fraction cases. The error resulted from a failure of staff to follow the virtual simulation protocol that assigned a reference point from which all other measurements

were to be made. Because the reference point was incorrect, subsequent radiation treatment field placements were also incorrect.

The existing quality assurance processes and the fact that most radiotherapy is given in multiple daily treatments meant that the error in virtual simulation for the six patients resulted in five close calls and only one uncorrected treatment error. Contributing factors that were identified in the subsequent root cause analysis are shown in Sidebar 11-2 (left).

These incidents undermined the confidence in the entire process and necessitated a major tightening in the regimen of training and the introduction of formal competency assessment. They subsequently had a profound effect on health care organizations in New South Wales, resulting in the initiation of a program of learning and quality improvement to prevent future errors and preserve patient safety. The program concerned all clinical staff because safe radiotherapy depends on a chain of interventions.

ORGANIZATIONAL LEARNING AND ACTION

In response to the findings of the root cause analysis, several remedial actions were taken, as shown in Sidebar 11-3 (*see* page 109).

The entire planning and simulation process was overhauled to remove inefficiencies and to add checking stages. In addition, competency certification was introduced for portal-imaging review, a list of competencies was established, and an imaging committee was created to oversee the introduction of imaging modalities and to improve imaging policies. An imaging policy was introduced that established procedures and tolerance limits for deviations. Instead of a single image being taken weekly, images were taken on the first three consecutive days so that random errors could be distinguished from systematic errors. Senior radiation therapists were given the

Sidebar 11-3. Remedial Actions Taken to Prevent Future Error

■ Notification of affected patients and appropriate physical and emotional follow-up and support offered*

■ Simplification of computerized tomography procedure

■ Education and certification of staff in the interpretation of verification images to improve documentation

■ Mandatory pretreatment of verification images by senior staff

■ Mandatory attendee of senior staff for all first treatments

* Disclosure is an important part of managing errors and near misses.

Source: Root Cause Analysis Findings, Liverpool Hospital, New South Wales, Australia. Used with permission.

task of checking images before single-fraction treatments, thus avoiding noncorrectable errors. A policy was instituted to refer incidents to higher levels of management, and radiation therapists were authorized to move treatment fields that exceeded defined limits.

These incidents also provided the impetus for the radiotherapy department to review its reporting of incidents. The subsequent discussion of repeat incidents or incidents that were considered serious and trend analysis reporting improved the learning from errors. A recent analysis has shown that for the three years during which this new system has been used, there has been a reduction in actual errors and an improvement in the department's reporting culture.[10] For the 688 reports received, the actual error rate decreased from 1% to 0.3% ($p < .001$) of treatment episodes per year. There were 3.5 times as many near misses reported as actual errors.

CONCLUSIONS

Radiotherapy is an essential part of cancer treatment, and advances in technology have resulted in better cure rates and less toxicity. Staff training has not always kept up with the demands of increased complexity. Errors have the potential to affect large numbers of patients because radiation effects may take years to appear. Risk profiling identifies steps in the process that are more risky and provides a framework for monitoring close calls and other incidents.

References

1. Delaney G., et al.: The role of radiotherapy in cancer treatment: Estimating optimal utilization from a review of evidence-based clinical guidelines. *Cancer* 104:1129–1137, Sep. 15, 2005.
2. Jacob S., et al.: Estimation of an optimal utilisation rate for palliative radiotherapy in newly diagnosed cancer patients. *Clin Oncol (R Coll Radiol)* 22:56–64, Feb. 2010. Epub Dec. 6, 2009.
3. Bogdanich W.: Radiation offers new cures, and ways to do harm. *New York Times,* Jan. 23, 2010. http://www.nytimes.com/2010/01/24/health/24radiation.html (accessed Sep. 15, 2010).
4. Donaldson L.: Reducing harm from radiotherapy. *BMJ* 334:272, Feb. 10, 2007.
5. The Joint Commission: Safely implementing health information and converging technologies. *Sentinel Event Alert* Issue 41, Dec. 11, 2008. http://www.jointcommission.org/SentinelEvents/SentinelEventAlert/sea_42.htm (accessed Sep. 15, 2010).
6. U.K. Department of Health: Radiotherapy: Hidden dangers. Chapter 5 in *On the State of Public Health: Annual Report of the Chief Medical Officer 2006.* London: Department of Health, 2007, pp. 35–39.
7. Shafiq J., et al.: An international review of patient safety measures in radiotherapy practice. *Radiother Oncol* 92:15–21, Jul. 2009. Epub Apr. 22, 2009.
8. World Health Organization: *Radiotherapy Risk Profile,* 2008. http://www.who.int/patientsafety/activities/technical/radiotherapy/en/index.html (accessed Aug. 4, 2010).
9. Donaldson L.J., et al.: Finding the Achilles' heel in healthcare. *J R Soc Med* 103:40–41, Feb. 2010.
10. Arnold A., et al.: The use of categorized time-trend reporting of radiation oncology incidents: A proactive analytical approach to improving quality and safety over time. *Int J Radiat Oncol Biol Phys,* in press. Epub Jul. 1, 2010.

CHAPTER 12

Health Information Technology: Look-Alikes in the Drop-Down Menu

Erika Abramson, M.D., M.Sc.; Rainu Kaushal, M.D., M.P.H.

CASE

A 30-year-old woman with HIV delivered a full-term baby boy, Baby X, at 5:00 P.M. (17:00). The mother had been followed closely by her obstetrician throughout the pregnancy and was maintained on the antiretroviral agent zidovudine, commonly referred to by the brand name AZT (the drug was originally known as *azidothymidine*). Zidovudine is routinely administered to HIV-positive women throughout their pregnancy and delivery and is also given to infants born to HIV-positive mothers within 6 to 12 hours after birth.

On admission to the well-baby nursery, Baby X was evaluated by a pediatric resident. After completing the baby's assessment, the resident began entering the baby's admission orders, using the hospital's computerized provider order entry (CPOE) system, which allows providers to enter a patient's orders electronically. The resident typed in *AZT*, which produced a drop-down menu listing both *AZT* (*zidovudine*) and *Aztreonam*. (Aztreonam is an antibiotic that is generally reserved for serious infections with organisms resistant to common antibiotics.) The resident inadvertently selected *Aztreonam*. Recognizing that aztreonam is not routinely administered to infants in the well-baby nursery, an astute pharmacist contacted the pediatric resident to clarify the order, and the order was

promptly changed. The infant received zidovudine at 10:00 P.M. (22:00). The pharmacist then reported the error in the hospital's voluntary reporting system.

Had the pharmacist not recognized the error, the baby might have mistakenly received aztreonam and not zidovudine. This could have significantly increased the baby's risk of acquiring congenital HIV as well as the risk of suffering potential side effects from unnecessary use of aztreonam.

ISSUES IN COMPUTERIZED PHYSICIAN ORDER ENTRY

At the hospital in which the case of Baby X occurred, a systematic review of voluntary reports, which is conducted monthly, led to the detection of an unusual trend in medication-related close calls that seemed to be directly associated with the hospital's CPOE system. These close calls included errors related to picking the wrong drug from a drop-down menu (as in this case), selecting the wrong patient, ordering medications with the incorrect unit (such as milligrams instead of micrograms) or dose, and improperly timing the start of a medication. There were also several tenfold errors (order-of-magnitude dosing errors).

Although CPOE has been shown in multiple studies to significantly reduce rates of medication errors and their subsequent harm, it can also have unintended consequences such as those described.[1-3] For example, Han and colleagues showed that mortality actually increased in a pediatric intensive care unit (ICU) immediately after a CPOE system was implemented.[4] Koppel et al. identified 22 situations in which CPOE facilitated prescribing errors,[5] and qualitative studies conducted in the United States, the Netherlands, and Australia by Ash and colleagues demonstrated a number of errors fostered by information technology (IT) systems.[6]

FORMING THE MEDICATION SAFETY TASK FORCE

At the hospital caring for Baby X, a multidisciplinary medication safety task force was created to address systematically the information learned from careful analysis of this report and other voluntary reports regarding CPOE–associated close calls. This task force, which was composed of attending physicians, resident physicians, nurses, nurse practitioners, pharmacists, and informaticists, was formed and headed by a director of quality and patient safety, with the support of senior administrative leadership.

The medication safety task force meets monthly to review and develop solutions for all medication-related voluntary reports as well as medication-related significant event reports. Significant event reports are detailed reports generated whenever harm occurs to a patient. The medication safety task force works closely with the formulary and therapeutics committee, which oversees the content of the CPOE dosing table that provides computer-generated dosing recommendations for providers during the prescription writing process. This ensures that any modifications to the CPOE dosing table can be rapidly enacted. In addition, one of the hospital's chief medical information officers is actively involved in the medication safety task force and ensures that changes to the hospital's CPOE system are consistent with other informatics policies within

the hospital, are carried out hospitalwide, and are disseminated to vendors. The director of the medication safety task force reports directly to the hospital's quality council, which discusses and prioritizes safety and quality issues.

INTERVENTIONS

The improvement process associated with the medication safety task force has led to more rapid identification of problems and implementation of solutions that are realistic within the context of provider work flow. During the course of two years, as a direct result of the task force's work, the hospital has been able to implement a number of IT and non–IT interventions to improve medication safety, as described in the following sections and as summarized in Table 12-1 (*see* page 113).

IT Interventions

The IT-based interventions have included changing screen displays so that information is presented more clearly, revising the clinical decision support warnings for providers to alert them better to order-entry errors, limiting the number of available formulations of a medication to reduce the likelihood of picking the wrong formulation, limiting the number of choices appearing on an ordering screen to decrease the likelihood of choosing the wrong medication from a drop-down menu, and expanding the available number of medications for which clinical decision support is available. Another intervention is adding so-called tall man lettering to order-entry screens, which involves displaying part of a medication name in capital letters to distinguish sound-alike/look-alike drugs (*see* Table 12-2, page 114). Tall man lettering might have prevented the error made in the case of Baby X.

Research has shown that the way in which a CPOE system is configured, including timing of alerts, pick lists and drop-down menu displays, and screen displays, can have an important

Table 12-1. Interventions to Improve Medication Safety

Interventions	Current Status of Intervention
Information Technology	
Changed screen displays to simplify ordering	Maintained
Revised clinical decision support warning language to better reflect potential for patient harm	Maintained
Limited medication formulation options	Ongoing: many seldom-used formulation options, particularly for high-risk medications, have been removed
Limited choices of medicines on ordering screen to help prevent "drop-down" errors	Ongoing: for many high-risk medications, the number of choices appearing on the order entry screen has been reduced
Expanded clinical decision support to additional medications	Ongoing
Use of tall man lettering	Maintained
Non-Information Technology	
Educational sessions for staff	
Departmentwide lectures and grand rounds	Maintained
Monthly conferences for residents and medical students, with topics drawn from the voluntary error reporting system	Maintained: these are led by the executive vice chair for education, the residency program director, and the associate program directors
Educational resources	
Laminated reference cards	Maintained: these are reviewed each year, revised if necessary, and handed out to all residents
Web-based tools	Maintained
Work-flow changes	
Intravenous drip orders entered by residents in the intensive care unit are double-checked by fellows and attendings at the time of medication ordering	Maintained: this expectation is part of the orientation for all incoming fellows and residents to the intensive care unit
Residents read back orders before entering into computerized physician order entry system for medications ordered during rounds	Maintained: this expectation is part of the orientation for all incoming fellows and residents to the intensive care units

Source: New York-Presbyterian Hospital, New York City. Used with permission.

impact on ease of system use, the way in which certain tasks are completed, and medication errors.[7] In addition, one of the limitations of CPOE systems is that clinical decision support, such as alerts for ordering errors, are often not perceived as useful because the benefit of clinically relevant alerts is lost in the high volume of clinically irrelevant alerts that are generated (a problem known as *alert fatigue*).[8] Thus, these are all important factors for organizations to address when analyzing medication errors related to health IT use.

Table 12-2. Examples of Tall Man Lettering for Sound-Alike/Look-Alike Drugs	
hydrALAZINE	hydrOXYzine
ceREBYX	ceLEBREex
vinBLASTine	vinCRIstine
chlorproPAMIDE	chlorproMAZINE
glipiZIDE	glyBURIDE
DAUNOrubicin	DOXOrubicin

Source: New York-Presbyterian Hospital, New York City. Used with permission.

In deliberations about the case provided, participants were reminded that *AZT*, given the confusion with aztreonam, was an error-prone abbreviation.[9] The appearance of *zidovudine* with *AZT* on the CPOE order-entry screen, as described in the close-call event, reflected an effort to reduce selection of the incorrect medication. There has been discussion about eliminating the ability to order *AZT* and instead to require providers to type in *zidovudine*, but no decision has been made.

Non-IT Interventions

The medication safety task force at the hospital caring for Baby X has developed a series of non-IT interventions that can be adopted by other organizations to improve medication safety. These interventions have included conducting educational sessions for staff members, developing educational reference materials, and changing work flow to standardize the communication of medication-related information.

The format of the educational sessions has varied, ranging from departmentwide lectures and grand rounds with a wide array of staff present to workshops geared solely toward residents and medical students which cover specific themes, such as ordering intravenous (IV) drips in ICUs. Monthly conferences are now also held for residents and medical students in which specific

medication errors drawn from the voluntary reporting system are discussed. In these conferences, led by the residency program director, system factors contributing to the errors are identified by the residents and medical students, and ways to prevent similar errors from occurring are discussed. Studies have shown that educational interventions can improve medication dose calculating and ordering by residents.[10] The residency program director is also a participant in the medication safety task force and can therefore bring ideas generated by the residents and medical students back to the medication safety task force for discussion.

Educational activities help raise awareness about the prevalence of medication errors, enable a broader audience beyond members of the medication safety task force to identify additional system weaknesses and generate solutions, and promote widespread dissemination of the task force's activities to address problems that have been identified. Providing effective feedback to staff is important to "close the loop" and ensure continued reporting in the future.[11] At the hospital at which the Baby X case occurred, this combination of activities has led to a doubling of voluntary reports generated in the past few years.

To complement the educational activities, educational resources have been developed for staff

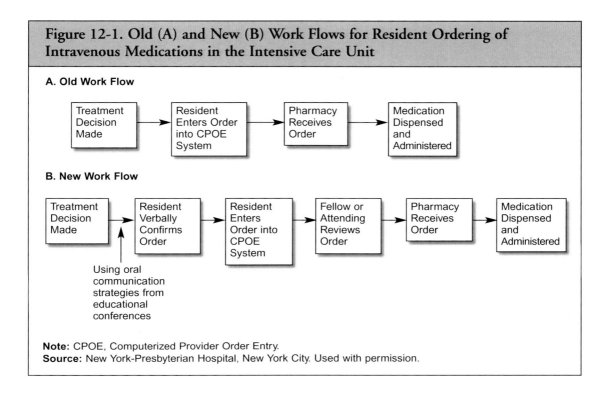

Figure 12-1. Old (A) and New (B) Work Flows for Resident Ordering of Intravenous Medications in the Intensive Care Unit

A. Old Work Flow

Treatment Decision Made → Resident Enters Order into CPOE System → Pharmacy Receives Order → Medication Dispensed and Administered

B. New Work Flow

Treatment Decision Made → Resident Verbally Confirms Order → Resident Enters Order into CPOE System → Fellow or Attending Reviews Order → Pharmacy Receives Order → Medication Dispensed and Administered

Using oral communication strategies from educational conferences

Note: CPOE, Computerized Provider Order Entry.
Source: New York-Presbyterian Hospital, New York City. Used with permission.

to use on an ongoing basis, often in direct response to some of the error patterns detected through the voluntary reporting system. For example, laminated reference cards, which provide decimal-unit conversion aids and the usual dose ranges of commonly used IV drips in the ICU, have been developed and distributed. In addition, Web-based tools have been developed that allow providers to enter a patient's weight and receive a printed list of medications with doses that are commonly used during a resuscitation. This list is placed at the patient's bedside to reduce the need for calculations to be performed in the middle of an emergency.

Work-Flow Changes. In addition, several work-flow changes have been implemented. For example, as shown in Figure 12-1 (above), all IV drip orders entered into the CPOE system by a resident working in the ICU must be double-checked by a fellow or an attending because residents frequently have less experience ordering these types of drugs, which can lead to mistakes

in the ordering process. In addition, all orders told to a resident by a fellow or attending must now be read back by the resident before being entered into the CPOE system, and staff have been educated about effective oral communication strategies for relaying information about medications.

CONCLUSIONS

Through identification and systematic analysis of errors, including close calls, health care organizations have an important opportunity to learn about system vulnerabilities and prevent a repeat of similar mistakes in the future. To deliver safer health care for patients, it is critical to educate staff about the importance of reporting close calls and developing practical, realistic IT and non-IT solutions.

References

1. Bates D.W., et al.: Effect of computerized physician order entry and a team intervention on prevention of serious medication errors. *JAMA* 280:1311–1316, Oct. 21, 1998.

2. Bates D.W., et al.: The impact of computerized physician order entry on medication error prevention. *J Am Med Inform Assoc* 6:313–321, Jul.–Aug. 1999.

3. Ammenwerth E., et al.: The effect of electronic prescribing on medication errors and adverse drug events: A systematic review. *J Am Med Inform Assoc* 15:585–600, Sep.–Oct. 2008. Epub Jun. 25, 2008.

4. Han Y.Y., et al.: Unexpected increased mortality after implementation of a commercially sold computerized physician order entry system. *Pediatrics* 116:1506–1512, Dec. 2005.

5. Koppel R., et al.: Role of computerized physician order entry systems in facilitating medication errors. *JAMA* 293:1197–1203, Mar. 9, 2005.

6. Ash J.S., Berg M., Coiera E.: Some unintended consequences of information technology in health care: The nature of patient care information system-related errors. *J Am Med Inform Assoc* 11:104–112, Mar.–Apr. 2004. Epub Nov. 21, 2003.

7. Khajouei R., Jaspers M.W.: CPOE system design aspects and their qualitative effect on usability. *Stud Health Technol Inform* 136:309–314, 2008.

8. van der Sijs H., et al.: Overriding of drug safety alerts in computerized physician order entry. *J Am Med Inform Assoc* 13:138–147, Mar.–Apr. 2006. Epub Dec. 15, 2005.

9. Institute for Safe Medication Practices (ISMP): *ISMP's List of Error-Prone Abbreviations, Symbols, and Dose Designations*, 2010. http://www.ismp.org/tools/error-proneabbreviations.pdf (accessed Aug. 9, 2010).

10. Nelson L.S., et al.: The benefit of houseofficer education on proper medication dose calculation and ordering. *Acad Emerg Med* 7:1311–1316, Nov. 2000.

11. Gandhi T.K., et al.: Closing the loop: Follow-up and feedback in a patient safety program. *Jt Comm J Qual Patient Saf* 31:614–621, Nov. 2005.

CHAPTER 13

Pediatrics: "Wrong Patient" Breast-Milk Administration in the Neonatal Intensive Care Unit

Michael L. Rinke, M.D.; Julie Murphy, R.N., B.S.N., I.B.C.L.C.; David G. Bundy, M.D., M.P.H.

CASE

Baby S was a 3-week-old infant born at 28 weeks' gestational age and cared for in a Level III neonatal intensive care unit (NICU) in an academic medical center. The baby had recently begun oral feeds with expressed breast milk through a nasogastric (NG) tube. Consistent with existing protocols in this 45-bed NICU, the infant's mother regularly labeled her own pumped breast milk and placed it in an open-top bin in a parent-accessible freezer in the breast pumping room. On one occasion, a number of the bins were rearranged because of patient discharges, and Baby S's mother mistakenly placed her milk in Baby J's bin. Baby J was a 4-week-old infant born with an omphalocele,* now status postrepair, who had been receiving expressed breast milk feeds for 8 days. Baby J's nurse took two bottles of milk out of Baby J's bin—one bottle was Baby J's and the second bottle was Baby S's. The nurse, attempting to feed her baby on time, did not check both bottles for two patient identifiers. The milk was warmed and given to Baby J's father, who proceeded to feed Baby J. Midway through the feed, Baby J's father noted the incorrect name on the bottle, and the feeding was stopped. The families

were independently notified of the error by an attending, and both mothers were tested for HIV, hepatitis B virus (HBV), hepatitis C virus (HCV), the human T-lymphocyte virus Type I/II (HTLV I/II), and cytomegalovirus (CMV). All test results were negative, and no known harm came to either baby. Although neither infant appeared medically harmed, the families' trust and confidence in the institution and its staff were damaged by this close call.

MISAPPROPRIATION OF EXPRESSED BREAST MILK

Misappropriation of expressed breast milk is a well-acknowledged safety risk in any children's hospital, with reported rates ranging from 0.07 to 0.14 errors per 1,000 feedings.[1–3] In a busy tertiary care NICU, this error rate equates to approximately one breast-milk misappropriation error every two months.[2] The actual numbers of misappropriations are higher, given that not all errors are discovered or reported. These errors may stem from the repetitive nature of the task (for example, feeding every infant every three hours), the apparent low acuity of this task in a high-intensity work setting (intensive care units and in-patient hospital wards), and the complex,

---

* Protrusion, at birth, of part of the intestine through a large defect in the abdominal wall at the umbilicus, the protruding bowel being covered only by a thin transparent membrane composed of amnion and peritoneum (*Dorland's Illustrated Medical Dictionary*, 26th ed. Philadelphia: WB Saunders, 1985).

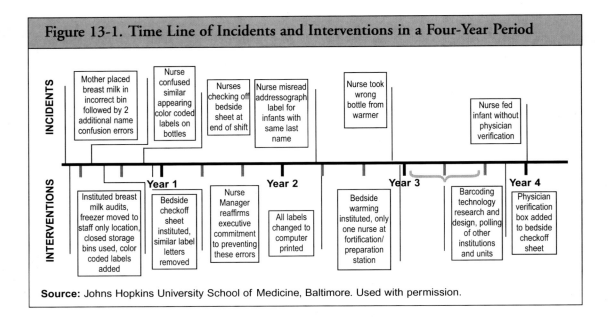

Figure 13-1. Time Line of Incidents and Interventions in a Four-Year Period

Source: Johns Hopkins University School of Medicine, Baltimore. Used with permission.

multistep work flow required to deliver breast milk to an infant safely.

INCIDENTS AND INTERVENTIONS

Existing literature suggests that eliminating breast-milk misappropriations can be a complex undertaking and may require multiple interventions.[2,4] Following the incident described in the case provided, the involved NICU strove during the next four years to reduce its rate of breast-milk misappropriation through process improvements and systems changes, as shown in Figure 13-1 (above) and Table 13-1 (*see* page 119) and summarized here. The initial incident was followed by two similar errors within a three-month period, creating momentum for change throughout the unit.

Initial Changes

Initial changes endorsed by the unit and supported by top-level management during monthly safety committee meetings included the following:

1. Moving the expressed–breast-milk freezer to a location accessible to staff only

2. Adding color-coded, infant-specific capital letters to breast-milk labels to aid in correct identification of milk

3. Storing bottles in closed bins

These quick fixes, along with audits of compliance, were implemented rapidly while additional system changes were considered.

Additional Incidents and Interventions

Before a more robust intervention could be implemented, additional errors occurred as nurses confused similarly looking letters on breast-milk labels (for example, *M* and *W* were easily confused and had to be made different colors). Some staff began to rely on this capital-letter label coding to the exclusion of using a patient's two recognized identifiers, such as full name and medical record number. A bedside check sheet was created to prompt each nurse, before feeding any patient, to identify the correct patient name, patient medical record number, current date, milk expiration date, and feeding time. Initially, this tool seemed promising to eliminate the error of giving the wrong breast milk to a baby. However, over time, errors

Table 13-1. Errors Discovered and Changes Made

Error Discovered	Change Made
Mother placed infant's milk in wrong bin in freezer.	1. Freezer moved to staff-only location 2. Color-coded labels added to breast milk 3. Bottles stored in closed bins 4. Audits instituted
Nurse confused similar-appearing color-coded letters on bottle.	1. Similar-looking letters removed 2. Bedside checkoff list created to confirm correct patient, feed, time before feeding
Nurse checked off bedside list for all feeds at end of shift.	1. Nurse manager reaffirmed executive commitment to eliminating errors
Nurse misread addressograph label for infants with the same last name.	1. All labels changed to computer printed
Nurse took wrong infant's breast milk from bottle warmer.	1. Each infant to receive bedside milk warming 2. One nurse/infant's milk at preparation/fortification area at any time

continued as staff began to complete the check sheet retrospectively for all feeds at the end of a shift. At this point, the senior nursing manager declared that using the check sheet "was not a choice for any nurse who wanted to work in the NICU." Performance temporarily improved with the institution of audits, but it waned again as time passed. In addition, after an error occurred that was attributed to the illegibility of carbon copy–type addressograph labels, addressograph-printed labels were replaced by computer-printed labels.

One common methodology for dealing with dangerous product administration, such as chemotherapy or blood products, is for two caregivers to independently check patient identifiers, amount, rate, and appropriateness before administration. This fix was discussed extensively for the continued errors in breast-milk misappropriation but was considered to be too onerous, given the large number of feeds provided daily and the interruption this would cause for other care processes. In addition, nurses expressed concerns that implementing double checks for breast-milk administration would decrease their effectiveness for blood products and other high-risk substances, reflecting provider fatigue.

The idea of two independent checks was reviewed once again, however, when a nurse placed a bottle in the milk warmer and stepped away to perform another task. A second nurse found the now-warmed bottle, removed it, and placed her own patient's bottle in the warmer. The first nurse returned, and in the belief that the second bottle was her patient's milk, fed the infant the breast milk of the second nurse's patient. At this point, independent milk warming at each patient's bedside was implemented, and staff were educated in allowing only one patient's milk and one nurse at the common milk preparation/fortification area at any time.

A rigorous process-mapping exercise was conducted, through which more than 35 steps were identified for the acquisition, storage, and delivery of breast milk. National neonatal message boards, pediatric conferences, and other comparable

NICUs were contacted to investigate potential improvements to this process. It was apparent that many other health care organizations were dealing with similar issues but that few of them had evidenced-based solutions. Other units within the index institution were polled regarding their abilities to handle similar situations, but no other area had such a large volume of administrations with such a high frequency of patients who were not able to talk or self-identify.

In Year 3, given the continued difficulties, a large-scale effort was launched, with executive backing, to develop a breast-milk bar-coding system. The system was intended to create a unique bar code for each bottle of breast milk and to pair an infant with his or her mother. Ideally, this system, in which nurses would scan infants and bottles immediately before feeding for confirmation, would prevent breast-milk misappropriation. A number of companies were contacted early in the breast-milk delivery-improvement process, and one was identified that promised a trial system within three weeks. Yet nine months passed before the bar-coding system was ready to go live.

A number of significant barriers were identified and overcome in preparation for this new system, as follows:

1. The company was experienced in connecting different products together through bar-coding technology but had to understand the existing NICU work flow and process map in order to create all the necessary linkages. For example, a mother of triplets needed to be able to provide milk to be scanned to any of her three babies. In addition, each bottle needed to have an embedded expiration date that varied, depending on whether the milk was frozen, fresh, thawed, or fortified. One bottle could require a computerized placeholder date for each of these events as it was pumped, refrigerated or frozen, thawed, fortified, and eventually fed to an appropriate infant. In addition, a new bottle or syringe label needed to be generated when a bottle was defrosted, fortified, or subdivided.

2. Bar-code bracelets had to be created, which would remain on a neonate with small extremities that were often manipulated for line placement and blood draws. The material of the bar-code band had to be appropriate, given the fragile skin integrity of a premature infant.

3. Formatting the infant band was a challenge because of the limited space on the small infant band.

4. Bar-code readers had to be obtained that could read through clear plastic isolettes, which were used to reduce the introduction of potential infections at feeding times. Other institutions have used bar-code labels placed on the outside of isolettes,[2] but it was felt that the potential for lost or incorrect labels was too high and would create more potential for errors if the labels were not placed directly on patients.

5. An effort was made to have the software interface with existing computing systems to avoid duplicate nurse charting of the feed in the bar-code device and on the computerized charting software.

6. The institution confronted the possible failures associated with bar-coding systems, given that the introduction of new technology does not alleviate all systems problems and can easily be "worked around."[5]

During this attempt to implement bar coding, additional errors were identified as patients and their mothers' breast milk were incorrectly transferred between the NICU, the pediatric intensive care unit (PICU), and the general pediatric floors. In addition, physicians in this NICU must approve each mother's request to breast feed on the basis of the initial breast-feeding questionnaire before feeding commences in order to prevent potentially harmful substances (for example, infections, medications, illicit drugs) from being transferred to the infant through breast milk. This approval item was added to each infant's bedside checklist to prevent nurses from missing this crucial step. Despite these preventive efforts, a nurse fed an infant breast milk from a mother whose breast-feeding questionnaire was not approved by a physician because of the mother's antiepileptic medications. The nurse saw an order to feed, saw that the infant had breast milk available, assumed that the breast milk was appropriate, and checked off all the boxes on the bedside checklist, without looking for the physician's approval of the questionnaire.

DISCUSSION

The initial breast-milk misappropriation close call described in the provided case grew into at least eight reported close-call near-miss breast-milk misappropriation events in the subsequent four years. Each event triggered significant staff investment in change and process improvement. To our knowledge, no patient has experienced medical harm from these errors, but family trust and staff morale have consistently suffered. Future directions include creating a centralized nutrition room with dedicated nutrition staff to

prepare single-dose feeds of breast milk, similar to medication administration in the pharmacy, and making the policy on breast-milk administration consistent between the NICU, the pediatric floors, and the PICU. The NICU also anticipates establishing a bar-coding system that is integrated into a hospitalwide bar-coding product designed to manage specimen collection and administration of medications and breast milk.

References

1. Drenckpohl D., Bowers L., Cooper H.: Use of the Six Sigma methodology to reduce incidence of breast milk administration errors in the NICU. *Neonatal Netw* 26:161–166, May–Jun. 2007.
2. Dougherty D., Nash A.: Bar coding from breast to baby: A comprehensive breast milk management system for the NICU. *Neonatal Netw* 28:321–328, Sep.–Oct. 2009.
3. Zeilhofer U.B., et al.: The role of critical incident monitoring in detection and prevention of human breast milk confusions. *Eur J Pediatr* 168:1277–1279, Oct. 2009. Epub Jan. 16, 2009.
4. Dougherty D., Giles V.: From breast to baby: Quality assurance for breast milk management. *Neonatal Netw* 19:21–25, Oct 2000.
5. Patterson E.S., Cook R.I., Render M.L.: Improving patient safety by identifying side effects from introducing bar coding in medication administration. *J Am Med Inform Assoc* 9:540–553, Sep.–Oct. 2002.

CHAPTER 14

Psychiatry: Mistaken Identity in a Patient with Schizophrenia

Geetha Jayaram, M.D., M.B.A.; Jennifer Meuchel, M.D.

CASE

Ms. Jane R. Smith, a 56-year-old woman, was brought to the emergency department (ED) at a large urban hospital on an emergency petition with a report of mood swings, erratic behavior, rapid speech, and delusions of grandeur. The emergency petition paperwork included her full name and date of birth, which were correctly documented as *Jane R. Smith, DOB: 7/4/48.*

The patient arrived in the triage area, where her name and date of birth were handwritten correctly on the triage documentation. By the time the patient reached the psychiatry area of the ED—the Psychiatry ED—she had been misidentified with an *incorrect* birth date of *3/17/58.* This incorrect date corresponded to a different Ms. Smith in the electronic medical record, a Ms. Jane S. Smith. The incorrectly identified patient was 10 years younger—aged 46—and had a history of HIV and hepatitis C and intravenous (IV) drug use. She also had a traumatically severed left fourth finger. She was followed in the medical center's HIV clinic. Chart review and interviews with staff members revealed a series of errors in the subsequent care of the patient. The psychiatric nurse, the ED resident, the psychiatric medical student, the admitting resident, the unit treating resident, and the attending physician all continued to see the patient as the incorrect Ms. Smith, being

unaware of the error that happened between triage and the psychiatry emergency care area.

During her ED and hospital stay, the patient repeatedly told many staff members that she never had HIV or hepatitis C or any other medical problems. She also repeatedly said she had never used drugs. Although her score on the Mini-Mental State Examination was 26 out of 30, no one took her protests seriously because the patient was thought to be delusional.

Initial laboratory studies included normal liver function tests, WBC (white blood cell) count, hematocrit, and platelet count. The CD4 (HIV helper cell) count in the previous month for Jane S. Smith (the incorrect patient) had been 114. However, no one repeated the current patient's HIV test.

The patient refused to provide any information to contact outside informants. She appeared confused, was grandiose, and did not appear to be a reliable informant. Her denial of her illness was attributed to her state of mind and possibly dementia. She was referred for cortical function testing to rule out HIV-related dementia. No evidence of the hospital personnel's attempts to contact the patient's family about the patient's putative HIV status were found (citing HIPAA [Health Insurance Portability and Accountability

Act] in the ED). The patient had refused to give permission to the staff to do so. Also, no one thought to ask the referring agency if it had records of the patient's HIV status.

The cortical function testing staff member who transported the patient for an evaluation noticed that the patient gave a different date of birth than what was in the record. The psychologist assumed that the patient was demented and did not call the floor to check on the date. Thinking that the patient was 46 years old, she then performed the cortical function testing and recorded results that were commensurate with HIV dementia and mild cognitive impairment. Later, after it was determined that the patient was actually 10 years older than was thought, the psychologist revised her evaluation in the chart.

The resident who performed a physical examination on the patient documented her evaluation accurately, noting crepitus in the lungs, but had no knowledge of the mix-ups and did not look for or record a missing fourth finger on the left hand. The magnetic resonance imaging (MRI) of the brain that was done was interpreted as small-vessel ischemia or, possibly, HIV disease.

The nurse on the unit recognized the patient from previous admissions and noted this in the record. However, she did not notice the discrepant medical record number and did not identify the previous admissions. The HIV clinic nurse was contacted to discuss the patients' case and to verify her treatment regimen, as described in the electronic patient record (EPR) for the incorrect medical record. The HIV nurse described the regimen but did not come to the unit to identify the patient. Antiretroviral treatment was begun.

The patient protested taking the HIV medication but was persuaded to do so. Each time the HIV medications were offered, she stated that she was not HIV-positive. Each time, she was overruled or gently persuaded to accept them. A phone call was made to the HIV clinic case manager, who

confirmed that the patient Jane Smith had in fact resided in their recovery house. However, she did not verify the patient's date of birth. Nor did the manager know that there was another patient with a similar name and diagnosis.

On hospital day 9, a day hospital worker noted the discrepancy between the patient's reported demographic number and that associated with her medical record number while obtaining authorization for the Schizophrenia Day Hospital. This was possible because he had access to two different databases: the ED database and the inpatient database.

The treating team explained the error to the patient and apologized. She was not angry. The hospitalization was not billed, and the patient was not sent any bills.

Possible damage resulting from antiretroviral medications was assessed. There were no immediate sequelae. The patient had no obvious HIV risk factors, and a subsequent HIV test was negative. The case was discussed with the director of the Schizophrenia Service. The fee for the hospitalization was waived. The flow of events in this case of mistaken identity is shown in Sidebar 14-1 (*see* pages 125–126). The process of care in the ED for the misidentified patient is illustrated in Sidebar 14-2 (*see* page 127). The patient's history and incorrect history are shown in Table 14-1 (*see* page 128).

FINDINGS AND CORRECTIVE ACTIONS

An incident review and a root cause analysis (RCA) were conducted, at which time it was noted that the radiology dictations still referred to the patient as a 46-year-old female with HIV.

Corrective action: This was followed up and corrected.

At the morbidity and mortality conference for residents and the performance improvement

Sidebar 14-1. Mistaken Identity: Flow of Events

Day 0

1:00 P.M. (13:00)—Ms. Jane R. Smith was a 56-year-old divorced female who was Emergency Petitioned from a crisis response center because of mood swings, erratic behavior, rapid speech, and delusions of grandeur. The Psychiatry emergency department (ED) paperwork included her full name and date of birth (7/4/1948).

2:10 P.M. (14:10)—The patient arrived in triage, where her name and date of birth were handwritten correctly on the triage documentation.

2:20 P.M. (14:20)—By the time the patient reached the Psychiatry ED, she had been misidentified with an incorrect birth date (3/17/1958) corresponding to a different patient—a Ms. Jane S. Smith in the hospital's electronic patient record (EPR). Ms. Jane S. Smith was then 46 years old, with a history of HIV and hepatitis C, followed in the HIV clinic.

2:30 P.M. (14:30)—Psychiatry ED nurse evaluated the patient.

3:15 P.M. (15:15)—The patient was examined by an ED resident. The history documented corresponded to the incorrect medical record number.

4:30 P.M. (16:30)—Psychiatric medical student interviewed the patient. The history documented corresponded to the incorrect medical record number.

5:30 P.M. (17:30)—Psychiatry ED resident evaluated the patient. The history documented included a traumatically severed left fourth finger, corresponding to the incorrect medical record number. The patient was described as grandiose, denying that she had HIV, hepatitis C, or any other medical problems. Mini-Mental State Examination 26/30 (–1 for orientation to floor, –3 for recall).

Initial laboratory studies included normal AST/ALT (aspartate aminotransferase/alanine aminotransferase), WBC (white blood cell count) 7,500, Hct (hematocrit) 34.5%, platelets 308,000.

6:30 P.M. (18:30)—The patient refused to provide any information in order to contact an outside informant. Rule out HIV dementia was included in the Axis I diagnoses.

7:30 P.M. (19:30)—The patient was examined by the ED attending, who agreed with admission.

Day 1

12:00 A.M. (00:00)—Night-shift Psychiatry ED resident evaluated the patient and agreed with a plan of inpatient admission for stabilization and observation.

12:00 A.M. (00:00)—Night-shift Psychiatry ED nurse received report and assessed the patient.

1:10 A.M. (01:10)—Report was given to Psychiatric admitting second-year resident and the floor nurse. The patient was admitted to the floor. The history documented on the resident's and nurse's admission notes correspond to the incorrect medical record number. The patient was placed in a single room because of a presumed history of methicillin-resistant *Staphylococcus aureus* (MRSA). The admitting nurse notes that the patient has previously been on the unit, although the incorrect medical record number identified no previous hospital admissions.

8:00 A.M. (08:00)—The patient's admission note was reviewed, and she was evaluated by the floor team on walk rounds. The patient denied any history of HIV and stated that she did not know of the HIV clinic.

Continued

Sidebar 14-1. Mistaken Identity: Flow of Events (continued)

Day 1 *(Continued)*

2:30 P.M. (14:30)—The HIV clinic nurse was contacted to discuss the patient's case and to verify her HAART (Highly Active Antiretroviral Therapy) regimen, as described in the EPR for the incorrect medical record number. The patient was started on an antiretroviral regimen of Trizivir, Atazanavir, and Ritonavir with Bactrim prophylaxis because of the most recent CD4 count of 114.

Day 2

The HIV clinic nurse visited the unit and discussed the case with the second-year resident. He did not visit the patient while on the unit nor see her face to face.

10:00 P.M. (22:00)—The patient questioned the HIV medication and asked if it was an antibiotic, then agreed to take it.

Day 3

TSH (thyroid-stimulating hormone) level of 45.93*—started on thyroid replacement.

11:30 A.M. (11:30)—Nurse's note indicates that the patient initially disagreed that she was HIV-positive. "When the time scale of the infection is explained, she accepts the possibility of being HIV-positive."

Day 5

3:00 P.M. (15:00)—Nurse's note indicates that the patient questioned her HIV medications. She appeared to remain confused about her HIV status and medications. The patient also repeated that she never used drugs. She denies ever living in the recovery house, although the HIV clinic case manager confirmed previous residence there on the phone (not knowing about duplicate names). Later, the patient continued to have many questions about HIV.

Day 6

MRI of brain—nonspecific periatrial white matter hyperintensity possibly due to small vessel ischemia or patient's HIV disease.

Day 8

Because of apparent cognitive limitations, neuropsychological testing was completed. The findings were suggestive of dysfunction in both frontal–subcortical and temporal lobe systems, consistent with a diagnosis of mild dementia. The initial evaluation had suggested that the findings were consistent with HIV dementia.

Day 9

While obtaining authorization for the Schizophrenia Day Hospital, the day hospital's screening nurse discovered a discrepancy in the patient's reported demographic information and that under the incorrect medical record number. The correct Ms. Smith was identified. Antiretroviral medications were discontinued, and there was no evidence of any associated side effects. Subsequently, the patient tested seronegative for HIV. She was immediately notified of the misidentification. It was explained to her that the antiretroviral medications had been incorrectly administered to her due to the error in initial identification.

*Normal TSH values range from 0.5 to 4.5 mU/L.
Source: The Johns Hopkins Hospital, Baltimore. Used with permission.

monthly meeting for attending physicians and unit managers, several important observations were made and addressed, as follows:

1. There were communication failures at the time of handoffs between treating staff members which were promoted by the absence of direct face-to-face communications. The initial identification error made by the patient data coordinator was perpetuated through a series of transitions to the inpatient unit, through the ED nurse and psychiatry resident, the admitting resident, and subsequent practitioners.

   Corrective action: Handoffs face to face are recommended, and residents pick up patients to be admitted in person.

2. The day hospital worker who discovered the misidentification error had access to both the hospital database and the ED database, which were not available to either the rest of the inpatient treating team or the Psychiatry ED.

   Corrective action: An electronic physician order entry system now obviates this need and prevents errors immediately.

3. There was a failure to conduct identity checks by use of three or more identifiers (two identifiers were the same): Although anecdotal evidence suggests that identification errors occur frequently,[1,2] such errors are infrequently noted by patient data coordinators and nursing personnel.

   Corrective actions: Name alerts are posted on charts in boldface and on boards in the staff meeting rooms, and the treating teams are advised of the possibility of error. In the EPR, the name alert appears readily and prevents the order from being entered until the name is acknowledged. The need for a photograph of the patient online has been recommended, and plans are in progress to fulfill this need.

Sidebar 14-2. The Process of Care in the Emergency Department for the Misidentified Patient

Patient comes to the emergency department (ED)—gets triaged by the ED nurse—is sent to the Patient Data coordinator who first looks at the database*—the patient is examined by the psychiatric nurse and ED resident*—additionally is interviewed by the medical student—is presented to the ED attending physician—is then admitted by the 2nd-year resident,* and interviewed by the admitting floor RN*—the patient is presented to the treatment team and attending psychiatrist and followed—labs are drawn, but HIV test is not repeated*—HIV clinic nurse is called and gives input without face to face with the patient*—the patient is sent to Neuropsychological Testing*—once treated, the patient is referred to the Schizophrenia Day Hospital—error is detected by access to 2 different databases†—error is communicated to all staff, HIV clinic staff, lab staff to correct error online, patient is told and not billed, and no sequelae occur.

* Denotes every missed opportunity for error pickup.
† Denotes error pickup.
Source: The Johns Hopkins Hospital, Baltimore. Used with permission.

---

4. There was a failure to respond to the patient's repeated protestations that she never used IV venous drugs or never was HIV-positive. Although we expect delusional patients in psychiatry, one must always confirm facts before deciding that the patient is delusional.

   Corrective actions: We teach residents to double-check the history independent of the previous interviewer. We encourage reviewing

Table 14-1. Patient's History and Incorrect History

Patient's History	Incorrect History*
I. Chronic schizophrenia Rule out schizoaffective disorder	I. BPAD I – manic with psychotic features Cocaine abuse
III. Tardive dyskinesia Hypothyroidism s/p Thyroidectomy Gastroparesis Iron deficiency anemia s/p Uterine fibroidectomy s/p Cervical polypectomy s/p Ventral hernia repair	III. HIV, CD4 114 (5/06) Hepatitis C Hypertension s/p Myocardial infarction History of asthma History of zoster History of syphilis Chronic back pain s/p MVC with severed left 4th finger and left orbit injury
Patient's Medications	Incorrect Medications
Prolixin 15mg po qhs Depakote 1000mg po qhs Synthroid 100mcg po qday Protonix 40mg po qday	Trizivir 1 tablet po q12hours Atazanavir 300mg po qday Ritonavir 100mg po qday Bactrim 160mg po qday

* As drawn from the medical record of Jane S. Smith.

Note. s/p, status/post (operative); po, by mouth; qhs, at bedtime; qday, every day; BPAD, bipolar affective disorder; MVC, motor vehicle collision; q12hours, every 12 hours.

Source: The Johns Hopkins Hospital, Baltimore. Used with permission.

old records and obtaining input from outside informants routinely.

5. There was a failure by staff to see the patient face to face instead of simply examining the record. In the case of face to face examination, the error would have been picked up as well. For this reason, psychiatric treating teams must ensure that they have an accurate history by attempting to call a care provider who knows the patient well or by repeatedly attempting to call family members. Although schizophrenic patients are unable to participate in their own care initially, it is not unusual for them to do so once they are treated. Slips and lapses resulting in the incorrect matching of patients during the registration process are a common cause of patient identification errors, particularly in the outpatient setting.[3–6] Also, HIPAA regulations are not applicable in emergency situations when a patient's life is at stake.

6. There was a failure to address fatigue and multitasking in the ED. Several studies have shown that multitasking creates an increased risk of error in the ED.[3] In psychiatric patients in particular, avoidance of errors compromising patient safety may be promoted by the use of input from family members and previous care providers. Also, residents and nurses must ask for help when overwhelmed with several acutely ill patients to reduce the problem of error.

ADDITIONAL CORRECTIVE ACTIONS

Several recommendations were proposed for improvements to prevent patient identification errors, as follows:

1. Use both date of birth and history number as identifiers, as well as a third identifier, such as mother's middle name for patients for whom there are duplicate names in the EPR directory. Currently, the electronic database lists similar-sounding names, with other details to facilitate accurate selection of patients. (Also, since the introduction of the physician order entry electronic order system, duplicates are eliminated by name alerts for all orders. In addition, the patient identification includes the middle name, medical record number, aliases, those patients with and without prior visits, and so on, to eliminate errors.)

2. Use an instant or digital camera to take pictures of patients, which would then be stored as part of the patient record to facilitate identification.

3. Use a smart card that accompanies the patient (in the record and that the patient also carries) with a gist of the patient's last treatment and discharge summary. This card can be read by a card reader at entry from any other source of care. Because of the cost of this intervention, it has not been pursued.

4. Make both patient databases available to all staff in the ED and the Department of Psychiatry. Currently, the systems are able to interface with one another, and the ED note is available in the physician order entry system. There is currently no need to look at two databases.

5. Use additional recognition aids for psychiatric patients, such as listing critical identification marks of each patient (such as the traumatically severed left fourth finger in the case pro-

vided). This could have served as a clear identification mark for that particular patient.

6. Encourage nurses and other providers, in addition to physicians, to alert the treatment team to possible unsafe practices. Although one nurse had documented knowing the patient in the chart, this nurse had not alerted the team to the possibility of misidentification.

7. Encourage person-to-person handoffs, which will prevent many avoidable errors.[4–6]

8. For delusional patients, consider using multiple identifiers. Nonetheless, any patient report that is out of range should not be ignored but should be checked. Although practitioners may be biased against psychiatric patients, particularly those with schizophrenia, it is incorrect to attribute all responses to illness and dismiss these patients as delusional. All facts need to be corroborated by an outside informant or care provider, especially details of medical illnesses in a cognitively impaired patient.

9. Encourage previous care providers to see the patient face to face to assist the treatment team.

CONCLUSIONS

Several lessons were learned from this close call about working with delusional patients and about data entry, checking for identity, and direct face-to-face handoffs. Among The Joint Commission's National Patient Safety Goals, the use of two patient identifiers is mandatory while providing care[7]*; Joint Commission International requires the same practice in its International Patient Safety Goal 1, "Identify the patient correctly."[8]† In this case, a third identifier was needed.

The National Patient Safety Goal on medication reconciliation (for example, communicating directly with the patient about medication and checking his or her home medication lists)[7] and

---

* Goal 1: Improve the accuracy of patient identification. NPSG.01.01.01. Use at least two patient identifiers when providing care, treatment, and services.

† Goal 1: Identify the patient correctly. The organization develops an approach to improve accuracy of patient identifications.

the standard (formerly also a National Patient Safety Goal) on handoff communication[7] would have been applicable. Patient-centered care would encourage processing patient input without bias. The current electronic order entry system prevents error but must be routinely used as prescribed.

References

1. Karp D.: The risk of hospitalist hand-offs. *Med Econ* 83:74, Jun. 2, 2006.
2. Valenstein P.N., Sirota R.L.: Identification errors in pathology and laboratory medicine. *Clin Lab Med* 24:979–996, Dec. 2004.
3. Laxmisan A., et al.: The multitasking clinician: Decision-making and cognitive demand during and after team handoffs in emergency care. *Int J Med Inform* 76:801–811, Nov.–Dec. 2007.
4. Groah L.: Hand offs: A link to improving patient safety. *AORN J* 83:227–230, Jan. 2006.
5. Naber D., Pincus H.: Hand-offs and trade-offs in psychiatric care. *Curr Opin Psychiatry* 18:672, Nov. 2005.
6. Mason D.J.: Shift to shift: Reclaiming patient "handoffs." *Am J Nurs* 104:11, Sep. 2004.
7. The Joint Commission: *2010 Comprehensive Accreditation Manual for Hospitals: The Official Handbook.* Oak Brook, IL: Joint Commission Resources, 2009.
8. Joint Commission International: *Joint Commission International Accreditation Standards for Hospitals*, 4th ed. Oak Brook, IL: Joint Commission Resources, 2010.

Event Reached the Patient, but Harm Was Mitigated

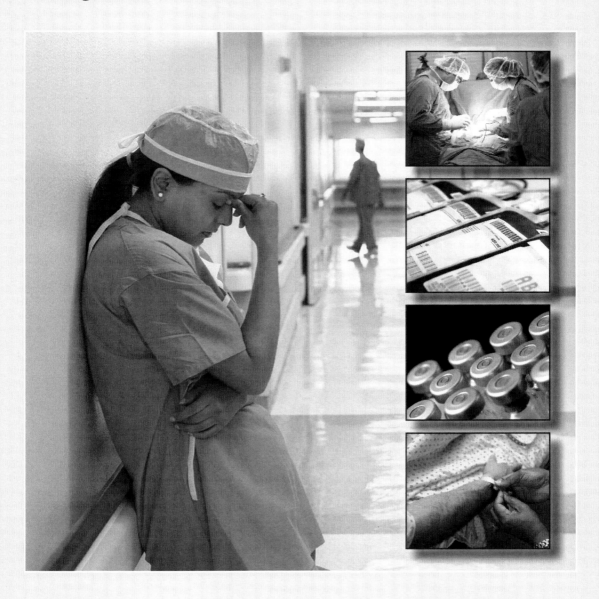

CHAPTER 15

Anesthesia: Administration of Sedatives to Patients Receiving Epidural Analgesia

Stephen Pratt, M.D.

Epidural analgesia (EA) is a common form of postoperative pain control in patients undergoing major abdominal or thoracic surgery. It offers pain relief that is superior to that of parenteral narcotics, whether administered intermittently by a nurse or by patient-controlled analgesia (PCA). EA has few adverse effects but can be associated with respiratory depression when neuraxial narcotics are included in the analgesic regime.[1–3] This is especially true when long-acting, hydrophilic narcotics (for example, morphine) are administered or when enteral or parenteral narcotics are co-administered with neuraxial narcotics.[4,5] A recent guideline published by the American Society of Anesthesiologists highlighted the concerns about respiratory depression with EA and identified strategies to prevent and monitor for this complication.[1]

CASES

The acute pain service (APS) within the hospital's department of anesthesia, critical care and pain medicine is responsible for managing all postoperative epidurals. The standard epidural solution is 0.1% bupivacaine with 10 mcg/mL of hydromorphone. The narcotic hydromorphone is used because of its relative hydrophilic nature compared with fentanyl, which facilitates pain control over a larger dermatomal area. However, it can also be sedating, especially in the elderly, and caution must be taken to monitor

for oversedation or respiratory depression. The higher degree of hydrophilicity may also facilitate rostral spread of the medication and thus increase the risk of respiratory depression.

Every patient who is admitted to the APS with postoperative EA has a standard set of orders written that includes the epidural medications to be administered, adjunct medications for treatment of pruritus or nausea, and a standard monitoring protocol (*see* Table 15-1, page 134).

No patient is to receive any enteral or parenteral sedatives, except as ordered by the APS. This is done to decrease the number of clinicians who can order these medications and, in so doing, reduce the risk of accidental overdose from multiple orders in this patient population at risk for respiratory depression.

However, during a two-year period, there were many instances in which surgical house officers wrote orders for sedatives in patients receiving EA. Despite the postoperative EA protocol, these medications were frequently delivered by the pharmacy and administered by the nursing staff. The sedating medications were most commonly ordered to assist the patients with sleep, but narcotics were occasionally ordered, most commonly as one-time, directly administered orders. Although this was generally a sporadic

Table 15-1. Standard Set of Orders for Postoperative Epidural Analgesia

Sedatives	NO OTHER NARCOTICS OR SEDATIVES may be given to patient unless ordered by Acute Pain Service.
Monitoring	Keep head of bed ≥ 30 degrees at all times
	Blood pressure and pulse rate Q15min x 2, then Q30min x 3, then Q4H for remainder of therapy AND after any dose increase
	Respiratory rate and sedation level Q30min x 4, then Q2H for the remainder of therapy AND after any dose increase
	Sensory level and motor function Q2H while patient is awake
	Pain score (at rest and with movement) Q2H while awake
	Postural BP/pulse prior to first ambulation

	Sedation Scale:
	    0 = NONE
	    S = SLEEP (normal, easy to arouse)
	    1 = MILD (occasionally sleepy, easy to arouse)
	    2 = MODERATE (frequently drowsy, easy to arouse)
	    3 = SEVERE (somnolent, difficult to arouse)
	    4 = UNRESPONSIVE

	Verbal Analogue: Scale Pain Score (0–10), 0 = No Pain, 10 = Worst Pain Possible
Activity	Patient must be accompanied at all times during ambulation
Fluids	Patient must have patent IV while epidural catheter is in place. Fluids as ordered by team; or lactated Ringer's solution to keep vein open.

Contact	Notify Acute Pain Service for the following:
	    A. SBP < _____ mmHg and/or P < _____ /min
	    B. Postural BP drop = 15 mmHg and/or HR _____
	    C. RR = 9/min
	    D. Sedation level = 3
	    E. Pain score of zero (0/10) at rest AND with movement
	    F. Inadequate analgesia or other problems related to the epidural

	Page Anesthesia STAT for:
	    A. Sedation level = 3 AND RR < 9/min
	    B. If patient is unresponsive
	    C. Numbness above nipples and/or inability to bend knees
	    D. If patient has syncope, circumoral numbness, or tinnitus, stop the infusion
	        and page anesthesia STAT

Note: Q, every; H, hour; BP, blood pressure; IV, intravenous (line); SBP, systolic blood pressure; P, pulse rate; HR, heart rate; RR, respiratory rate.

Source: Beth Israel Deaconess Medical Center, Boston. Used with permission.

event that could be resolved with specific feed-back to the house officer writing the order, it occurred up to four times per month. Ultimately, two patients experienced respiratory depression that required treatment and additional monitoring after receiving additional narcotics. Fortunately, no patient was harmed by the additional seda-tives. Given the recurrent nature of this problem and the potential for devastating consequences from respiratory depression, the hospital under-took a patient safety initiative to eliminate seda-tive orders by non-APS physicians.

INTERVENTION

Identifying Contributing Factors

A multidisciplinary work group, with represen-tation from the departments of surgery and anesthesia, perioperative and postoperative nursing, the hospital Department of Health Care Quality, and the pharmacy, was convened to design a solution to the problem of co-admin-istration of sedatives and neuraxial narcotics during EA. The first step was to understand why this was occurring despite the fact that the exist-ing written protocol stated explicitly that only the APS was to order any additional sedatives. The group met several times and solicited input from the surgical house officers. Frank discus-sion was encouraged to help elucidate the roots of the problem. Three contributing factors were identified, as follows:

1. It became clear that most surgical house offi-cers did not know about the protocol associ-ated with EA. In addition, they did not know about the potential dangers of administering sedating medications to patients who are receiving continuous epidural narcotics.

2. The surgeons expressed a strong interest in being able to maintain the authority to care for their patients. This included the ability to administer medications for sleep.

3. Nurses often felt caught in the middle between members of the surgery and anesthe-sia departments. The APS anesthesia staff

take calls from home and were often not physically present in the hospital when the surgical residents wrote orders for the sedat-ing medications in these patients. The nurses were thus frequently confronted with the real physical presence of a surgical house officer demanding that his or her order be carried out versus the abstract concerns of the APS resident at home who expected the protocol to be followed. Given this situation, it is not surprising that the nurses often administered the medications despite the protocol.

Corrective Actions

Understanding the roots of the problem helped to direct three corresponding corrective actions, as discussed in the following sections:

1. ***Computerized provider order entry (CPOE) process.*** The hospital implemented a process in the CPOE system to prevent surgical staff from ordering inappropriate sedating medica-tions in patients receiving EA. This was more difficult than expected because simply identi-fying which patients had an epidural infusion was not easy. Although most patients receive the hospital's standard epidural solution for postoperative pain relief (0.1% bupivacaine and 10 mcg/mL of hydromorphone), some receive nonstandard solutions. Some of the solutions are special orders and thus are not easily amenable to routine computer queries. The project ultimately was able to receive support from the information technology (IT) staff to solve this problem by searching for the epidural route of administration in any postoperative patient.

A list was then created of medications that should not be administered to patients receiv-ing EA without approval from the APS (*see* Table 15-2, page 136). These medications were grouped by category so that if a new medication was added to the formulary under each category, it would automatically be added to the list of prohibited medications.

Table 15-2. List of Medications Not to Be Administered to Patients Receiving Epidural Analgesia Without Approval from the Acute Pain Service	
Narcotic analgesics	Morphine, hydromorphone, fentanyl including fentanyl patch, oxycodone, methadone, levorphanol, oxymorphone, meperidine, codeine, hydrocodone, opium, propoxyphene, sufentanil, tramadol, buprenorphine, butrophanol, nalbuphine, pentazocine
Ataractics-tranquilizers	Alprazolam, clorazepate, diazepam, oxazepam, buspirone, meprobamate
Sedative non-barbiturate	Chloral hydrate, dexmedetomidine, flurazepam, lorazepam, midazolam, pentobarbital, temazepam, triazolam, zolpidem, zaleplon
Anti-anxiety agents	Chlordiazepoxide

Source: Beth Israel Deaconess Medical Center, Boston. Used with permission.

Finally, the IT staff created a pop-up window that alerts any staff members trying to order a prohibited medication for a patient with EA. This window alerts the ordering physician to the fact that he or she was attempting to order a medication prohibited in patients receiving EA: "You have ordered a medication that requires APS approval or override in patients receiving epidural analgesia." It also requires that the ordering physician answer one of three questions in order to continue, as follows:

1. I have spoken to Dr. _____ from APS, and they agree with this order.
2. D/C [discontinue] epidural infusion. I will manage pain control. APS to D/C epidural catheter.
3. I am from the APS.

This system was created and tested in the virtual patient environment,* and input and buy-in were sought from other stakeholders—specifically, members of the orthopedics and gynecology departments who had not been involved in the work group. A comprehensive educational campaign was then undertaken to ensure that the housestaff and nurses from the affected services knew about the new system. This was done through repeated e-mails, announcements at staff meetings, face-to-face education by the APS quality assurance nurse, and input from the appropriate residency directors.

2. ***Determination of medications that surgeons could safely administer.*** The hospital determined what medications the surgeons might be able to administer safely to patients receiving EA so they could maintain their desired autonomy over their patients' care without increasing risk. Diphenhydramine (Benadryl) was not included in the prohibited list, and the surgeons were allowed to write for this mediation as a "sleeper."

3. ***Education of surgical housestaff.*** The hospital improved education to the surgical housestaff about the hazards of postoperative EA. The director of the APS lectures to the incoming first-year surgical residents about general topics in acute pain management and specific issues related to EA. In addition,

---

* A replica of the standard CPOE program that uses fabricated patients (for example, "Kermit Frog").

information about the safe care of patients receiving EA was added to the resident in-service packets for surgical services with a high postoperative epidural use rates.

RESULTS

The pop-up system was well received by all surgical services, as were the resident lectures and in-service packets. In the first year after implementation, there was only one case identified of inappropriate medications being ordered by a surgical house officer, and no cases of respiratory depression occurred among patients receiving EA. There are failures within the system, most notably miscommunication between the ASP and surgical house officers about what care is safe. However, these are resolvable with simple communication between the parties involved.

DISCUSSION

Respiratory depression is a known complication of neuraxial narcotic administration, with an incidence rate of up to 7%.[6,7] Risk factors include obesity, obstructive sleep apnea, coexisting disease and advanced age, the use of hydrophilic narcotic medications such as morphine, and the co-administration of enteral or parenteral narcotics.[1,4–6] Recent literature suggests that under well-controlled circumstances, additional parenteral or enteral narcotics might safely be administered to patients receiving EA. In one study, Anghelescu et al. found only one case (0.85%) of respiratory depression among 117 pediatric patients who received simultaneous epidural and systemic narcotics. This case was related to a dosing error in a small child.[2] The hospital's system was created, in part, because of concerns that having multiple services ordering sedating medications in the high-risk population receiving EA might increase the chance of a medication error caused by concurrent administration of multiple orders.

The hospital's experience demonstrated several important points in using a close call to help improve patient safety, as follows:

1. It is important to have a quality assurance system that is able to identify these cases. The institutional culture of safety must be such that clinical staff actively look for potential adverse events and close calls. Providers must also feel that it is safe to report their own close calls. In the system in question, the APS staff monitor each patient's medical administration record on a daily basis to look for potential concerning medications.

2. It is helpful to use a formal approach to understand the root causes of the problem. The open discussion between nursing, pharmacy, anesthesia, and surgical staff helped them to better understand one another's positions and to determine the root causes of the problem. This, in turn, helped to direct the corrective actions.

3. The institution must have adequate resources and must make solving those problems that are identified a priority, even when no patient harm has occurred. In this case, significant IT resources were required to develop the pop-up in the CPOE system.

4. The corrective action must include a well-designed implementation plan to ensure that all clinicians who might be affected by the improvements are apprised of the new processes. The hospital undertook a rigorous education campaign to ensure that staff knew about the new CPOE system and that surgical house officers were better educated about the risks of postoperative epidural analgesia.

The hospital recently experienced another close call in the same patient population. A patient receiving postoperative EA was written a prescription for, and nearly received, a dose of clopidogrel (Plavix). A recently published guideline by the American Society of Anesthesiologists[8] indicates that an epidural catheter should not be placed or removed for seven days after *stopping* clopidogrel ingestion. Had this close call not been caught, the patient might have needed to keep his epidural for a week. The hospital plans to use a similar process to the one described previously to limit the administration of anticoagulants in patient receiving postoperative EA.

References

1. American Society of Anesthesiologists Task Force on Neuraxial Opioids, et al.: Practice guidelines for the prevention, detection, and management of respiratory depression associated with neuraxial opioid administration. *Anesthesiology* 110:218–230, Feb. 2009.
2. Anghelescu D.L., et al.: The safety of concurrent administration of opioids via epidural and intravenous routes for postoperative pain in pediatric oncology patients. *J Pain Symptom Manage* 35:412–419, Apr. 2008. Epub Mar. 4, 2008.
3. Carvalho B.: Respiratory depression after neuraxial opioids in the obstetric setting. *Anesth Analg* 107:956–961, Sep. 2008.
4. Gustafsson L.L., Schildt B., Jacobsen K.: Adverse effects of extradural and intrathecal opiates: Report of a nationwide survey in Sweden. *Br J Anaesth* 54:479–486, May 1982.
5. Weinger M.: Dangers of postoperative opioids. *Anesthesia Patient Safety Foundation Newsletter* 21:61–68, Winter 2006–2007.
6. Horlocker T.T.: Practice guidelines for the prevention, detection and management of respiratory depression associated with neuraxial opioid administration: Preliminary report by ASA Task Force on Neuraxial Anesthesia. *ASA Newsl* 71:24–26, Jun. 2007.
7. Shapiro A., et al.: The frequency and timing of respiratory depression in 1524 postoperative patients treated with systemic or neuraxial morphine. *J Clin Anesth* 17:537–542, Nov. 2005.
8. Horlocker T.T., et al.: Regional anesthesia in the patient receiving antithrombotic or thrombolytic therapy: American Society of Regional Anesthesia and Pain Medicine Evidence-Based Guidelines (Third Edition). *Reg Anesth Pain Med* 35:64–101, Jan.–Feb. 2010.

CHAPTER 16

Emergency Medicine: Medication Displacement in an Automated Medication Dispensing System

Sommer Gripper, M.D.; Elizabeth Fang, Pharm.D., B.C.P.S.; Sneha Shah, M.D.; Melinda Ortmann, Pharm.D., B.C.P.S.; Michelle Patch, R.N., M.S.N.; Jordan Sax, M.D.; Julius Cuong Pham, M.D., Ph.D.

CASE

A 45-year-old woman presented to the emergency department (ED) at an academic medical center for chest pain. The patient complained of "crushing" chest pain that radiated to her back and woke her from sleep. She reported having experienced two other episodes earlier in the day, before arrival at the ED. While being evaluated in the ED, she appeared clinically stable, with normal vital signs.

The patient's past medical history was significant for hypertension and tobacco use. She reported taking hydrochlorothiazide daily for her hypertension, as well as ibuprofen, as needed, for pain. The patient also reported an allergy to penicillin. No significant surgical or family history was noted. Her review of systems was positive for chest pain, shortness of breath with exertion, nausea, and back pain. Aside from this review of systems, the patient's physical examination was unremarkable. Initial vital signs were as follows—temperature: 37°C; pulse: 82 bpm; blood pressure: 150/90 mmHg; O_2 saturation: 100% on room air.

On the basis of the patient's examination, the most concerning differential diagnoses of consequence included aortic dissection and acute coronary syndrome (ACS). The patient's initial electrocardiogram (EKG) reading was normal sinus rhythm with ST depression in V5–V6,

which was concerning for ischemia. She was evaluated with a computerized tomography (CT) angiogram, which did not show any evidence of vascular aneurysm or dissection. On the basis of a high suspicion of ACS, the patient was treated with oral (PO) aspirin, sublingual nitroglycerin, and intravenous (IV) morphine, with mild improvement in her pain. The patient's first series of cardiac enzymes revealed significantly elevated total creatine kinase (CK), MB fraction, and CK index and a troponin of 10ng/mL. Her repeat EKG showed ST elevation in V5–V6.

At this time, the interventional cardiology team was activated. The patient started treatment with continuous IV heparin, PO clopidogrel, and IV metoprolol x 3 doses. After one dose of metoprolol, staff noted that the patient's cardiac rhythm converted to supraventricular tachycardia, with a heart rate of 170 bpm and an increased systolic blood pressure that peaked at 190 mm/Hg. The patient was administered a second dose of IV metoprolol, without effect. IV adenosine was then administered, without success. Next, IV diltiazem was administered to the patient, lowering the pulse to 110 bpm. She was subsequently started on a diltiazem infusion.

On further review of the medications administered to the patient, ED staff found that IV terbutaline had been inadvertently administered instead of IV metoprolol. After the error was identified, the nursing staff went to the automated medication dispensing system (AMDS) and confirmed that the metoprolol storage compartment contained both metoprolol and terbutaline, mixed in the same compartment. The cardiology team was apprised of the situation. The patient was transferred to the cardiac catheterization laboratory without further event and ultimately did well. The family and the patient received full disclosure of the medication error by both physicians and nursing staff.

BACKGROUND

Medication errors contribute to significant patient morbidity and mortality.[1] Approximately 6.5% of hospital admissions are associated with medication errors, and an additional 5.5% are associated with close calls.[2] In the ED, the medication error rate can be as high as 60% of patients.[3] EDs are predisposed to medication errors because of high patient census,[4] sudden interruptions in work flow, miscommunication between providers and nurses during critical situations, and the need for continuous multitasking among staff.[5] In this case, an incorrect medication was inadvertently administered to a patient by a nurse. This fits a common profile of voluntarily reported medication errors in the ED, where nurses are most likely to be involved (54% of medication errors), and the errors are most likely to occur at the administration step in the medication process (36%) and during the busiest shift (3:00 P.M. [15:00]–11:00 P.M. [23:00]; 42%). In addition, an incorrect medication is the third most common type of medication error (11%).[6]

Several technological advances have been developed to decrease the risk of medication administration errors. One tool that can help mitigate some of this risk and reduce such errors is an AMDS. Approximately 83% of hospitals in the United States have implemented AMDSs as part of their medication safety strategy.[7] AMDSs can help improve the accuracy of medication inventory, billing, and administration, but they are not a fail-safe system and can produce medication errors as well. In Pennsylvania, approximately 15% of medication errors are attributable to automated dispensing cabinets (ADCs), one type of ADMSs.[8] In the ED, AMDSs contribute to approximately 3.6% of medication errors.[6,8] AMDSs can themselves contribute to medication errors because (1) they may not necessarily include a pharmacist review/double check of the medication before it is administered, (2) medication displacement—medications located in an incorrect inventory location—can occur within the AMDS, and (3) nursing staff can inadvertently remove medication from the incorrect compartment. In most inpatient units, when an order is placed, a pharmacist checks it against the patient's allergies, liver and kidney function, comorbid diseases, and drug interactions to ensure the safety of administration. In the ED, this responsibility is often left to the physicians and nurses to check their own actions in urgent and emergent situations.

Medication displacement, which is one of the many potential risks associated with AMDS use, significantly contributed to the medication error in this case. Medication displacement can occur in several different ways, including incorrect stocking of an AMDS by pharmacy staff, physical shifting of medications between storage compartments or "pockets" because of weak storage barriers, and incorrect return of medications to the AMDS by nursing staff. Look-alike packaging for different medications and the same medications with labeling variations from different manufacturers can contribute to all of these problems.

Although there are different brands of AMDSs marketed, most share similar features. Often, an AMDS is composed of several different types of pockets within a single cabinet. The variety in pocket size, shape, and accessibility allow the institution to customize the machine and maximize space to meet that institution's needs.

Figure 16-1. Examples of Different Automated Medication Dispensing Systems (AMDSs)

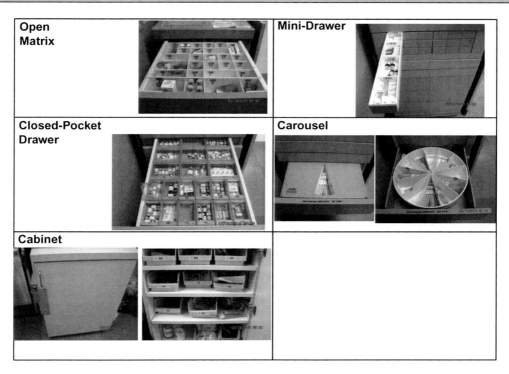

Source: The Johns Hopkins Hospital, Baltimore. Used with permission.

Various AMDS pocket types for the organization include the following, as shown in Figure 16-1 (above):

- *Open matrix:* All medications within the drawer are accessible to the user, but each medication is separated by an individually pocketed barrier.

- *Mini-drawer:* The mini-drawer is a smaller version of the open matrix drawer.

- *Closed-pocket drawer:* This commercially available drawer consists of a matrix of closed pockets, and only the pocket of the medication slated for removal opens.

- *Carousel:* The entire drawer opens, but only the carousel slice with the medication is visible and accessible.

- *Cabinet:* Freestanding medication bins are stored in an open closet/refrigerator.

AMDSs that rely heavily on open-matrix and mini-drawer configurations generally have more functional storage capability but are also predisposed to many of the potential displacement errors discussed previously.

INVESTIGATION AND ACTION TAKEN

When reviewing the storage configuration of the AMDS machine involved, it was noted that both medications in question—IV terbutaline and IV metoprolol—were stocked in the same open-matrix drawer in close proximity. During the next several months, multiple medication displacement errors were found in other AMDSs in the ED, suggesting that this risk of medication error was common and required some systemic interventions. The first possibility was that the barriers of the storage pockets in the open-matrix drawer were moveable, allowing medications to shift underneath the storage barriers between pockets. Medications may have also shifted over the storage barriers between pockets during medication removal. To mitigate medication shift, the AMDS pockets were reinforced to increase their structural integrity. Although this may reduce the risk of medication shifts within the open-matrix drawer, it also limits the ability to make any future changes to the drawer configuration.

A second possible cause of medication displacement was a stocking error from the pharmacy. Before this event, the pharmacy used several methods to restock the AMDS. The AMDSs were stocked either by choosing a single item at a time, which allows drawers to open individually for restocking, or by choosing a list of medications at one time, which allows multiple drawers to open in sequence. To minimize variability and decrease stocking errors, the single-item approach to restocking the AMDs was implemented. In addition, carrying the same medication supply from different manufacturers might have contributed to the stocking error. Although a variation in medication supply is not always avoidable, the differences in packaging, coloring, and labeling could increase confusion, particularly when multiple manufacturers of the same medication are stocked within the same AMDS pocket. The pharmacy continued to strive for consistency in medication manufacturer.

Third, the open-matrix drawer itself might have created a higher-risk storage environment. Users might have inadvertently removed medications from the incorrect bin. Therefore, open-matrix drawers were converted to closed-pocket drawers when possible. These newly implemented closed pockets were preferentially filled with medications thought to be of high risk to the patient, as well as any look-alike/sound-alike medications. The addition of these drawers to AMDSs also reduced the potential for stocking errors. By

allowing only a single pocket, rather than a complete medication drawer, to open at one time, the likelihood that medications are stocked in an incorrect storage bin is reduced. These cumulative interventions were associated with a 37% decrease in medication displacement over the ensuing several months.[9]

Fourth, medications being returned inaccurately to the AMDS by ED staff might have led to medication displacement. In this case, a terbutaline vial may have been inadvertently placed into the metoprolol pocket when medications were returned directly to the AMDS. To mitigate this risk, medications were no longer allowed to be returned directly to the AMDS machine. Medications are returned to a "medication return" bin (similarly to library books) and are later restocked by pharmacy personnel.

Finally, the pharmacy made plans to implement AMDS medication bar coding, which holds promise for reducing medication displacement due to restocking errors. Scanning with a medication bar-coding system would help ensure that the correct medication, dose, and dosage form are stocked in the appropriate AMDS compartment.

No amount of automation/technology can replace medication checks at the bedside before administration. For medication administration, the "five rights" must be ensured: right patient, right medication, right dose, right route, and right frequency. In this case, the emergent nature of the patient's condition and multitasking both contributed to medication error. These conditions are commonplace in the ED. ED clinicians must balance the vigilance required to prevent medication errors while ensuring that patients receive timely treatment.

CONCLUSION

Medication errors are associated with morbidity and mortality and can occur at any time during the administration process, including physician ordering, verbal orders, medication retrieval, and medication admixture and administration. Emergent situations and high-stress environments, such as those encountered in EDs, can predispose staff to lapses in consistent administration practices, which may lead to medication errors. Implementing safer automated technologies can decrease medication errors. Some examples of these would be to separate medication return bins and certain types of restrictive bins within the AMDS (carousel or closed-pocket drawers). Regardless of the type of process improvement implemented, technology cannot completely eliminate the need for consistent procedures for medication verification.

References

1. Bates D.W., et al.: The costs of adverse drug events in hospitalized patients. Adverse Drug Events Prevention Study Group. *JAMA* 277:307–311, Jan. 22–29, 1997.

2. Bates D.W., et al.: Incidence of adverse drug events and potential adverse drug events. Implications for prevention. ADE Prevention Study Group. *JAMA* 274:29–34, Jul. 5, 1995.

3. Patanwala A.E., et al.: A prospective observational study of medication errors in a tertiary care emergency department. *Ann Emerg Med* 55:522–526, Jun. 2010.

4. Kulstad E.B., et al.: ED overcrowding is associated with an increased frequency of medication errors. *Am J Emerg Med* 28:304–309, Mar. 2010.

5. Croskerry P., et al.: *Patient Safety in Emergency Medicine*, 1st ed. Philadelphia: Lippincott Williams & Wilkins, 2009.

6. Pham J.C., et al.: National study on the frequency, types, causes, and consequences of voluntarily reported emergency department medication errors. *J Emerg Med*, in press. Epub Sep. 25, 2008.

7. Pedersen C.A., Schneider P.J., Scheckelhoff D.J.: ASHP national survey of pharmacy practice in hospital settings: Dispensing and administration—2008. *Am J Health Syst Pharm* 66:926–946, May 15, 2009.

8. Paparella S.: Automated medication dispensing systems: Not error free. *J Emerg Nurs* 32:71–74, Feb. 2006.

9. Fang E., et al.: Evaluation of the displacement of medications in automated dispensing cabinets in an adult emergency department (unpublished manuscript). Baltimore, Jun. 10, 2010.

CHAPTER 17

Obstetrics: Pulmonary Edema Following a Failed Handoff

Susan Mann, M.D.; Stephen D. Pratt, M.D.

Labor and delivery (L&D) units are complicated care settings in which caregivers historically care for complex patients while working in relative isolation. Staff are often unaware of the competition for resources or of the acuity of other patients on a unit. This close-call case illustrates a lack of coordination of care between disciplines and a failure to provide a structured handoff from the L&D setting and L&D providers to the postpartum setting and its providers.

CASE

The patient was a 33-year-old G_1P_0 (primigravida [first pregnancy]) admitted at 8 weeks in labor to an academic medical center. She was scheduled to have a Cesarean delivery because of a previous myomectomy. The patient underwent an uncomplicated Cesarean delivery of a male infant at 5:35 P.M. (17:35)—weight 8 lb. 5oz. (3,795 g) and Apgar scores of 9^1 and 9^5. The estimated blood loss was 800 cc, and she received 2,000 cc of crystalloid intraoperatively. At 11:10 P.M. (23:10) there was a note by the obstetric resident that the patient had decreased urine output, and she was given three fluid boluses of 500 cc each. On examination, the patient had bibasilar rales after having received 5,340 cc in eight hours. A hematocrit was ordered, which demonstrated a decrease from 30% preoperatively to 26.9%. A chest x-ray was

ordered because her oxygen (O_2) saturation had decreased. The preliminary reading was normal, but the final report was pulmonary edema. The patient was given furosemide and had a significant diueresis. She was transferred to the postpartum floor in good condition eight hours after delivery and had excellent urine output and normal oxygen saturation.

There was no mention of the fluid issues to the postpartum physicians or nurses caring for the patient. The patient did well until postoperative day 4, when she developed chest pressure and an elevated blood pressure of 160/90 mmHg. She was treated with labetalol, and her repeat blood pressure was 140/90 mmHg. The provider who evaluated the patient was unaware of the issues during L&D. The patient was sent for venous Doppler studies of the lower extremities, which were negative, and the patient demanded to be discharged. She was urged to remain hospitalized to monitor her blood pressure, but she requested discharge. She agreed to see her obstetric provider the next day and was discharged, but she developed significant shortness of breath at home that evening. She was admitted with pulmonary edema to another hospital.

The patient recovered uneventfully thereafter but wrote a letter to the State Department of Public Health (DPH) regarding her concerns about the care she received while hospitalized for the delivery of her child. This complaint triggered an external review by the DPH as well as an internal review by the quality assurance (QA) committee of the department of obstetrics and gynecology.

INTERVENTION

Contributing Factors

A root cause analysis (RCA) of this case identified four contributing factors, as follows, three of which concerned the absence of a standardized process of care:

1. There was a lack of a standard process of care for patients recovering from anesthesia while on L&D units. The nurses caring for the postoperative patients would frequently "catch" whichever physician was nearby to evaluate the patient. These providers often did not know what treatments had already been rendered to the patient or the "big picture" plan of care. In essence, there was no clear leader of the team of providers, which included both obstetricians and anesthesiologists, for patients in the L&D postanesthesia care unit (PACU). A lack of standardized care in obstetric PACUs has recently been identified as a significant problem in the United States.[1] Most mothers are cared for by perinatal nurses who frequently have had no specific training in PACU care. In addition, these nurses often have other responsibilities that require them to leave the patient's bedside, sometimes to care for laboring patients outside the PACU.[1] This is especially problematic in the face of recent data demonstrating that a large percentage of anesthesia-related deaths occurs in the recovery period.[2]

2. There was also an absence of a standard approach to the obstetric patient with decreased urine output. Although hypovolemia is the most common cause of oliguria after Cesarean delivery, there are many other potential causes, including postrenal obstruction, intrinsic renal dysfunction from preeclampsia, hormonal impact of oxytocin use, and cardiac dysfunction. None of these were considered in the case described. In retrospect, this patient likely had a mild hypertensive disorder of pregnancy, which contributed to both her oliguria and her subsequent pulmonary edema. Hypovolemia is less commonly the cause of oliguria in the patient with preeclampsia, even if clinical signs indicate an apparent prerenal etiology.[3]

3. There was a lack of a standardized handoff of care between disciplines caring for the patient initially treated in L&D and then in the postpartum area. The attending obstetrician caring for the patient on the postpartum unit did not know about the oliguria, pulmonary edema, or need for diuresis in the PACU. The management of postoperative fluids and the response to the hypertension and desaturation on the postpartum floor would likely have been different if this information had been known. The Joint Commission requires hospitals to have a process for handoff of care and suggests that the handoff communication include the patient's condition, care, treatment, medications, services, and any recent or anticipated changes to any of these (Standard PC.02.02.01, Element of Performance 2).[4] The use of structured language, such as the Situation–Background–Assessment–Recommendation (SBAR) technique, has been suggested as a way to ensure that all relevant information is transferred.[5]

4. Individual care deficiencies by the attending obstetrician and systems issues were identified. Within the obstetrics and gynecology department's QA process, one of three peer review categories is assigned to each case with respect to the individual quality of care, as determined by consensus of the QA committee members. The first option is "no deficiency in care," and no further action is taken. The second option is "opportunity for improvement," in which a provider receives a letter indicating what may have been done

differently, often related to documentation. The third option is "deficiency in the care provided," and these cases are referred to the executive committee in the obstetrics/gynecology department for review and resolution. In this case, the physician was sent a letter citing an opportunity for improvement. The committee felt that a chest x-ray should have been obtained before discharge because this may have changed the course prior to her discharge and prevented the emergent hospitalization.

Corrective Actions

After the RCA was completed and the case was reviewed by the QA committee, the case was referred to the quality improvement (QI) committee to address the system issues identified. This multidisciplinary committee has representation from obstetrics, L&D, and postpartum nursing; anesthesiology; neonatology; and other ad hoc services, as needed. It is charged with overseeing the quality and safety processes on L&D and the postpartum unit. This committee dealt with each of the issues identified.

Consistency of Care. Several steps were taken to improve the consistency of care in the L&D PACU and the postpartum floors. First, the anesthesia staff were identified as the primary care providers while patients are in the acute recovery phase. This does not mean that the anesthesiologist must deal with all issues that arise in the PACU. Some issues (for example, maternal hemorrhage) clearly require a multidisciplinary approach, and others (difficulties with breast feeding) are not in the anesthesiologist's purview at all. However, all issues should be communicated to the anesthesiologist so that one clinician has an overall view of the patient and can act as leader.

Second, to better standardize the management of oliguria, the team developed an oliguria guideline for obstetric patients (*see* Figure 17-1, page 148). This was developed specifically for man-

agement of preeclamptic patients, for whom the cause and management of oliguria can be complex, but it can be used for any patient with decreased urine output. The primary goal of the guideline was to allow clinicians to treat the most common cause of oliguria—hypovolemia—and to encourage a more thoughtful, multidisciplinary approach if these initial steps are not effective. Concerns that might preclude the safe additional administration of intravenous fluids are reviewed if urine output does not improve after two fluid challenges. For example, the anesthesiologist might indicate that the patient has a particularly difficult-looking airway and that volume overload leading to pulmonary edema and the need for emergent intubation would be life threatening. Alternatively, the obstetrician may raise concerns about placental function in an undelivered patient with oliguria and indicate that even mild maternal hypoxemia from volume overload might precipitate an emergent Cesarean delivery. Such concerns about additional fluid challenges would require that additional diagnostic tests be performed or that urgent delivery be considered.

After the QA committee had considered the case and the QI committee developed the oliguria guideline, case-based learning was used to promote guideline implementation. The case (and its outcome) and the guideline were presented at departmental grand rounds followed by a question-and-answer process to clarify the guideline. Similar education occurred in the anesthesia and nursing departments.

Multidisciplinary Teamwork and Communication. The importance of communication in the PACU was emphasized. The L&D unit has implemented formal team training based on crew resource management,[6] which has created team structures and processes of care. Within this structure, the fact that the PACU is a high-risk area was emphasized, and multidisciplinary communication was improved.

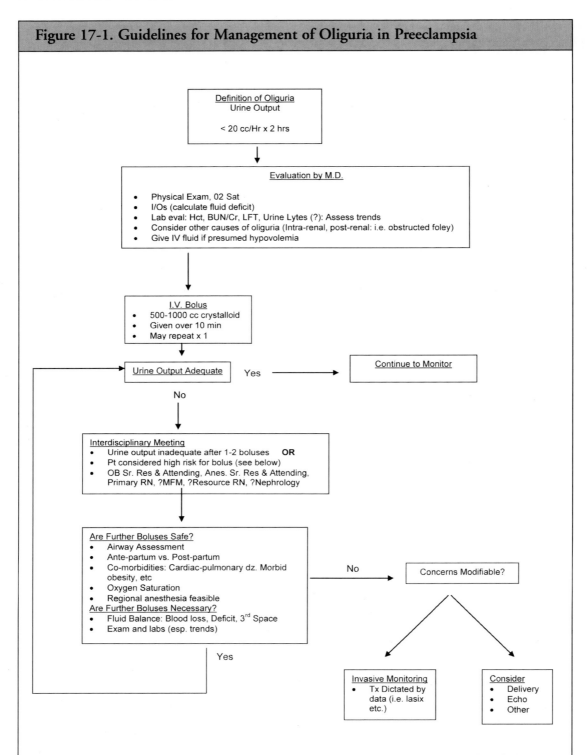

Figure 17-1. Guidelines for Management of Oliguria in Preeclampsia

Note: Hr, hour; M.D., physician; O2 sat, oxygen saturation; I/O, input/output; Hct, hematocrit; BUN/Cr, blood urea nitrogen/creatinine; LFT, liver function tests; IV, intravenous; pt, patient; OB, obstetrics; Sr., senior; Res, resident; Anes., anesthesia; RN, registered nurse; MFM, Maternal-Fetal Medicine; dz., disease; Tx, treatment.

Source: Beth Israel Deaconess Medical Center, Boston. Used with permission.

Multidisciplinary briefings are now held before every Cesarean delivery so that potential postoperative problems can be anticipated and discussed.

In addition, the development of obstetric-specific triggers designed to force multidisciplinary communication is in process. The use of obstetric-specific triggers has been demonstrated to improve care and obstetric outcomes,[7] and obstetric-specific triggers are distinct from the triggers already in place within the medical center designed to prevent cardiopulmonary arrest. The obstetric triggers are designed to get the appropriate clinicians to the bedside while emergent obstetric events are unfolding. To date, we have developed triggers for fetal bradycardia, which call the obstetric, nursing, and anesthesia staff; for maternal hemorrhage; and for oliguria. According to one of the identified intraoperative triggers, a second attending is called if the patient has received two units of blood and additional blood loss is expected or if a patient needs to return to the operating room from the postoperative recovery area. Surgical sign-out from the operating room, a standardized process where concerns are identified for recovery and shared with the team, is also in the developmental stage.[8] Other triggers are currently being developed for the antepartum floor.

Finally, to improve communication between L&D and the postpartum team, handoff processes were clarified and defined. The handoff of care for nursing included a faxed report and verbal exchange between L&D and postpartum care. Particular attention is paid to patients who have had to initiate the oliguria protocol. Attendings have a verbal exchange and review patients with one another in a systematic way, both electronically and verbally, to allow an opportunity for questions. In the 24 months since the occurrence of the case provided, no cases of close calls or patient harm attributable to L&D/postpartum handoffs have occurred.

CONCLUSIONS

This case allowed the opportunity to identify problems and create solutions for patients in the L&D PACU through identifying roles, establishing protocols, and improving handoffs of care. The process of performing an RCA, creating a system improvement, using the QA and QI committees, and educating staff on changes in policies through case-based learning helps to introduce and implement changes to improve patient care.

References

1. Wilkins K.K., et al.: A survey of obstetric perianesthesia care unit standards. *Anesth Analg* 108:1869–1875, Jun. 2009.
2. Mhyre J.M., et al.: A series of anesthesia-related maternal deaths in Michigan, 1985–2003. *Anesthesiology* 106:1096–1104, Jun. 2007.
3. Lee W., Gonik B., Cotton D.B.: Urinary diagnostic indices in preeclampsia-associated oliguria: Correlation with invasive hemodynamic monitoring. *Am J Obstet Gynecol* 156, Jan. 1987. http://www.jcrinc.com/NPSG-2-Improve-the-effectiveness-of-communication-among-caregivers (accessed Apr. 11, 2010).
4. The Joint Commission: *2010 Comprehensive Accreditation Manual for Hospitals: The Official Handbook.* Oak Brook, IL: Joint Commission Resources, 2009.
5. Joint Commission Resources: *Passing the Baton—Use of the SBAR Tool—May 21, 2009.* http://www.jcrinc.com/2009-Archived-Audio-Conferences/SBAR-Tool-Archive/1679/ (accessed Apr. 11, 2009).
6. Pratt S.D., et al.: John M. Eisenberg Patient Safety and Quality Awards. Impact of CRM-based training on obstetric outcomes and clinicians' patient safety attitudes. *Jt Comm J Qual Patient Saf* 33:720–725, Dec. 2007.
7. Gosman G.G., et al.: Introduction of an obstetric-specific medical emergency team for obstetric crises: Implementation and experience. *Am J Obstet Gynecol* 198:367.e1–367.e7, Apr. 2008.
8. Haynes A.B., et al.: A surgical safety checklist to reduce morbidity and mortality in a global population. *N Engl J Med* 360:491–499, Jan. 29, 2009. Epub Jan. 14, 2009.

CHAPTER 18

Radiology: A Chance Discovery of Retained Sponges

Anthony Fotenos, M.D., Ph.D.; John Eng, M.D.

CASE

Ms. H is a middle-aged woman who underwent urgent aortic and mitral valve replacement, placement of an ascending aortic graft, placement of an interposition graft to coronary artery bypass, and placement of an intra-aortic balloon during the course of an all-day surgery.

Ms. H had a history of severe aortic and mitral valve stenosis, as well as coronary artery disease and noncardiac comorbidities. Postoperatively, the patient's mediastinum was packed and her sternotomy left open due to hypotension and difficult hemostasis. On postoperative day (POD) 3—a Saturday—the patient returned to the operating room (OR) for sternal closure and pack removal, which was performed by a different surgeon. Intraoperative foreign body radiographs were obtained to confirm removal of all packed sponges. A first-year radiology resident covering the OR described the radiographs over the phone to the radiologic technologist (RT). The RT returned to the OR and reported the examination as negative (no foreign body). A written report of the examination was not made until Sunday morning, POD 4, when it was incidentally discovered within the radiology image archive by a senior attending radiologist. The attending radiologist noted the persistent retention of two postoperative sponges. He immediately alerted the surgeon who had closed

the patient on Saturday. The patient returned to the OR that same afternoon for retrieval of the retained surgical sponges. Her postoperative course was notable for prolonged respiratory failure secondary to *Hafnia alvei* and *Enterobacter* pneumonia, brief pulseless electrical activity (PEA) arrest on POD 7, and dysphagia requiring placement of a percutaneous gastrostomy tube. The patient eventually made a full recovery and was discharged on POD 47, after a long course of inpatient rehabilitation.

Background

Retained surgical objects, particularly retained sponges, can cause death.[1] Legally, when harm from retained surgical objects occurs, the doctrine of *res ipsa loquitur* ("the thing speaks for itself") applies, meaning defendants in these cases are assumed negligent unless they can prove otherwise. In 2005, The Joint Commission added "unintended retention of a foreign object in a patient after surgery or other procedure"[2] to its list of sentinel events that require hospitals to conduct a root cause analysis, develop an action plan, implement improvements, and monitor outcomes.[3] Yet despite the importance of this medical error, the system for preventing retained surgical objects has not changed significantly since the widespread incorporation of radiopaque material in sponges more than 50 years ago. The prevailing system relies on a "three-legged stool" of responsibility, placing responsibility on surgeons to inspect wounds before closure, on OR technologists and nurses to count objects before and after they are used, and on radiologists to detect these objects when they are retained.

Much of the literature on retained surgical objects reflects the perspective of surgeons and OR staff, who receive the radiologist's interpretation in the simplest binary form: retained object positive or negative. The present case, which describes retained chest sponges that were initially missed, demonstrates the multifactorial backstory and vulnerabilities of that deceptively simple, binary product.*

IDENTIFICATION OF FAILURE POINTS

Table 18-1 (*see* page 153) lists the major workflow steps and lists questions for each step that one might ask to gain insight into the overriding question of whether a foreign body interpretation was provided quickly, clearly, and correctly. In the sequence of tasks that must be accomplished for the successful execution of a foreign body examination, responsibility shifts from RT (acquires and processes images) to radiology resident (interprets and generates preliminary report) to radiology attending (reads over and finalizes report). Many of the less obvious sources of variability, such as 1, 2, 4, 14, 15, 16, and 20 in Table 18-1, hinge on the constantly rotating relationship of who is responsible for what images in radiology departments. For example, at the institution in question, radiologists' work flow depends on reading lists that grow as imaging requests are fulfilled and shrink as reports are dictated and digitally signed using the department's speech recognition software.

The assignment of housestaff and attendings to reading lists changes, often daily or even twice daily. The reading lists are grouped according to a combination of modality, anatomy, equipment location, and time of day. Thus, a resident on the body computerized tomography (CT) rotation might be responsible for covering all nononcological outpatient body CTs acquired between 8:00 A.M. (8:00) and 5:00 P.M. (17:00) during a weekday, but while on call the same resident would cover all CTs, ultrasounds, and emergency department (ED) radiographs acquired between midnight (0:00) and 8:00 A.M. (8:00). The significance of this personnel arrangement for detecting retained surgical objects is that the staff in the OR cannot count on one phone number or reading room to reach a known radiologist around the clock. Conversely, the lists on which radiologists and RTs work do not sort themselves by clinical priority. Interruption, by pager, phone call, or walk-in, is frequently required to move the most time-sensitive examinations to the top of the work list.

The variability entailed by this personnel arrangement played a major role in the shortcomings of the present case. In particular, the second-year RT covering the OR on the Saturday of the closure operation was unable to contact the attending radiologist covering inpatient radiographs because, unknown to the RT, the Saturday attending radiologist was physically located in the mammography reading room and not the inpatient reading room as usual. In addition, the examination was not entered into the radiology information system (RIS) immediately after being obtained as per protocol, so it did not appear on the Saturday radiologist's work list. (It was incidentally discovered in the imaging

---

* Some might argue that the present case represents an adverse event due to medical error and not a close call, because the patient was forced to return to the OR to have the missed sponges removed. On the other hand, the missed sponges were reported on the initial, albeit belated, report of the attending radiologist. The sponges were promptly removed, and the patient did not suffer any adverse outcome from the additional operation, nor did the additional operation contribute to the patient's complicated postoperative course. Therefore, this case is probably best characterized as on the borderline between a close call and an adverse event.

Table 18-1. Typical Work Flow for Obtaining a Radiograph for a Potential Retained Surgical Object

Radiology request is generated in operating room (OR) and communicated to radiologic technologist (RT).	1. Correct request generated in the OR? 2. RT available?
RT exposes imaging plate(s) in OR.	3. RT trained in the imaging policy for foreign body examination? 4. RT's work list manageable at the time of examination? 5. Radiograph technically adequate (kVp, mAs, distance, grid ratio)? 6. Positive control image technically adequate (correct surgical objects, kVp, mAs)? 7. Signal-to-noise not overly limited by obesity and/or known apparatus? 8. Lateral views provided?
RT processes imaging plate(s) and transmits image(s) to image archive.	9. Radiographs processed correctly?
RT calls radiology resident for verbal report.	10. Radiologist available?
Radiology resident loads image(s) from image archive and generates a verbal report.	11. Radiologist trained in interpreting foreign body exams? 12. If report provided verbally, did recipient acknowledge understanding?
RT communicates verbal report to OR personnel.	13. Was radiograph available for examination and discussion with surgeon?
RT registers exam in radiology information system (RIS).	14. Correct exam information placed in RIS?
RIS adds exam to appropriate work list(s).	
Radiology resident selects exam from work list, loads image(s) from image archive, and generates preliminary written report in RIS using speech recognition technology.	15. Unread radiograph appears on reading list covered by a radiologist? 16. Radiologist's work list manageable at time of examination? 17. Normal sequence of displaying, examining, and reporting images followed?
RIS adds preliminary report to attending radiologist work list.	
Attending radiologist selects preliminary report from work list, loads image(s) from image archive, and verifies the report.	18. If resident provided preliminary read, is attending radiologist aware? 19. Radiologist familiar with reason for exam? 20. If critical finding, did radiologist follow protocol for prompt verbal communication with ordering physician?

Figure 18-1. Digital Anteriorposterior (AP) Chest Radiograph

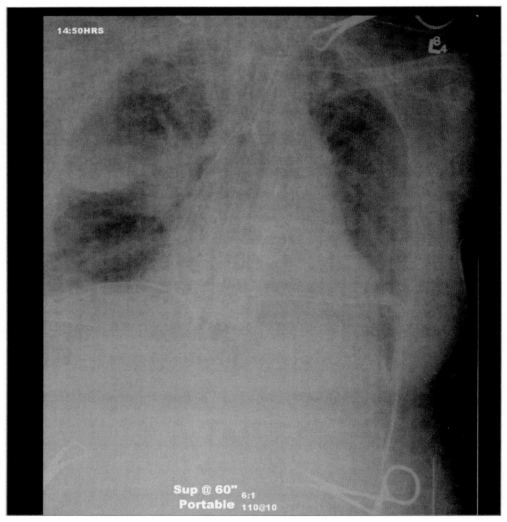

AP chest radiograph demonstrates retained surgical sponge in the medial right costophrenic angle.
Source: Copyright © Johns Hopkins, 2010. Used with permission.

archive by a different attending radiologist on Sunday.) The only radiologist the RT was able to contact at the time of the intraoperative exam on Saturday was the first-year radiology resident physically located in the ED reading room. At the request of the inquiring RT on the phone, the resident examined the digital anteriorposterior (AP) chest radiograph (Figure 18-1, above) and the accompanying positive control image

(*see* Figure 18-2, page 155). The positive control image is a nonstandard image introduced into the foreign body protocol to demonstrate the radiographic appearance of the possibly retained objects identified by an incorrect sponge count; in this case, a sponge and laparotomy pad were imaged (*see* Figure 18-2). The resident used nonstandard terminology ("suture" and "ribbon" markers) to describe the

Figure 18-2. Accompanying Positive Control Image

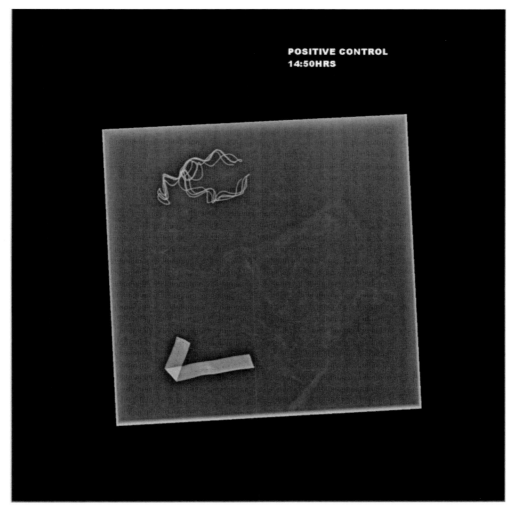

POSITIVE CONTROL
14:50HRS

Positive control radiograph demonstrates appearance of possibly retained sponge (top) and laparotomy pad (bottom).
Source: Copyright © Johns Hopkins, 2010. Used with permission.

findings in the chest radiograph and did not specifically express the presence of a "sponge." The RT informally repeated parts of this description and communicated a negative finding to the surgeons in the OR. The resident did not generate a written report of the examination. He did not contact the attending radiologist. The senior attending radiologist who eventually provided a written interpretation the next day

(Sunday) was actually not on any work schedule but occasionally volunteers his time on weekends to help with the considerable inpatient volume. In summary, failure points included items 10, 12, 14, 15, and 18 (Table 18-1) related to work schedules, reading lists, and report formats. Although these failure points may sound arcane to nonradiologists, they were central to the present case.

The case also exposed three latent errors that are vulnerable to exaggeration by inexperience: items 11 (resident training), 19 (familiarity with patient history), and 17 (examination sequence; Table 18-1). First, the resident training program does not offer pre-call testing, and foreign body examinations are not part of the didactic curriculum of orientation and morning conferences. Second, the patient in the present case had a complex medical and surgical history, with initial postoperative images demonstrating numerous lines and tubes and intra-aortic balloon, open sternotomy, and intentionally placed intrathoracic sponges. The RT calling the ED resident could not have been expected to know or communicate this complex history, and the time pressure to provide a real-time response may have limited the radiologist's ability to extract the relevant information from the electronic medical record and other clinical sources. Third, such interruption and time pressure can also cause some radiologists, especially those with less experience, to deviate from the disciplined, thorough, and time-consuming search pattern necessary to look at all the relevant information contained in images and to understand and communicate its significance.

Finally, the case illustrated several factors known to increase the risk of retained surgical objects (items 7 and 8, Table 18-1). First, the value of the lateral chest radiograph for detecting pericardial sponges has been reported,[4] but a lateral view was not obtained in the present case because it is not considered standard practice. Second, a landmark case-control study of risk factors for retained surgical objects identified emergent procedures, unplanned surgical changes, and higher body-mass index—all factors present in this case—as factors associated with an 8.4- to 1.1-fold increase in risk of retention.[5]

CORRECTIVE ACTIONS

In response to this case, changes in the system of foreign body readings were made. RTs are now required to contact only attending radiologists

for real-time interpretation of foreign body examinations. A Web site is being developed to provide integrated, up-to-date listings of covering radiologists. Policies to encourage direct communication between surgeon and radiologist are also being explored. The positive control protocol designed to illustrate the radiographic appearance of missing objects will be maintained on every foreign body examination, although this practice is not common in peer institutions. Labeling the positive controls using standardized surgical vocabulary would have facilitated communication in the present case. To learn the radiographic appearance and terminology of a wide variety of surgical instruments and sponges, interested readers may consult the pictorial essay by Wolfson and colleagues[6] or consult a useful Internet resource provided by the University of California at San Francisco.[7]

Some centers have adopted technological innovations, such as bar coding of sponges, to prevent postoperative retention. The use of bar coding has increased the sensitivity for miscounts and the total time devoted to counting (8.6 minutes without bar coding and 12.0 minutes with, on average), but no study has yet been powered to detect an effect on retained sponges.[8–10] Currently available technological solutions would seem to have been unlikely to help in the present case. Indeed, despite the multiple efficiencies of digital imaging and remote access, the work flow and communication errors this case illustrates probably would not have happened in an earlier time when limited technology required side-by-side consultations between radiologists and clinicians in central viewing locations. As we look forward, we would do well to remember the value of human relationships within systems that operate optimally to prevent error.

References

1. Hyslop J.W., Maull K.I.: Natural history of the retained surgical sponge. *South Med J* 75:657–660, Jun. 1982.

2. Joint Commission on Accreditation of Healthcare Organizations: *Comprehensive Accreditation Manual for Hospitals: The Official Handbook,* Update 4, 2005. Oakbrook Terrace, IL: Joint Commission Resources.

3. Dagi T.F., et al.: Preventable errors in the operating room—Part 2: Retained foreign objects, sharps injuries, and wrong site surgery. *Curr Probl Surg* 44:352–381, Jun. 2007.

4. Scott W.W., Beal D.P., Wheeler P.S.: The retained intrapericardial sponge: Value of the lateral chest radiograph. *AJR Am J Roentgenol* 171:595–597, Sep. 1998.

5. Gawande A.A., et al.: Risk factors for retained instruments and sponges after surgery. *N Engl J Med* 348:229–235, Jan. 16, 2003.

6. Wolfson K.A., et al.: Imaging of surgical paraphernalia: What belongs in the patient and what does not. *Radiographics* 20:1665–1673, Nov.–Dec. 2000.

7. University of California–San Francisco School of Medicine, Department of Radiology & Biomedical Imaging: *Imaging of Retained Surgical Objects in the Abdomen/Pelvis.* http://www.radiology.ucsf.edu/patients/objects (accessed Aug. 6, 2010).

8. Greenberg C.C., et al.: Bar-coding surgical sponges to improve safety: A randomized controlled trial. *Ann Surg* 247:612–616, Apr. 2008.

9. Egorova N.N., et al.: Managing the prevention of retained surgical instruments: What is the value of counting? *Ann Surg* 247:13–18, Jan. 2008.

10. Christian C.K., et al.: A prospective study of patient safety in the operating room. *Surgery* 139:159–173, Feb. 2006.

CHAPTER 19

Geriatrics: Improving Medication Safety in the Nursing Home Setting—The Case of Warfarin

Jerry H. Gurwitz, M.D.; Terry Field, D.Sc.; Jennifer Tjia, M.D., M.S.C.E.; Kathleen Mazor, Ed.D.

CASE

An 85-year-old female nursing home resident with a history of atrial fibrillation, stroke, dementia, and hypertension was receiving chronic therapy with warfarin. Her primary care provider had been dosing her warfarin to maintain her at an International Normalized Ratio (INR) of 2–2.5. One evening, a nurse called a covering physician to indicate that the patient had developed a fever. The patient was initiated on antibiotic therapy to treat a presumed urinary tract infection. The next morning, the primary care provider was called with the previous day's INR, which was 1.75. The daily warfarin dosage was increased from 4 mg to 5 mg per day. The provider was not notified of the antibiotic ordered the previous evening by the covering physician. One week later, the INR came back at 13.8, and a different covering physician was notified. That evening's warfarin dose was held. An INR the following day was 16.1. No bleeding had been noted by the nursing staff. The primary care physician was notified, and oral vitamin K was administered for three days, with a reduction in the INR to 0.9. The patient's primary care provider wrote in the nursing home record that "warfarin will not be reinitiated because anticoagulation has been difficult to control for unclear reasons."

ANALYSIS

An analysis of the case reveals a number of important observations:

1. The covering physician, who was not familiar with the patient, was not informed that the patient was being treated with warfarin (and also did not ask).

2. An important drug interaction (warfarin–antibiotic) was not recognized by the nursing staff.

3. The primary care provider was not notified of the antibiotic ordered by the covering physician—important information that would have informed decision making regarding subsequent dosing and monitoring of warfarin.

4. No one ever recognized that the high INR levels were actually the result of multiple errors.

5. In the end, the patient was denied warfarin therapy, which if managed appropriately would substantially reduce her risk of a disabling stroke related to atrial fibrillation.

WARFARIN SAFETY IN THE LONG TERM CARE SETTING

An increasing body of research has provided compelling evidence of safety problems with warfarin therapy in the long term care setting. As many as 1.6 million Americans, most of whom are elderly, currently reside in nursing homes, and approximately 12% receive chronic anticoagulant therapy with warfarin. Concerns related to the risks of warfarin anticoagulation therapy are intensified in the long term care setting because elderly residents of nursing homes are among the most frail patients in the geriatric population.[1–3] The prevalence of medical conditions for which warfarin is indicated increases with advancing age, yet the management of anticoagulation therapy with warfarin in this population can be especially challenging. Factors such as aging, comorbid conditions, diet, and interacting medications can affect the pharmacodynamics and pharmacokinetics of warfarin, thus making dosing and monitoring more complex in older patients.[4] Although oral direct thrombin inhibitors and other new oral agents hold promise as less-complicated anticoagulants, warfarin is likely to remain a commonly employed treatment in the care of many frail elderly patients for the foreseeable future.

A recent study assessed the safety of warfarin therapy in 25 nursing homes located in the state of Connecticut.[1] Outcomes of interest included close calls, which were defined as incidents in which the INR value was ≥ 4.5 and no injury to the patient occurred but in which an error in warfarin management was identified. (The case provided meets this definition.) According to this study definition, not all INR values of ≥ 4.5 were considered to be close calls because high INRs can occur with no obvious cause, despite careful dosing and monitoring of warfarin. The 4.5 threshold level for the INR was chosen because various studies have demonstrated that the risk of intracranial hemorrhage increases dramatically with INRs above this level.[5,6] Under this definition, a rate of 6.6 close calls per 100 resident-months on warfarin therapy was observed. In addition, a rate of 5.4 preventable warfarin-related injuries (primarily bleeds) per 100 resident-months was found.

Errors in warfarin management were determined to occur most commonly at the prescribing and monitoring stages of warfarin management.

Monitoring errors include inadequate laboratory monitoring of warfarin therapy and a delayed response to high INR levels. Prescribing errors include wrong dose (with respect to the INR) and a known drug interaction.

If the findings of this study are generalized to all U.S. nursing home residents on warfarin, as many as 34,000 fatal, life-threatening, or serious warfarin-related injuries per year can be expected to occur, the majority of which may be preventable. Close calls are even more common. Many nursing home residents on warfarin are frequently subjected to a very high risk of bleeding because of high INR values caused by errors in warfarin management.

These distressing high rates of preventable warfarin-related injuries and close calls highlight the need for effective strategies to improve warfarin safety in the nursing home setting. Unfortunately, leading-edge, high-technology–based strategies to alleviate problems in prescribing and monitoring of warfarin are not currently amenable to incorporation into most nursing homes. For example, the information technology infrastructure required to support computerized provider order entry (CPOE) with clinical decision support is almost nonexistent in the majority of nursing homes in the United States.[7,8] Few long term care facilities have implemented such systems because of cost, complexity, and logistical challenges as well as uncertainty about how effective these systems actually are for reducing drug-related injuries after implementation.[9] However, even if systems-level changes such as CPOE with clinical decision support are not feasible at the present time, efforts to improve the effectiveness of communication between nursing staff and physicians about the use of warfarin therapy deserve consideration. Physicians spend very little time in the nursing home setting, and therapeutic decision making commonly occurs over the telephone during brief conversations between physician and nurse, as apparent in the provided case.

IMPORTANCE OF COMMUNICATION AMONG HEALTH CARE PROVIDERS

As in the case provided, many of the safety issues concerning the use of warfarin in the long term care setting are associated with suboptimal communication between nursing staff and physicians. Clear and complete communication between health care providers is a prerequisite for safe patient management and is a key component of The Joint Commission's National Patient Safety Goals for long term care.[10] Communication failures are at the root of more than 60% of sentinel events reported to The Joint Commission.[11] Communication between health care workers is an essential component of information flow in all health care settings, and growing evidence indicates that errors in communication have an impact on patient safety.[12] A recent study explored the barriers to optimal nurse–physician communication on the telephone related to health care delivery in the nursing home setting.[13] "Feeling hurried by the physician" was the most frequent barrier reported by nurses, followed by "having difficulty reaching the physician." Respondents indicated that nurses needed to be brief and prepared with relevant clinical information when communicating with physicians and that physicians needed to be more open to listening.

Nurse preparedness is a key target for improving the effectiveness of nurse–physician communication in the long term care setting, especially related to the care of patients receiving warfarin. Clear communication about patients receiving warfarin may improve quality of care and patient outcomes, as illustrated in the case. Tools that provide a structure for telephone communication and that inform the content of the key clinical information necessary for reporting various clinical scenarios to physicians are essential to improving clinical communication. Such tools may help overcome differences in communication styles between nurses and physicians that may be a major factor contributing to interdisciplinary communication difficulties and failures.

USE OF STRUCTURED COMMUNICATION TECHNIQUES

Structured techniques such as Situation–Background–Assessment–Recommendation (SBAR), which format communication into a highly distilled–content and quick-delivery format, are increasingly being used within various health care settings to address the challenges both of providing complete content and time constraints.

Recently, an SBAR-based approach to improving nurse–physician communication related to residents on warfarin in nursing homes was implemented in the state of Connecticut.[14] The overall initiative included customized methods of identifying and highlighting residents taking warfarin in the nursing home, systematic procedures for tracking and communicating INR results, a targeted training program for nursing staff focused on using the SBAR approach for telephone-based communication, and message templates (SBAR forms) to standardize telephone communication about nursing home residents on warfarin between the nursing staff and the physician (*see* Figure 19-1, page 162).

Nurses were encouraged to collect information and consider their own assessment of the nursing home resident's situation before placing calls to physicians to report (1) INR values, (2) indicators of possible adverse events in residents receiving warfarin, and (3) infections such as urinary tract infections that may lead to the prescribing of interacting medications. The SBAR approach may provide a promising alternative or supplement, and it may complement other interventions that have been developed to improve warfarin management, including the use of computerized dosing algorithms, specialized anticoagulation services, and pharmacist-based management.

Figure 19-1. Situation–Background–Assessment–Recommended Action (SBAR) Template for Telephone Communication for Resident on Warfarin

Telephone communication for resident on warfarin

Date: _____ Time: _____

Originator of call: _____ **I am calling about warfarin patient <resident name >, one of Dr. <MD name>'s patients at <nursing home>.**
The issue I am calling about *(select from the following options)* is:

New INR Result	Change in Condition	Fall without injury/ Minor skin tear

INR result: _____	☐ fall with potential injury
	☐ skin tear with potential complication
	☐ fever
	☐ ANY bleeding or bruising
	
	☐ other injury:
	☐ other medication issue:
	
	☐ abnormal UA test results
	
	☐ abnormal chest Xray results
	
	☐ other, specify:
		☐ fall
		  ☐ no injury noted
		  ☐ no bleeding/bruising
		
		☐ skin tear
		  ☐ no redness noted
		  ☐ no drainage
		  ☐ size: apx ____ cm
		If calling for one of these situations, skip to the Recommended Action section

Situation

Last 2 INR test results

INR Date	INR	Dosing Pattern		Date from	Date to
_____	_____	Current _____	mg	_____	_____
_____	_____	Previous _____	mg	_____	_____

Indication for warfarin: ☐ AFIB ☐ DVT/PE ☐ MECHANICAL HEART VALVE ☐ OTHER _____

Other important medications the resident is taking (any in past 3 days):
  ☐ antibiotics:
  ☐ NSAIDs (e.g. ibuprofen, motrin, piroxicam, indocin, meloxicam, etc):
  ☐ aspirin or Plavix (clopidogrel)

Background

☐ No concerns

☐ I'm uncomfortable about this patient because: ☐ high INR   ☐ bleeding/bruising   ☐ other
        ☐ low INR

Assessment

Say what you think would be helpful or needs to be done, which might include:
  ☐ No new orders needed

  INR/Warfarin Recommendations
  ☐ Tell me if the warfarin dose should be changed or held
  ☐ Tell me when to repeat the INR   ☐ In 3 days?   ☐ In 7 days?   ☐ Other?

  Other Recommendations
  ☐ Tell me whether to order an antibiotic
      ☐ If so, should we adjust the warfarin dose?
          ☐ When should we schedule the next INR test?
  ☐ Tell me whether to order other tests

  ☐ Should we send the patient to the emergency department?

When do you want us to call again (or under what conditions)?

ENTER ALL ORDERS DIRECTLY ONTO THE PHYSICIAN ORDER SHEET

Response from MD or office
Who responded: _____ Date: _____ Time: _____

Recommended Action Based on Nurse Assessment

Signature _____ Date_____

Note: Training materials are available at Centers for Education and Research on Therapeutics: *Clinician-Consumer Health Advisory Network: Warfarin Communication Toolkit for Nurses.* http://www.chainonline.org/content.cfm?content_id=1395 (accessed Oct. 29, 2010). INR, international normalized ratio; UA, urinalysis; apx, approximately; AFIB, atrial fibrillation; DVT/PE, deep vein thrombosis/pulmonary embolism; NSAID, nonsteroidal anti-inflammatory drug; MD, physician.

Source: Meyers Primary Care Institute, Worcester, Massachusetts. Used with permission.

Because quality of communication has the potential to affect quality of medication management in nursing homes, an innovative, low-technology intervention to improve use of warfarin in nursing homes by implementing structured communication seems especially attractive. SBAR establishes a standardized structure for medical communication, ensuring that critical information that directly affects clinician decision making is transmitted in a predictable and reliable manner. Its use is particularly well suited to telephone communication in the nursing home, where medication management involves the critical flow of information between nursing staff and off-site physicians. Frequently, decisions about warfarin dosing and INR measurement are made during brief telephone conversations with inadequate information about prior INR values, warfarin doses, and interacting medications. The SBAR template guides the nurse through communication in a consistent fashion, using standard language. This low-technology approach may ultimately serve as a model for improving the safety of other medications associated with high rates of preventable adverse drug events and close calls (for example, antipsychotics) and for improving the overall safety of frail elderly patients residing in nursing homes, who are at very high risk for medication-related problems.[15]

References

1. Gurwitz J.H., et al.: The safety of warfarin therapy in the nursing home setting. *Am J Med* 120:539–544, Jun. 2007. Epub Apr. 26, 2007.
2. McCormick D., et al.: Prevalence and quality of warfarin use for patients with atrial fibrillation in the long-term care setting. *Arch Intern Med* 161:2458–2463, Nov. 12, 2001.
3. Gurwitz J.H., et al.: Atrial fibrillation and stroke prevention with warfarin in the long-term care setting. *Arch Intern Med* 157:978–984, May 12, 1997.
4. Gurwitz J.H., et al.: Aging and the anticoagulant response to warfarin therapy. *Ann Intern Med* 116:901–904, Jun. 1992.
5. Hylek E., Singer D.E.: Risk factors for intracranial hemorrhage in outpatients taking warfarin. *Ann Intern Med* 120:897–902, Jun. 1, 1994.
6. Fang M.C., et al.: Advanced age, anticoagulation intensity, and risk for intracranial hemorrhage among patients taking warfarin for atrial fibrillation. *Ann Intern Med* 141:745–752, Nov. 16, 2004.
7. Rochon P.A., et al.: Computerized physician order entry with clinical decision support in the long-term care setting: Insights from the Baycrest Centre for Geriatric Care. *J Am Geriatr Soc* 53:1780–1789, Oct. 2005.
8. Subramanian S., et al.: Computerized physician order entry with clinical decision support in long-term care facilities: Costs and benefits to stakeholders. *J Am Geriatr Soc* 55:1451–1457, Sep. 2007.
9. Gurwitz J.H., et al.: Effect of computerized provider order entry with clinical decision support on adverse drug events in the long-term care setting. *J Am Geriatr Soc* 56:2225–2233, Dec. 2008.
10. The Joint Commission: *2008 National Patient Safety Goals—Long-Term Care Program.* http://www.jointcommission.org/PatientSafety/NationalPatientSafetyGoals/08_ltc_npsgs.htm (accessed Jun. 17, 2009; site now discontinued).
11. The Joint Commission: *Sentinel Event Statistics.* http://www.jointcommission.org/SentinelEvents/Statistics (accessed Sep. 24, 2010).
12. Schmidt I.K., Svarstad B.L.: Nurse–physician communication and quality of drug use in Swedish nursing homes. *Soc Sci Med* 54:1767–1777, Jun. 2002.
13. Tjia J., et al.: Nurse–physician communication in the long-term care setting: Perceived barriers and impact on patient safety. *J Patient Saf* 5:145–152, Sep. 2009.
14. Field T.S., et al.: Randomized trial of a warfarin communication protocol for nursing homes: An SBAR-based approach. *Am J Med*, in press.
15. Gurwitz J.H., et al.: The incidence of adverse drug events in two large academic long-term care facilities. *Am J Med* 118:251–258, Mar. 2005.

CHAPTER 20

Laboratory Medicine/Pathology: Improving Diagnostic Safety in Papanicolaou Smears

Lee Hilborne, M.D., M.P.H.; Maria Olvera, M.D.; Dereck C. Counter, M.B.A.; Toni L. Kick, Ph.D.; Stephen C. Suffin, M.D.

CASE

Ms. G, an ostensibly well 39-year-old woman, recently relocated to a city where she has no physician. She presented to Dr. O with the intent of establishing a doctor–patient relationship. She had no significant contributory history. She was newly divorced and had not been sexually active for 10 months. Dr. O is a family medicine physician who has been in solo practice for 24 years.

As part of the evaluation, Dr. O performed a Papanicolaou (Pap) smear using one of the standard liquid-based cytology processes. The Pap smear was sent to the local medium-sized hospital clinical laboratory that Dr. O has used for years. The Pap smear was read by a certified cytotechnologist and cytopathologist as showing atypical glandular cells (AGCs). There were no squamous cell abnormalities. Although the laboratory offers human papillomavirus (HPV) testing, Dr. O did not request this test.

The report was received by the medical assistant in Dr. O's office, who was instructed to triage reports—to file most cases but to show Dr. O any case that suggested a possible squamous cell abnormality (for example, atypical squamous cells of uncertain significance [ASCUS], a low- or high-grade squamous epithelial lesion [SIL], or any report with the word *carcinoma*). If the

medical assistant was unsure, she was instructed to ask Dr. O. However, because there was no mention of squamous atypia, the medical assistant filed the report and anticipated that Ms. G would return the following year for a routine visit. Ms. G assumed that because she did not hear anything from Dr. O's office, there was nothing in her laboratory findings that required any follow-up.

About two months later, Ms. G was involved in a car accident. She was taken to the local hospital that had performed her previous Pap smear. A workup for serious injury resulting from the accident was negative. However, the emergency department (ED) physician spotted the previous Pap results in the hospital laboratory information system and asked Ms. G about the follow-up to her recent Pap smear. Ms. G indicated that she had not heard back from Dr. O and that she had therefore assumed that everything was okay.

Ms. G was discharged from the ED with a recommendation that she see Dr. O within the next week and that there be a complete assessment of her abnormal Pap smear by a gynecologist. On the basis of the initial findings, the gynecologist repeated the Pap smear and also performed a complete colposcopic examination, took several cervical biopsies, and performed an endocervical curettage. The curettage and biopsy were sent to a larger laboratory trusted by the gynecologist. The ectocervical biopsies showed mild squamous atypia consistent with HPV, yet the endocervical curettage was positive for an endocervical adeno-carcinoma. The Pap smear specimen was ana-lyzed for HPV and found to be positive for high-risk HPV subtypes. Ms. G underwent definitive treatment for the carcinoma, and at three years she has had no evidence of recurrence.

BACKGROUND

Laboratory diagnostics play a key role in guiding patient care and ensuring that patients receive the right evaluations and treatments. Given that up to 60% to 70% of clinical decisions are influ-enced by laboratory tests,[1] it is safe to conclude that many close calls and errors in clinical practice involve, to some degree, laboratory diagnostic testing.

Providing safe, high-quality, and effective labora-tory services is not new to the laboratory profes-sion. In fact, the importance of examining and reducing errors and close calls was recognized early on by the laboratory profession when it began to examine analytical quality. In the 1920s, the American Society for Clinical Pathology began a voluntary proficiency testing (PT) program that was the predecessor of the College of American Pathologists' current PT program.[2] The proficiency testing program focuses primarily on analytic quality, the second of the three phases of what is now known as the *total testing process*.[3,4]

The total testing process is a cyclical process that provides a framework for assessing the quality of laboratory services.[4] The process is divided into three main phases, as follows:

1. In the initial or pre-analytic phase, the need for a test is determined, the test is ordered, and the patient is identified; the specimen is then collected and transported to the laboratory.

2. Next, the specimen is prepared and then ana-lyzed during the analytic phase.

3. In the final, or postanalytic, phase, the results are reported to the individual who ordered the test, and appropriate action or interven-tion is undertaken.

Raab and colleagues, who evaluated the frequen-cies of cancer diagnostic errors, extrapolated their findings to the entire United States and concluded that, at a minimum, every year 150,000 patients have a Pap smear–gynecologic histology diagnostic error, and another 155,000 have a nongynecologic (for example, urinary tract, lung, breast cytology–histology correla-tions) diagnostic error.[5]

Opportunities for close calls and errors—and performance improvement—exist in all phases of the total testing process. Because of the com-mitment of laboratories to, and their success in, improving quality, the greatest opportunities for improvement now exist in the pre- and postana-lytic phases, which account for 46%–68% and 19%–47% of errors, respectively.[6–11] Although the laboratory has nearly complete control of the analytic phase, the pre- and postanalytic phases involve the interaction of the laboratory with its "clients."

ATYPICAL GLANDULAR CELLS IN CLINICAL PRACTICE

The mean reporting rate in the United States for AGC on Pap tests is 0.3%.[12,13] Although cervical squamous cancer has declined during the past several decades, HPV-related glandular lesions have increased.[14] Collection by liquid-based cytology methods has also increased the fre-quency of detection of AGC on Pap tests com-pared with conventional screening. Although reflex HPV DNA testing is unacceptable for use in guiding definitive treatment of AGC,[15] it can be helpful in the initial workup of AGC in the detection of precancerous/cancerous lesions, especially in women younger than 50 years of age.[16]

Although in most studies the majority of AGC on Pap smears turns out to be negative for histologic abnormalities, the clinically significant minority (29%–38%) represents a variety of high-grade lesions—most commonly squamous lesions (highlighting the difficulty in accurate classification of AGC, as was reflected in the case provided), followed by endometrial lesions, endocervical lesions, and, least commonly, nonuterine lesions.[12,17,18] Other studies have reported significant pathology in up to 83% of AGUS (atypical glandular cells of undetermined significance) cases, depending on the study criteria used in the classification.[12,19] However, there are significant differences by age group in predicting the most likely sites for disease. In addition, there are also statistically significant differences associated with the different modifiers (for example, favor neoplasia, favor endometrial origin) used to describe AGC. Regardless of these factors, the 2006 American Society for Colposcopy and Cervical Pathology (ASCCP) consensus guidelines for AGUS lesions in all women are the same, including multiple modalities to address the many possibilities.[15] All AGUS subcategories (except atypical endometrial cells) are followed by colposcopy, endocervical sampling, HPV DNA testing, and (if > 35 years of age or at risk) endometrial sampling. Initial management of atypical endometrial cells includes both endocervical and endometrial sampling, with subsequent colposcopy if no lesion is identified.

On investigation, data show a discrepancy between the number of Pap smears that have AGUS and subsequent histologic sampling.[20] This may be due to the limited information available to investigators, with short follow-up—typically averaging six months—observed in the published literature. The data are limited with respect to whether untimely follow-up occurred because of patient noncompliance or clinician failure to recall the patient. Some studies suggest that this is due to a combination of providers' lack of familiarity with the guidelines and

"patients' reluctance to undergo these somewhat invasive and painful procedures."[20(p. 1067)]

Given the rarity of an AGC diagnosis, lower-volume nongynecology providers are less likely to encounter patients with AGC. When they do, they may simply treat AGC as if the diagnosis was ASCUS or remain undecided regarding treatment and plan to repeat the Pap smear at the next routine interval to see if the abnormality resolves. Frequently, women without risk factors have their Pap smears rereviewed by a second cytopathologist to confirm the initial AGUS diagnosis, potentially eliminating the need for further intervention other than repeating the Pap smear. However, this should be done only after initial management according to the guidelines and not as an alternative to following the guidelines (for example, to avoid patient discomfort).

In the case provided, the medical assistant, not having seen an AGC case before and not having been told specifically to flag this diagnosis for further review, was unable to recognize the AGC category as a flag for further follow-up. Anecdotal results were gathered from telephone calls to the offices of 22 physicians whose patients received diagnoses of AGC. Although most patients received follow-up at three months, there were five patients for whom the offices had neither followed up nor made plans for timely follow-up either by the physician or by referral to a specialist. On the basis of previous studies, one would expect to find one or two of these five patients harboring significant disease. Four of these five patients were seen by a primary care physician in community practice; one patient was seen by an obstetrician/gynecologist. These anecdotal findings suggest how important it is that physicians and other providers who refer Pap smears to laboratories understand the spectrum of diagnoses and the necessary follow-up for resultant findings.

In addition, Ms. G did not follow up with her primary care physician to make sure that her results were within the established reference ranges. As part of national and international efforts to improve the safety of health care, patients are encouraged to follow up when they have diagnostic tests. The Agency for Healthcare Research and Quality lists 20 tips for patients to help prevent medical errors; one of those tips is "If you have a test, don't assume that no news is good news. Ask about the results."[21]

Glandular lesions can present major challenges in all three phases of the total testing process, as follows:

1. *Pre-analytic:* Difficulty in obtaining an adequate screening sample, especially in endocervical glandular lesions located high in the endocervical canal

2. *Analytic:* Cytologic interpretation, including conveying information in a way that is understandable to the reader

3. *Postanalytic:* Interpretation of the management algorithm (for example, false-negative colposcopy examination and lack of familiarity with the guidelines for follow-up)

WHAT CAN LABORATORIES, CLINICIANS, AND PATIENTS DO TO PREVENT CLOSE CALLS IN SIMILAR CASES?

The close call in this case was related to a postanalytic error. Specifically, although the clinician provided an adequate sample and history and the laboratory released a report with a clear diagnosis, the patient did not initially receive the follow-up that guidelines indicate she should have received. Evidence from one hospital suggests, at least for clinical laboratory testing, that only 55% of the results for urgent laboratory tests requested by an ED were accessed in a timely manner.[22] Although the exact numbers may differ for cytology results, it is reasonable to assume that not all findings will receive the critical review and assessment they warrant.

Improving communication between laboratories and clinicians is central to improving patient safety related to laboratory use.[3,23,24] As more and more tests become available, clinicians are increasingly ordering laboratory assays outside their field of primary expertise or are receiving interpretations that reflect new understanding of disease. Clinicians may therefore lack the knowledge base to correctly order and interpret tests.[25] Inappropriate use of laboratory tests and incorrect application of the results can result in poor patient management, increased cost, and adverse clinical outcomes.[26] Laboratories and clinicians must together realize that the total testing process concludes only after the clinician has reviewed and responded to the test results.

With respect to reports with high-risk diagnoses, a number of options exist to ensure that patients receive timely follow-up. Laboratories can telephone physicians to ensure that the report is received, understood, and reviewed. Some laboratories have implemented anatomic pathology "critical values" to parallel those used for critical clinical laboratory results.[27] Although initial studies of anatomic pathology critical values show that they have not included atypical glandular lesions on the critical lists, this is one strategy to ensure communication with the clinician without dramatically increasing call frequency. Some laboratories provide a comment with a recommendation for the usual next steps in management (for example, consider tissue sampling of the endocervix/endometrium if clinically appropriate). Laboratories may also elect to summarize ASCCP guidelines on reports of patients whose Pap smears contain AGC. Whereas many clinicians appreciate this information on laboratory reports, others caution that any guidance should be of a general nature to avoid a situation where a definitive recommendation is made that may be contraindicated in a given setting, either because of the patient's condition or the patient's personal preferences. It is also incumbent on those rendering diagnoses to use standard and consistent terminology to ensure that interpretation is not clouded by obscure terms.[5] For example, in the case provided, the laboratory elected to consistently include the following phrase on all its laboratory reports:

> AGC are identified in this cytology specimen. The exact clinical behavior of these cells cannot be conclusively determined from this procedure. They may be of little consequence; however, they may be suggestive of an underlying neoplastic process. If clinically indicated, timely definitive evaluation is necessary to resolve the nature of our findings.

The hospital pathologists have a good relationship with members of their medical staff. The provided case was also presented at a medical staff patient safety conference.

Finally, laboratories that are part of closed practices (for example, staff-model health maintenance organization, academic center), wherein patients who receive an initial diagnosis are likely to receive follow-up from the same institution, can review their records to determine whether abnormal findings have in fact prompted necessary follow-up.

Many industry-leading laboratories and other health care organizations use, for example, the Six Sigma methodology to systematically improve quality, eliminate defects, and drive processes toward perfection.[28] At the core of Six Sigma is variation reduction. The general medical treatment process involves multiple interactions between patients, physicians, nurses, laboratories, assistants, and administrative staff. The opportunity for variation is present in any multiple-interaction process. With respect to the case provided, formal performance improvement methods could improve communication between laboratories and clinicians by reducing the variation in terminology (AGC category), process (understanding necessary follow-up), calculations (management algorithm interpretation),

sampling (adequate screening sample), and individuals (not seeing the diagnosis before).

CONCLUSIONS

Laboratory medicine—both anatomic pathology and clinical pathology—provides an important link in ensuring high-quality, effective patient care. To fully realize the contributions that laboratory diagnostics has to offer for reducing the risk of close calls or actual patient harm, laboratories must work closely with their clinical colleagues to make sure the right tests are ordered, that analyses are performed accurately and timely, and that patients receive the follow-up required on the basis of the findings reported and the patient's individual needs and preferences.

References

1. Forsman R.W.: Why is the laboratory an afterthought for managed care organizations? *Clin Chem* 42:813–816, May 1996.
2. Rodriguez F.H. Jr., Ball J.R.: The American Society for Clinical Pathology: The pathology society of "firsts." *Lab Med* 38:595–601, Oct. 1, 2007.
3. McCay L., Lemer C., Wu A.W.: Laboratory safety and the WHO World Alliance for Patient Safety. *Clin Chim Acta* 404:6–11, Jun. 2009. Enub Mar. 18, 2009.
4. Boone D.J.: Opening Remarks. Institute on Critical Issues in Health Laboratory Practice: Managing for Better Health, Atlanta, Sep. 24, 2007.
5. Raab S.S., et al.: Clinical impact and frequency of anatomic pathology errors in cancer diagnosis. *Cancer* 104:2205–2213, Nov. 15, 2005.
6. Plebani M., Carraro P.: Mistakes in a stat laboratory: Types and frequency. *Clin Chem* 43(8 Pt. 1):1348–1351, 1997.
7. Bonini P., et al.: Errors in laboratory medicine. *Clin Chem* 48:691–698, May 2002.
8. Plebani M.: Errors in laboratory medicine and patient safety: The road ahead. *Clin Chem Lab Med* 45(6):700–707, 2007.
9. Carraro P., Plebani M.: Errors in a stat laboratory: Types and frequencies 10 years later. *Clin Chem* 53:1338–1342, Jul. 2007. Epub May 24, 2007.
10. Lippi G., et al.: Preanalytical variability: The dark side of the moon in laboratory testing. *Clin Chem Lab Med* 44(4):358–365, 2006.
11. Plebani M.: Errors in clinical laboratories or errors in laboratory medicine? *Clin Chem Lab Med* 44(6):750–759, 2006.
12. Schnatz P.F., et al.: Clinical significance of atypical glandular cells on cervical cytology. *Obstet Gynecol* 107:701–708, Mar. 2006.

13. Nora L.C., et al.: Cytomorphological criteria, subclassifications of endocervical glandular cell abnormalities, and histopathological outcome: A frequency study. *Diagn Cytopathol*, 38:806–810, Nov. 2010. Epub Jan. 8, 2010.

14. Chute D.J., Lim H., Kong C.S.: BD FocalPoint slide profiler performance with atypical glandular cells on SurePath Papanicolaou smears. *Cancer Cytopathol* 118:68–74, Apr. 25, 2010.

15. Apgar B.S., et al.: Update on ASCCP consensus guidelines for abnormal cervical screening tests and cervical histology. *Am Fam Physician* 80:147–155, Jul. 15, 2009.

16. Zhao C., Florea A., Austin R.M.: Clinical utility of adjunctive high-risk human papillomavirus DNA testing in women with Papanicolaou test findings of atypical glandular cells. *Arch Pathol Lab Med* 134:103–108, Jan. 2010.

17. Sharpless K.E., et al.: Dysplasia associated with atypical glandular cells on cervical cytology. *Obstet Gynecol* 105:494–500, Mar. 2005.

18. Zhao C., et al.: Histologic follow-up results in 662 patients with Pap test findings of atypical glandular cells: Results from a large academic womens hospital laboratory employing sensitive screening methods. *Gynecol Oncol* 383–389, Sep. 2009.

19. Wood M.D., Horst J.A., Bibbo M.: Weeding atypical glandular cell look-alikes from the true atypical lesions in liquid-based Pap tests: A review. *Diagn Cytopathol* 35:12–17, Jan. 2007.

20. Massad L.S., et al.: Histologic correlates of glandular abnormalities in cervical cytology among women with human immunodeficiency virus. *Obstet Gynecol* 114:1063–1068, Nov. 2009.

21. Agency for Healthcare Research and Quality: *Patient Fact Sheet: 20 Tips to Help Prevent Medical Errors.* 2000. http://www.ahrq.gov/consumer/20tips.pdf (accessed Apr. 25, 2010).

22. Kilpatrick E.S., Holding S.: Use of computer terminals on wards to access emergency test results: A retrospective study. *BMJ* 322:1101–1103, May 5, 2001.

23. Plebani M., Lippi G.: To err is human. To misdiagnose might be deadly. *Clin Biochem* 43:1–3, Jan. 2010. Epub Jul. 14, 2009.

24. Plebani M., Lippi G.: Improving the post-analytical phase. *Clin Chem Lab Med* 48:435–436, Apr. 2010.

25. Kratz A., Laposata M.: Enhanced clinical consulting—Moving toward the core competencies of laboratory professionals. *Clin Chim Acta* 319:117–125, May 21, 2002.

26. van Walraven C., Naylor C.D.: Do we know what inappropriate laboratory utilization is? A systematic review of laboratory clinical audits. *JAMA* 280:550–558, Aug. 12, 1998.

27. Pereira T.C., et al.: A multi-institutional survey of critical diagnoses (critical values) in surgical pathology and cytology. *Am J Clin Pathol* 130:731–735, Nov. 2008.

28. Gras J.M., Philippe M.: Application of the Six Sigma concept in clinical laboratories: A review. *Clin Chem Lab Med* 45(6):789–796, 2007.

Index